TRANSCENDENCE BY PERSPECTIVE

TRANSCENDENCE BY PERSPECTIVE

Meditations on and with Kenneth Burke

Edited by Bryan Crable

Parlor Press
Anderson, South Carolina
www.parlorpress.com

Parlor Press LLC, Anderson, South Carolina, USA

Printed in the United States of America

S A N: 2 5 4 - 8 8 7 9

Library of Congress Cataloging-in-Publication Data

Transcendence by perspective : meditations on and with Kenneth Burke / edited by Bryan Crable.
    pages cm
  Includes bibliographical references and index.
    ISBN 978-1-60235-528-6 (pbk. : acid-free paper) -- ISBN 978-1-60235-529-3 (cloth : acid-free paper) -- ISBN 978-1-60235-530-9 (adobe ebook) -- ISBN 978-1-60235-531-6 (epub) -- ISBN 978-1-60235-588-0 (kindle) -- ISBN 978-1-60235-532-3 (ibook)
  1. Burke, Kenneth, 1897-1993--Criticism and interpretation. 2. Transcendence (Philosophy) in literature. 3. Social justice--Philosophy. 4. Social change--Philosophy. I. Crable, Bryan, 1970- editor.
  PS3503.U6134Z93 2014
  818'.5209--dc23

                        2014030388

Front cover image by Björn Simon. http://islanddesign.de/. Unsplash. Public Domain
Cover design by David Blakesley
Copyediting by Jeff Ludwig
Indexing by Meagan Blakesley
Printed on acid-free paper.

1 2 3 4 5
First Edition

Parlor Press, LLC is an independent publisher of scholarly and trade titles in print and multimedia formats. This book is available in paper, hardcover, and digital formats from Parlor Press on the World Wide Web at http://www.parlorpress.com or through online and brick-and-mortar bookstores. For submission information or to find out about Parlor Press publications, write to Parlor Press, 3015 Brackenberry Drive, Anderson, SC 29621, or e-mail editor@parlorpress.com.

CONTENTS

ACKNOWLEDGMENTS

Putting together an edited volume like this is impossible without the support and tireless efforts of a number of people. In one respect this is obvious—and requires nothing more than a quick glance at the table of contents; as the editor of this collection, I am indebted to all of the scholars who have allowed me to include their work in the book, for both their intellectual labor and their patience as this volume moved through the publication process. Yet, I would also like to recognize others to whom I owe a great debt; it is no exaggeration to say that this book would not exist without them.

First, since this volume grew out of the Seventh Triennial Conference of the Kenneth Burke Society, I must thank Robert Wess, then-president of the KBS. He was not only helpful in the planning of the conference, but he was also a key interlocutor as I worked to hash out the conference theme. In planning the conference, I also unabashedly picked the brain of Jack Selzer, since he had so successfully hosted the KBS Triennial at Penn State in 2005. Members of the Burke family, especially (but not only) Michael Burke and Julie Whitaker, were also generous with their time, both before and during the conference—and their participation in the conference events will always be one of my happiest memories of the 2008 conference. Throughout much of the two-odd years working on the conference, George Boone was invaluable as my graduate assistant; the success of the conference is, in part, a testament to his dedication, intelligence, and good nature. Dan Earle, also a graduate assistant, also played an invaluable role in designing the print and multimedia materials for the conference. Finally, though, I must express my most sincere gratitude to Fr. Kail Ellis, OSA, now Villanova University's Vice

President for Academic Affairs, but then Dean of the College of Liberal Arts and Sciences. His support, financial and otherwise, made it possible for me to actually realize the vision I had for the conference. Its success is directly due to his willingness to offer his, and the College's, support.

Although I initially imagined otherwise, creating an edited volume from a conference is no easy matter. For this reason, I am incredibly indebted to David Blakesley for his willingness to offer me a contract for the volume, his patience as delays set in, and his work on the manuscript after I submitted it to Parlor Press. I am also very grateful to Jeff Ludwig for his outstanding work copyediting the volume, and to Meagan Blakesley for creating the index. Although Jeff is not responsible for any arguments readers might have with the content between the covers, he is definitely responsible for smoothing out the many rough places that might otherwise have distracted the reader from said content.

Finally, I want to end with an homage to love. There are many lovers of Burke (or "KB," as many fondly say) in the world, and this volume will hopefully speak to them, adding something new to their encounters with this incredible artist, critic, and theorist. As Burke would (I think) remind us, though, the love of ideas and the love of another are not the same. For making that point abundantly clear to me, I want to thank my partner, in moon observations and in life, Billie.

TRANSCENDENCE
BY PERSPECTIVE

INTRODUCTION
BURKEAN PERSPECTIVES ON TRANSCENDENCE: A PROSPECTIVE RETROSPECTIVE

Bryan Crable

> *Might there not also be the qualitative importance of beginning, middle, and end? That is: should we not attach particular significance to the situations on which the work opens and closes, and the events by which the peripety, or reversal is contrived? Hence, along with the distinction between opposing principles we should note the development from what through what to what.*

—Kenneth Burke, *Philosophy of Literary Form*

Pay attention to beginnings and endings, Kenneth Burke often reminded his readers, since they tell us much about what lies between them. Are the words explicitly chosen as equivalent to each other to open and close a book? Are they opposites? Is there a maturation or development in the movement from the former to the latter? Is there a transformation in the motivation required to shift from one term to the next? Convinced of the insight generated by this line of questioning, Burke applied it no less frequently to his own work than to the work of others; it was a self-reflexive tendency that reflected and celebrated his emphasis on the necessarily symbolic dimensions of our embodied, human existence.[1] In true Burkean fashion, then, it is appropriate to introduce the essays collected in this volume—essays celebrating the thought and work of Kenneth Burke—by reflecting upon the question of beginnings and endings.

In one sense, this question is rather straightforward; after all, the end (the volume in your hands) lies in its beginning. This volume grew out of papers submitted to and presented at the Seventh Triennial Conference of the Kenneth Burke Society, held at Villanova University in the summer of 2008. Similarly, the title of this volume, as well as the thematic unity of its contents, originated from the conference theme for the Seventh Triennial. In planning the conference, I tried to embrace the unity in Burke's diversity by suggesting the inherent connection between two of Burke's central concepts: *perspective* and *transcendence*. In connecting the two, after conversation with then-KBS President, Robert Wess, I settled upon a particular attitude toward the relationship between these terms: "transcendence by perspective."

This theme called on Burkeans across the disciplines (and, as it turned out, across the world) to explore the relevance of Burkean thought for the transcendence of conflicts, whether enduring (as in America's "racial divide") or ephemeral (as in humanitarian crises as they are spelled out across a wide variety of journalistic outlets). The result was a conference program filled with papers and panels that engaged, in their various incarnations, the pressures of symbolicity, the multiple dimensions of perspective, and the possibilities of transcendence. These panels and papers were complemented by central conference events, including: keynote speaker John S. Wright, a noted American Studies and African-American Studies scholar and author of this volume's first chapter; three featured presenters, including Cheree Carlson, Michael Hyde, and Robert Perinbanayagam; and five conference seminars. From the music of Tom Chapin to eulogies for three recently deceased colleagues— Bernard Brock, Leland Griffin, and William Rueckert—the Seventh Triennial featured diverse opportunities for engagement with various dimensions of the conference theme and also with Burke's enduring relevance.

The conference's end marked yet another beginning for this volume. Afterwards, conference attendees and participants were invited to reflect upon the conference theme and to submit their work for inclusion in a summarizing volume. As I selected the essays that would form the chapters of this volume, I found that they challenged my thinking in some significant ways. Most seriously, I discovered that the conference theme required an additional complication—I had been too simplistic in my discussion of these two key Burkean terms. In my explication of the conference theme, I recognized that I had not fully differentiated two different understandings of "transcendence." This is how I had initially defined and described the theme:

For Burke, the concept of "transcendence" addresses vital concerns of community—including our all-too-common struggles over unity and division. One of the hallmarks of Burke's work is a deep-rooted suspicion of entrenched antagonism, of the bitterly contested either/or. Confronting a Western tradition mired in dualisms, and a social world fractured along binaristic lines, Burke traced these all-too-common symptoms to their source in the human symbolic condition and, not content simply with this diagnosis, he also sought a cure: the disciplined cultivation of transcendence via "ultimate" terms (Burke, 1969, pp. 186–189). Thus, for Burke, transcendence is impossible without a thoroughgoing understanding of our perspectival, symbolic existence. As Burke writes in *Attitudes Toward History*, "When approached from a certain point of view, A and B are 'opposites.' We mean by 'transcendence' the adoption of another point of view from which they cease to be opposites" (Burke, 1984a, p. 336). Although inspired in part by his reading of Plato, Burke's vision of transcendence avoids the pitfalls of the transcendental, but instead is grounded solidly in the necessity of our embodied symbolicity. In Burke's skilled hands, transcendence becomes not the elimination of perspective, of partisanship, but the embrace of transcendence by perspective—because only by rigorously acknowledging the symbolic nature of perspective can we move beyond the stagnant stalemate of reified social, political, and philosophical binaries.

In reflecting further upon the essays submitted, I realized that in this framing of the conference theme, I had problematically equated discussions of transcendence in 1937 and in 1950, in *Attitudes Toward History* and *A Rhetoric of Motives*, respectively. In part, the conference theme's discussion of transcendence reflected the state of my own scholarly interests at the time—specifically, my exploration of Burke's Platonic meditations in the *Rhetoric*.[2] Unbeknownst to me at the time, James Zappen (2009) was working a similar vein in Burke's work. His detailed examination of the *Rhetoric* led him to differentiate between Burke's early, Hegelian/Marxist vision of transcendence, and his later, Platonic account of "dialectical-rhetorical transcendence" (pp. 280–281).

Pushed by my post-conference encounter with Zappen's argument, and by the different senses of transcendence animating the chapters submitted for this volume, I quickly found that completing this edited book required returning to the Burkean corpus. My rereading further convinced me that Burke's writings contained multiple—not exactly opposing, but certainly not equivalent—conceptions of transcendence. Although I do not exactly quarrel with Zappen's view of transcendence, returning to the Burkean corpus has led me to broaden my focus, from Burke's rhetorical theory to his thought as a whole. By doing so, I suggest that we can locate three versions of transcendence within Burke's body of work: (1) transcendence as a curative method; (2) transcendence as a dialectical process; and (3) transcendence as our human condition. This argument certainly has implications for Burkean scholarship; it suggests one route whereby we can trace the development (from what, through what, to what) of Burke's thought. These three types of transcendence also help illuminate the essays in this volume and the continued relevance of Burkean examinations of global, social, and personal conflict. Before arriving at such a conclusion, let us start with a more detailed discussion of Burke's trio of transcendences.

TRANSCENDENCE AS CURATIVE METHOD

Burke's earliest discussions of transcendence appear, understandably enough, in his first published work of criticism, *Counter-Statement*. However, as befitting both Burke's early aestheticism and the subject matter of the book, Burke treats transcendence as an aspect of the poetic or aesthetic process.[3] Describing the emergence of art from the raw materials of experience in "Psychology and Form," Burke (1968) famously writes: "Art, at least in the great periods when it has flowered, was the conversion, or transcendence, of emotion into eloquence, and was thus a factor added to life" (p. 41). In this formula, to transcend is to convert (to translate or transform) material from one realm into another—from "emotion into eloquence." Similarly, within "The Poetic Process," Burke returns to this account of transcendence in his definition of art; he refers again to the essential role played by the process of translation and transformation, as when the artist converts his or her emotion or experience into a symbol (pp. 54–56). This early text, then, spends little time theorizing transcendence, but it does touch upon transcendence as central to producing a work of art.

Burke's next published book, *Permanence and Change*, shifts away from this early aestheticism, and toward concerns more directly symbolic and political. The text develops a robust theoretical framework, one that locates the uniqueness of human life in the dialectical interplay of language and embodiment. Burke's emphasis here on the importance of symbolicity in human life leads him also to emphasize, even champion, the importance of perspective. According to Burke, as symbolic beings, we never engage reality directly, on its own terms. On the contrary, we learn how to be *oriented* to the world; we learn a systematic, interlinked set of interpretations of the world around us, and thus equip ourselves to act within it. As Burke (1984b) explains:

> Our minds, as linguistic products, are composed of concepts (verbally molded) which select certain relationships as meaningful. Other groups may select other relationships as meaningful. These relationships are not *realities*, they are *interpretations* of reality—hence different frameworks of interpretation will lead to different conclusions as to what reality is. (p. 35)

"Orientation," he tells us, "is thus a bundle of judgments as to how things were, how they are, and how they may be" (p. 14).

The problem, Burke points out, lies in the comprehensive nature of our orientations; since they equip us so thoroughly for action, it is difficult for them to be challenged from without. The result, Burke argues, is that human beings are more persistent in their problematic interpretations of the world than the simplest of animals. Just as a chicken's response to a ringing bell makes it easier to slaughter, "People may be unfitted by being fit in an unfit fitness" (Burke, 1984b, p. 10). All contrary or unexpected messages, events, or stimuli are first experienced and engaged in light of the orientation that would be challenged and, as a result, "A way of seeing is also a way of not seeing" (p. 49). Within *Permanence and Change*, Burke proposes the concept of "perspective by incongruity" as a way to systematically loosen such congealed orientations and prevent the successes of our symbolic frameworks from becoming consequential liabilities. However, he has an additional, related goal in this text: to theorize the process of conversion from one orientation to another while retaining a symbolic and perspectival account of human life. Burke's perspective by incongruity does not underestimate the entrenched nature of perspectives, but it nonetheless begins to sketch a path toward individual and social change.

As a result, I locate the foundation of Burke's first view of transcendence in *Permanence and Change*—in Burke's attempt to theorize the birth of opposing or competing perspectives. In this text, Burke points to the symbolic roots of our interpretations of social reality—the orientations that produce our differing views of (and commitments to) the past and the future. However, it was only two years later, in *Attitudes Toward History* (*Attitudes*), that Burke *explicitly* addresses the problem of perspective as one of transcendence. Compare, for example, the three explicit mentions of transcendence in *Permanence and Change* with the dozens in *Attitudes Toward History*, the specific definitions of the term offered in the latter with the passing (and much less systematic) use in the former. These quantitatively different treatments of transcendence reflect subtle, thematic differences between these two texts.[4]

Permanence and Change presents a diagnosis of then-contemporary American society, locating the origins of the clash of perspectives between (to use Burke's examples) Marxists and capitalists, or psychoanalysts and neurotics. *Attitudes*, however, focuses less upon the possibility of conversion from one perspective to another—the subject of much discussion in *Permanence and Change*—than upon human beings' symbolic resolution of conflict.

Given the welter of perspectives that populate an individual's environment (from his or her earliest moments of experience) in this later text, Burke does not deny the fractured and evolving character of social and political life. He also recognizes that human beings, as they form their adult perspectives on the world, are driven to create syntheses that unite the disparate elements of their symbolic and non-symbolic environments. Individuals, on Burke's account, confront both a multitude of conflicts and the possibility (necessity, even) of symbolically resolving such conflicts. It is this process of symbolic resolution that Burke discusses as transcendence.

Moreover, he makes it clear that the kind of transcendence he describes is much more than the aesthetic process of conversion described in *Counter-Statement*. Indeed, the definition of transcendence from *Attitudes* is so clear that it is often cited as Burke's (1984a) primary definition of the term: "When approached from a certain point of view, A and B are 'opposites.' We mean by 'transcendence' the adoption of another point of view from which they cease to be opposites" (p. 336). The Hegelian flavor of this definition is evident throughout the text, since Burke describes transcendence as the symbolic merging of opposites—he talks about it as a kind of symbolic "bridging" of the divide between opposing principles, values, identities, or factions (pp. 80, 92).

It is important to note that Burke consistently locates this symbolic bridging *at the level of the individual*. Within *Attitudes*, transcendence is explicitly defined as a matter of individual integration—even "salvation." The drive toward transcendence, Burke explicitly argues, is not a symptom of capitalist society, or of a particular social or economic arrangement; it is not, in other words, a feature of human life that could be eliminated by restructuring social and/or economic life. On the contrary, transcendence is an endemic feature of existence as a symbol user. As Burke (1984a) phrases this point, "the process of transcendence" is "basic to thought" (p. 86).

Burke supports and develops this argument through a discussion of three basic prompts, or "stimuli," toward transcendence in human life. The first involves "the many kinds of conflict among values implicit in a going social concern" (Burke, 1984a, p. 179). These conflicts can, under particular conditions, produce crises for individual members of a society. Such crises are best averted or resolved by symbolic acts of bridging, allowing individuals to say an overarching "yes" or "no" to the prevailing social order. Even absent such a crisis, an individual may be stirred to an act of transcendence by the dissonance between individual experience and the demands of the community. Here we witness the effort "to bridge the gap between his private impulses and the social norms," an effort particularly evident in the life and work of the artist (p. 180). One need not be an artist, though, to feel these promptings toward transcendence. Burke (1984a) argues that there lies within all human beings an embodied source of transcendence: "Man is 'dualistic' at least in the sense that his sleeping self is radically dissociated from his waking self. Each morning and each night, he crosses and recrosses a threshold, thereby changing his identity" (p. 180). This produces, according to Burke, a need to symbolically bridge the gap between "the rational experience of waking life" and "the incongruous perspectives of sleep" (p. 180).

Together, these three sources of conflict or dissonance suggest the power of and the drive toward transcendence in human life: "Even if you remove the class issue in its acuter forms," Burke (1984a) concludes, "you still have a disparate world that must be ritualistically integrated" (p. 184). Transcendence, in *Attitudes*, is thus described as natural; it is as characteristic of humans as our capacity to learn and to use symbols. Just as important, Burke portrays transcendence as *curative*, as a method of making the individual symbol-user at home within his or her world, of creating unity from the divisive materials of human experience. Burke explains this method quite precisely within the text, emphasizing its perspectival (or attitudinal) character. He famously writes, "When objects are not in a line, and you would have them in a line without moving them, you may put them into a line by shifting your angle of vision" (p. 224). As with the definition of transcendence quoted earlier, Burke's emphasis here is upon attaining a perspective from which differences can be overcome, the disparate brought into alignment, and the discordant made harmonious. Within the text, he often describes this process in Hegelian terms: "Prayer 'transcends' a given conflict (involving a yes and no) when it adopts a 'higher' point of view from which the opponents are found to merge" (p. 326). Here again I emphasize the personal or individual nature of these discussions; Burke's text describes the method by which symbol-users can reconcile the divisive elements of life, and thereby achieve symbolic integration.

This method is not without its drawbacks. Most seriously, Burke stresses that these acts of transcendence produce a symbolic, non-material resolution of discord. Burke's (1984a) discussion of acceptance nicely captures this point: "One confronts contradictions. Insofar as they are resolvable contradictions he acts to resolve them. Insofar as they are not resolvable, he symbolically erects a 'higher synthesis,' in poetic and conceptual imagery, that helps him to 'accept' them" (p. 92). As this quotation indicates, symbolic acts of transcendence are not necessary insofar as one is able to otherwise eradicate the conflicts that one faces. To the extent that conflict or dissonance is not addressable, symbolic transcendence enables an individual symbol-user to instead adjust his or her point of view—to bring the differing elements into alignment. Yet, such an act of transcendence provides only a temporary solution. As Burke notes, "Since the transcendence of conflicts is here contrived by purely symbolic mergers, the actual conflicts may remain. And in 'untranscendental moments,' they may again make their pressure felt"—leading to a need to repeat the act of transcendence (p. 180). Transcendence, Burke tells us, may be a curative method, but it remains a remedy in need of constant re-application.

Toward the end of *Attitudes*, just after his famous definition of the process of transcendence, Burke (1984a) introduces an interesting distinction:

> This is, at present, the nearest approach we can make to the process by verbal means. As a matter of fact, such verbalizations completely slight an all-important qualitative ingredient . . . that makes all the difference between a true transcendence and the empty acquisition of the verbal paraphernalia. (pp. 336–337)

In his brief attempt to sketch the difference between a "true" and "empty." or (merely) "verbal." transcendence, Burke appeals to the complexity of the comic frame. He argues that the comic is itself a transcending symbolic framework, one that (he suggests) provides the "true" transcendence missing from other frames of acceptance and rejection. Further, he uses the terms "transcendence upward" and "transcendence downward" to suggest the qualitative difference between these frames—although, he notes that these terms are "at best bungling approximates" (p. 337).[5] While Burke does not develop this distinction in greater detail, it foreshadows something new. Even as he summarizes his view of transcendence as cure, Burke points toward a different treatment of the concept, one that allows him to evaluate—even hierarchize—symbolic acts of transcendence. As a result, *Attitudes* finds Burke grappling with transcendence as an individual problem, but as also pointing toward the author's "next stage" (to borrow a Burkean phrase): an account of transcendence as less a method of adjustment than a dialectical *process*.

TRANSCENDENCE AS DIALECTICAL PROCESS

Burke's dissatisfaction with his earlier conception of transcendence was first announced, appropriately enough, in Burke's "thirty-minded" essay collection, *The Philosophy of Literary Form* (*PLF*). As George and Selzer (2007) point out, although a portion of the volume dated from the early 1930s (and thus prior to *Permanence and Change* and *Attitudes*), the "many essays in *PLF* that were written late in the decade . . . point to concerns that Burke would develop in his later criticism and theory, after the tumultuous 1930s were history" (p. 183). One of the most important of these late-decade pieces was the eponymous lead essay, as it heralded a new direction in Burke's thought about language, art, and human motivation.

In discussing this text, Burkean scholars typically point to a few key features of the essay, such as its introduction of language as "symbolic action" (e.g., Burke, 1973, pp. 8–18), or its distinction between dream, prayer, and chart (Burke, 1973, pp. 5–7). For the purposes of this introductory chapter, I wish to instead highlight the essay as a shift away from Burke's earlier conceptions of transcendence. Admittedly, this topic consumes less of Burke's explicit attention than these other matters, but the text makes it clear that, by the end of the 1930s, Burke had become dissatisfied with his earlier, more Hegelian, conception of transcendence.

In a treatment of the complex relationship between criminality and the work of art, Burke unpacks the ambiguity lurking within the Latin term *sacer*. He notes that is not simply the root of the English "sacred," since the word could equally be used to describe a criminal. Burke (1973) suggests that we translate the term as "untouchable" or as "power[ful]," since both terms (especially the latter) suggest the ambiguity and ambivalence that unites the sacred and the profane, good power and bad power (p. 55). In unpacking this point, Burke draws upon the relationship between chord and arpeggio:

> [I]f A is in the same chordal structure with B and C, its kindred membership must be revealed by narrative arpeggios. That is, its function as an associate will be revealed by associational progressions in the work itself (as you find a progression from A to B to C in one place, from A to C to B in another, from B to A in another, etc.). The *ambivalent* notion of *sacer* will be more fruitful for leads here than a less dialectical essentializing that reduces the whole matter to either a "good" or "bad" alone. (pp. 58–59)

Rather than looking within a work of art for a synthesizing attitude—one that unites opposites in a single term—Burke proposes looking within the work for its characteristic transformative developments, from one term to another. Here Burke begins to suggest his dialectical leanings and emphasize process over state, to suggest temporal unfolding over eternal simultaneity—the movement of an arpeggio through a series of notes (a "dialectical" approach) rather than the concurrent sounding of dissonant tones within a single chord (an "essentializing" approach).

As the essay continues, Burke again cites this arpeggio-chord distinction to critique Hegel and his disciples. The problem with the Hegelian view, Burke (1973) argues, is that it collapses two senses of time, the eternal and the unfolding. The result is the characteristically Hegelian opposition of thesis and antithesis:

> In the arpeggio of biological, or temporal, growth, good *does* come out of evil . . . But when you collapse the arpeggio of development by the nontemporal, nonhistorical forms of logic, you get simultaneous "polarity," which adds up to good and evil as consubstantial. Now if one introduces into a chord a note alien to the perfect harmony, the result is a discord. But if you stretch out that same chord into an arpeggio having the same components, the discordant ingredient you have introduced may become but a "passing note." (p. 99)

Indeed, Burke states, attention to this distinction is the key to a more dialectical (in the non-Hegelian sense) conception of transcendence: "'Transcendence' is the solving of the logical problem [of opposition] by stretching it out into a narrative arpeggio, whereby a conflicting element can be introduced as a 'passing note,' hence not felt as discord" (pp. 99–100).

Although, within the text, Burke directs this critique at Hegel, it is no less an indictment of his own early writings. "The Philosophy of Literary Form" indicates Burke's shift away from the definition of transcendence presented in *Attitudes*. He sketches a conception of transcendence grounded not in the eternal simultaneity of synthesis—the uniting of opposites in a single term—but in the arpeggio, in the unfolding process that both traces and produces a transformation. As Hegelian might, as Burke argues, attempt to unite the opposing forms of "Yes" and "No" with a synthetic "Maybe." Instead, Burke re-describes this as a development from one pole to the other *through* the intermediary step of "Maybe." As he notes, "though this total form, as collapsed into a 'simultaneity,' still gives you the quality of 'Maybe,' as drawn out it gives you a transcendence, *from* quality 'Yes' *to* quality 'No'" (Burke, 1973, p. 100).

Note that, in this passage, Burke (1973) describes the movement from "Yes" to "No" as a *movement* from one *quality* to another. Instead of depicting transcendence as a bridging, here Burke describes it as a "radical change in quality" (p. 99). This phrase, I believe, is key to understanding this account of transcendence as a substantial revision of Burke's earlier (Hegelian) emphasis upon an individual's method of adjustment. Instead of discussing transcendence as a synthesizing or merging of opposites (the curative adjustment to conflict), in "The Philosophy of Literary Form" Burke discusses the term as a transformation in quality—a radical alteration that occurs through the temporal development from starting point to ending point. Fittingly, Burke's break with his early views was heralded in the pages of this transitional collection, but not made complete until the arrival of his next major work: *A Grammar of Motives.*

Reflecting Burke's attitude toward the horrors of war—specifically World War II, as it coincided with his writing of the text—*Grammar of Motives* (*Grammar*) was given the motto *Ad bellum purificandum*, or "Towards the Purification of War" (Burke, 1969a, p. 319; cf. Weiser, 2008). Although there is much that can be said about this motto, Burke puts it rather simply: Might we find a way, through the systematic analysis of our symbolic existence, to create a more humane social order? In his attempt to substitute a reflexive clash of words for the clash of arms and armies, Burke undertakes a careful, even exhaustive, examination of our linguistic resources. Although it is certainly the case that perspectival differences can lead to conflict (as Burke emphasizes in his early works), in *Grammar*, Burke strives to organize competing perspectives into a unifying dialogue—even as he evaluates the defects, blind spots, and problematic tendencies lurking within these particular symbolic frameworks.

As he famously asks in the book's opening sentence, "What is involved, when we say what people are doing and why they are doing it?" (Burke, 1969a, p. xv). Although the subject of motives tends to steal the attention of readers, the emphasis here should be placed on the word "say" within the passage. Burke is not interested in anything more (or less) mysterious than what we typically *say* about motives, our conversion of existential situations into characteristic symbolic forms. As Burke phrases it, "our concern is primarily with the analysis of *language* rather than with the analysis of '*reality*'" (p. 317). Our words betray more than our motives; they betray *us*, Burke argues, because they display the limitations and defects of our customary terminologies. Our symbol systems provide the resources we draw upon when we interpret and respond to events, persons, and situations. Although each of us, as Burke points out in *Attitudes*, is driven to establish a (more or less) unified perspective on the world, these symbolic structures are not necessarily adequate, adaptive, or even functional. Given the changing nature of the situations we confront, our necessarily limited, symbolically derived perspectives may be as easily a source of conflict and error as are success and harmony; we can easily be "trained to draw the lines at the wrong places, interpreting both private and social situations in woefully inaccurate terms" (p. 101).

Further, Burke argues that we cannot root out and correct the inaccuracies and inadequacies in our vocabularies unless we are attentive to the symbolic nature of perspective. Otherwise said, we cannot remain within the limited confines of a particular terminology if we hope to combat our tendency to "draw the lines at the wrong places." What is needed, Burke contends, is less one more perspective than a *perspective on (or of) perspectives* (Crable, 2000). In other words, only a radically symbolic perspective can evaluate the sources of limitation, error, and aggression implicit within particular vocabularies:

> Language being essentially human, we would view human relations in terms of the linguistic instrument. Not mere "consciousness of abstracting," but *consciousness of linguistic action generally*, is needed if men are to temper the absurd ambitions that have their source in faulty terminologies. (Burke, 1969a, p. 317)

Further, according to Burke, the kind of perspective he calls for requires a *dialectical* approach to the study of language: "We believe that an explicit approach to language as a dialectical structure admonishes us both what to look for and what to look out for, as regards the ways of symbolic action" (p. 313).

These twin beliefs lead Burke to adopt an unlikely ally within the *Grammar*: Plato. Although, to most twentieth century thinkers, Plato's writings epitomize dogmatism and essentialism, Burke (1969a) offers a counter-reading of the philosopher's work, stating that

> nearly everything that this greatest of dialecticians says of "heaven" can be profitably read as a statement about *language* . . . . Even the doctrine of heavenly "archetypes" is sound enough, if read as a statement about the relationship between class names and names for the individuals thus classified by a common essence. (p. 253)

Interpreted in this way, Burke argues that we can see in Plato's dialogues the outline of a powerful, and thoroughly symbolic, dialectical method. Further, Burke explicitly connects this method to the concept of transcendence, since he argues that the Platonic dialogue "was designed to produce a form wherein the end transcended the beginning," providing a "way of development through the cooperative competition of divergent voices" (p. 253).

Indeed, near the end of the text, Burke (1969a) pushes the point further, arguing that "the nature of transcendence or transformation" is "embodied in Plato's dialogues": "For not only do they *plead for* transcendence; they are themselves so formed that the end transcends the beginning" (p. 421). Platonic dialogues, Burke explains, both advocate and reflect the twin movements of the "Upward Way" and "Downward Way." They trace the movement from a plurality of competing voices, through increasing levels of abstraction, to the arrival at a new, unifying principle—one found at the root of the subject matter being considered. Therefore, as Burke summarizes, within these dialogues

> you are taken on the Upward Way to a vision of the One . . . And when you return to the world of diversity, you consider it in terms of the new principle encountered en route, whereupon it is viewed in a transcendent light. (p. 428)

Within *Grammar*, Burke identifies the Platonic journey "Upward" and then "Downward" as the dialectical method *par excellence*, the temporal unfolding that produces the qualitative transformation that Burke (at this point in his career) identifies as transcendence. Moreover, Burke suggests that this method is the key to his "perspective of perspectives" and to his attempt to draw competing, individual (persuasive but "faulty") vocabularies into a productive, transformative dialogue.

Not surprisingly, given its subject matter, this reading of the Platonic dialectic reappears within Burke's follow-up volume, *A Rhetoric of Motives* (*Rhetoric*). *Rhetoric* was designed to complement *Grammar* by extending its studies of our linguistic resources into the rhetorical realm—into the "Human Barnyard," the journalistic/advertisement-filled/political "Scramble," the combative scene for the "competitive use of the cooperative" (Burke, 1969a, p. 442). Although *Rhetoric*, as a project, evolved a great deal between its inception and its publication, Burke's reliance upon Plato remained a constant feature (Crable, 2009). Indeed, one might argue that the Platonic dialectic plays an even more important role within this text than in its predecessor. Within *Rhetoric*, Burke not only describes the Upward and Downward Ways, but he takes readers on this Platonic journey in order to arrive at the "perspective of perspectives" necessary to transcend the divisive rhetorical realm.

Classically, as Burke (1969a) points out, rhetoric is rooted in opinion and belief, and not in knowledge. Yet, the Platonic dialectic offers a method by which this starting point can be transcended. It outlines a process of qualitative transformation from origin to destination:

> Perhaps, as a first rough approximate, we might think of the matter thus: Bring several *rhetoricians* together, let their speeches contribute to the maturing of one another by the give and take of question and answers, and you have the *dialectic* of a Platonic dialogue. But ideally the dialogue seeks to attain a higher order of truth, as the speakers, in competing with one another, cooperate towards an end transcending their individual positions. (p. 53)

The route "up" and "down," in other words, is a transformative one; its starting and ending points differ not just in content, but also in quality. Through the disciplined process of the Platonic dialectic, Burke argues, one methodically produces a qualitative change: from conflicting opinions to "a higher order of truth."

To firmly and fully ground this dialectical process within his symbolic framework, Burke links the Platonic method to a tripartite hierarchy of terms: positive, ultimate, and dialectical. All words, according to Burke, fall into one of these three terministic "orders." Positive terms, as Burke (1969b) defines them, are words that "name par excellence the things of experience, the *hic et nunc*" (p. 183). These terms—that refer unambiguously to the non-symbolic realm of sensory perception—are thus rather limited in scope. Dialectical terms, Burke's second order of terminology, instead comprise "the order of *action* and *idea*. Here are words for *principles* and *essence*" (p. 184).[6] Burke notes that such terms can be likened to titles, since they entitle, encapsulate, or name a situation that itself contains a host of positive terms. Furthermore, because these dialectical terms entitle a wealth of positive details, Burke tells us that they are also prone to conflict—since they are countered by opposing titles or principles that entitle the same set of conditions quite differently. Burke uses the dialectical titles of "feudalism," "capitalism," and "socialism" to illustrate this point.

If we did not have recourse to another realm of terminology, Burke contends, we would be stuck with the inevitability of dialectical conflict. Opposing titles would confront one another as warring members of parliament, content with nothing less than total victory over their adversaries. Under such conditions, although a compromise might, at times, be brokered, it would be at least somewhat unsatisfactory to all involved. Fortunately, Burke argues, we have an alternative: the "ultimate" order of terms. An ultimate term, according to Burke (1969b), is not simply another principle, but the "principle of principles," a term that is able to arrange the competing voices of the dialectical realm into an ordered whole. In other words,

> the "ultimate" order would place these competing voices themselves in a *hierarchy*, or *sequence*, or *evaluative series*, so that, in some way, we went by a fixed and reasoned progression from one of these to another, the members of the entire group being arranged developmentally with relation to one another. (p. 187)

According to the process that Burke sketches within the text, just as dialectical terms are "in a different order of vocabulary" than positive terms, the ultimate order is not an alternate principle or idea, but something altogether different, "a new level of motivation, motivation *beyond* the ideas, not present in the dialectical reduction to pure ideas" (p. 200). For this reason, Burke describes the ultimate order of terms as *mythic*, as the archetypal origin of dialectical ideas and (positive) sensory images. Here again, Burke echoes the Upward Way of the Platonic dialogue as an active process that moves from sensory images to ideas to myth—from the materials of sensation, through the agon of concepts, to the mythic, archetypal image that harmoniously arranges or orders these opposing principles (cf. Crable, 2009; Zappen, 2009).

The advantage of this dialectical process, Burke writes, is twofold. First, the link between the positive and the dialectical realms retains Burke's earlier account of the origin of differing perspectives or vocabularies—the symbolic constitution or entitlement of the non-verbal realm. Unlike Burke's earlier work, here the appropriation of Platonic materials is additionally designed to *transform* the clash of partisan principles or vocabularies. As Burke (1969b) puts it, the end result of this dialectical method is "an ultimate order whereby ideas would transcend sensory images, and mythic images would in turn transcend ideas. The final stage would be reached through a moral and intellectual development, through processes of discipline and initiation" (p. 203).

This is the full import of the link between the dialectical and the ultimate orders of terminology. Burke contends that his Platonically-inspired dialectical process includes—even requires—the limited, clashing vocabularies of the dialectical realm. However, rather than leave these opposing vocabularies to their endless wrangling, Burke engages them in order to transform them, and a unifying, mythic origin or ancestor arises from these warring principles. By locating the mythic image that transcends the partiality of faction, Burke's (1969b) Platonic dialectic ensures that "The voices would not confront one another as somewhat disrelated competitors that can work together only by the 'mild demoralization' of sheer compromise; rather, they would be like successive positions or moments in a single process" (p. 187).

This ultimate order, Burke (1969b) argues, thus "transcend[s] the bias of the competing rhetorical partisans"; it "introduce[s] a new level of motivation, motivation *beyond* the ideas not present in the dialectical reduction to pure ideas" (p. 200). In other words, the ultimate order produced by Burke's Platonic dialectic cannot be reduced to any of the terms that produced it. The ultimate is a vocabulary whose *quality* has been transformed through the disciplined movement of the Upward Way. It is no longer another limited symbolic framework for entitling the human or natural world; it is no longer another partisan voice within the cacophony of dialectical opposition. On the contrary, the ultimate is a terminology that *transcends* the terminologies of the other two realms. By systematically placing competing rhetorical vocabularies into a harmonious order—and thereby tracing a developmental progression from partiality to inclusion—Burke's dialectical journey within *Rhetoric* generates the "principle of principles" that *Grammar* had first outlined. Rather than adding simply another vocabulary of human motivation, Burke uses Plato to create a productive, transcending order from the "faulty terminologies" that offer a limited perspective upon social life and interaction.[7]

However, as Burke points out earlier, in *Grammar*, the stages sketched above represent only half of the process. The full value of this Upward journey is felt on the way Downward—when the mythic image transforms the world of action and sensation. Indeed, the transcendence produced through Platonic dialectic is not static, but active; the mythic image provides a transforming vision of the dialectical and positive orders that it both harmonizes and grounds—an insight that offers new possibilities for action. Although Burke had originally hoped to develop such a Downward Way within *Rhetoric*, the main text ends just at the point where this process would have begun: He closes the main portion of the text with a vivid depiction of his own mythic image, "pure persuasion" (Burke, 1969b, pp. 293–294; cf. Crable, 2009).

As Burkean scholars have begun to discover, Burke envisioned, but never completed, a rhetorical "devices" book that would have provided the second half of this dialectic, using *Rhetoric*'s "principle of principles" to transform our view of the rhetorical realm (Williams, 2001). Further, as is widely known, Burke had originally envisioned a third volume in his *Motivorum* project: *A Symbolic of Motives* (*Symbolic*).[8] There are, of course, many possible theories regarding these successors to *Rhetoric* (Rueckert, 1982, 2001; Thames, 2007; Wess, 2007; Williams, 2001). It is not my primary intent to add to this particular portion of the ongoing conversation, but I think it significant that we see a concurrence of events in Burke's career, including Burke's struggle to conclude the *Motivorum* series, including the "devices" project and *Symbolic*; and Burke's development of an altogether different conception of transcendence. Although there might be no more than coincidence linking these aspects of Burke's mid- to late career, I believe that Burke's work in *Rhetoric* and later, in *Symbolic,* led him to an unexpected alteration of his account of transcendence and, with it, a new set of scholarly priorities. In the years following the publication of *Rhetoric*, Burke began to think about transcendence as less a dialectical method than as our all-too-human *condition*.

TRANSCENDENCE AS EXISTENTIAL CONDITION

At one point within *Rhetoric*, while tracing the "Upward" stages of the Platonic journey, Burke pauses to note that human social life is filled with small instances of transcendence—that even our relentless pursuit of commodities can be understood as a search for transcendence. However, Burke

(1969b) also suggests that these everyday moments are indicative of something more profound, that transcendence is deeply rooted within human existence:

> [W]hen we use symbols for things, such symbols are not merely a reflections of the things symbolized, or signs for them; they are to a degree a *transcending* of the things symbolized. So, to say that man is a symbol-using animal is by the same token to say that he is a "transcending animal." Thus, there is in language itself a motive force calling man to transcend the "state of nature" (that is, the order of motives that would prevail without language, Logos, "reason"). (p. 192)

Burke returns to this point later in the text, after arrival at his mythic image of "pure persuasion." In describing this "principle of principles," Burke adds that it points beyond rhetoric, toward something more fundamental: "the nature of language itself, the 'rationality' of *homo dialecticus*, of man as a symbol-using animal whose symbols simultaneously reflect and transcend the 'reality' of the nonsymbolic" (p. 275). The main text of *Rhetoric* breaks off not long after Burke's musing on this link between language, transcendence, and human existence, but that does not mark the end of Burke's reflections on the subject. Following the publication of *Rhetoric*, as Burke worked on the manuscript for "Poetics, Dramatistically Considered" (one iteration of *Symbolic*), he again grappled with the meaning of transcendence, returning to this profound link between language and transcendence.

Within "Poetics, Dramatistically Considered," Burke explicitly defines his dramatistic treatment of poetics in terms of catharsis. Burke also acknowledges the need to distinguish between catharsis and transcendence, explaining why the penultimate section of the manuscript is entitled "Platonic Transcendence" (Williams, 2001, p. 22). These pages of "Poetics" offer an account of transcendence that is very familiar to readers of *Grammar* and *Rhetoric of Motives*. Burke (2001c) himself underscores the continuity between this discussion and his previously published volumes: "The resources and forms of dialectic have been discussed so often in these *Motivorum* books, we shall here try merely to sum up" (p. 70). Following this statement, he offers a sketch of the Platonic Upward and Downward Ways, again discussing this as a method of transcendence—a transformation from sensory image to idea, and from competing ideas to a unifying, mythic image (pp. 70–73).

This brief treatment of transcendence appears to have left Burke at least somewhat dissatisfied. As Williams (2001) indicates, while working on the revision and completion of "Poetics" in mid-1955, Burke wrote a lengthy reflection on Ralph Waldo Emerson's essay, *Nature*—pages that he considered central to his project in *Symbolic* (p. 13). Rueckert (2001) emphasizes that this work on Emerson was conceptually vital to Burke's account of poetics: "The Emerson essay is primarily devoted to making an essential distinction between catharsis and transcendence, a distinction that is essential to Burke's theory of tragedy and catharsis" (p. 105). Although the essay appears (for some reason) not to have been included in Burke's plans for the "Poetics" manuscript (Rueckert, 2001; Williams, 2001), Burke found it significant enough to warrant its inclusion within *Language as Symbolic Action*, where it appeared in rather unchanged form (Rueckert, 2001, pp. 122–123). Within this essay, published under the title "I, Eye, Ay," Burke outlines a new account of transcendence, one that is at the root of the forms of transcendence depicted in his earlier works. Moreover, this third conception of transcendence builds upon Burke's passing comment in *Rhetoric* and, I argue, sets the stage for much of Burke's later work.

Burke's (1966) essay on Emerson opens with a contrast between "dialectical transcendence" and "dramatic catharsis"; although often treated as synonymous, he contends that they are not the same, that "transcendence is a rival kind of medicine" to catharsis (p. 186).[9] As part of his effort to differentiate these easily-confused concepts, Burke utilizes both conceptions of transcendence that appear in his earlier work. For example, he draws upon the appendix to *Attitudes*, titled "The Seven Offices," and describes transcendence as "a sheerly terministic, or symbolic function," as the creation of "a terminology designed to *bridge* . . . disparate realms" (p. 187). Within the essay's pages, Burke also identifies transcendence in the "cooperative competition" of the Platonic dialectic, the transformation produced by the unifying term that unites the divisive voices of the social world (pp. 188–191).

However, within "I, Eye, Ay," Burke also recontextualizes both of these earlier positions through invoking a more fundamental conception of transcendence. Thus, Burke (1966) does not abandon the Platonic dialogue, the transformative journey Upward and Downward; he notes, "Transcendence, as we shall see, is best got by processes of dialectic" (p. 188). Similarly, he does not reject his earlier emphasis upon the power of symbolic bridge-building. Early in the essay, he notes that "Viewed as a sheerly terministic, or symbolic function, that's what transcendence is: the building of a *terministic bridge* whereby one realm is *transcended* by being viewed *in terms of* a realm 'beyond' it" (p. 187).[10]

In the passage quoted above, Burke suggests that there is a common thread that unites these two accounts: the inspiriting of the *here and now* by something *beyond*. This, I believe, is the key to Burke's (1966) third conception of transcendence, one that uses the "beyond" to combine the Platonic and the pontifical:

> In dialectical transcendence, the principle of transformation operates in terms of a "beyond." It is like our seventh office, the "priestly" function, in that it pontificates, or "builds a bridge" between disparate realms. And insofar as things here and now are treated in terms of a "beyond," they thereby become infused or inspirited by the addition of a *new* or *further* dimension. (pp. 189–190)

Here, in Burke's revised definition of transcendence, we hear echoes of his early emphasis upon the reconciliation of divided elements. We also see an oblique reference to the transformative vision produced by the dialectical (Downward) journey of the Platonic dialogue. For Burke, both of these exemplify the human drive toward transcendence, understood as a transformative connection between the "here and now" and the "beyond."

Much of Burke's essay is, understandably enough, focused upon the presence of this type of transcendence within Emerson's essay. However, Burke offers us more in these pages than a literary analysis of one canonical figure. What is notable about Emerson, Burke tells us, is not the presence of transcendence in Emerson's discussion of nature, but the *thoroughness* of his exploration of it. This is why Burke (1966) insists that "the design here being discussed is employed in all sorts of terministic schemes" (p. 191). After pointing to works by Joyce, Chaucer, and Virgil that similarly display the workings of transcendence, Burke ends with a summarizing definition of the term. This definition emerges from Emerson's essay, but Burke extends it to cover a wide range of human activity: "That is the pattern. Whether there is or is not an ultimate shore towards which we, the unburied, would cross, transcendence involves dialectical processes whereby something HERE is interpreted *in terms of* something THERE, something *beyond* itself" (p. 200).

Understood in this sense, Burke argues, transcendence surrounds us—it is an ever-present feature of human symbol-use. This is because, according to Burke, this kind of transcendence is endemic to language itself. In a sweeping passage that concludes the essay on Emerson, Burke (1966) offers a compelling vision of the symbolic origin of transcendence:

> The machinery of language is so made that, either rightly or wrongly, either grandly or in fragments, we stretch forth our hands through love of the farther shore. Which is to say: The machinery of language is so made that things are necessarily placed in terms of a range broader than the terms for those things themselves. And thereby, in even the toughest or tiniest of terminologies, terminolo-

gies that, on their face, are far from the starry-eyed Transcendental-
ism of Emerson's essay, we stretch forth our hands through love of a
farther shore. (p. 200)

To be a language-user, Burke believes, is to be marked by transcendence, to
view "HERE" in terms of "something THERE, something *beyond* itself."
Whether we do it "grandly or in fragments," we *do* reach for the "farther
shore" of the beyond. In this, Burke tells us, we are but following the promptings of language, that transcend the non-symbolic realm that it speaks and
writes *about*. Indeed, I argue that we can see, in much of Burke's late work,
a concern with transcendence in this more existential sense: as a stretching
toward the "beyond," the "love of a farther shore," that is rooted in our human (symbolic) condition.

Of course, one of the challenges posed by Burke's late body of work is its
eclecticism in both form and content. Unlike the early or middle periods of
his career, there is only one complete book to consider, *The Rhetoric of Religion*, though it, like the later *Dramatism and Development*, is quite unlike his
earlier books, since it was crafted from a series of lectures. The other primary
volume from this period of time, *Language as Symbolic Action*, is a collection
of essays—some, but not all, dating from Burke's work on the *Symbolic of
Motives*—that range from philosophy of language to literary criticism, and
much in between. Beyond these works, we have a range of essays, reviews,
lectures, and interviews published from the 1950s into the early 1980s, many
of which touch upon radically disparate subjects. Indeed, when one adds to
this list the manuscripts and essays comprising the never-published *Symbolic*,
it only adds to the difficulty of summarizing this period of Burke's career.
I also believe that we can bring order to, or even unite, much of this late
work under Burke's third conception of transcendence, this symbolically-
induced stretching toward the "beyond." Therefore, I want to end my review
of transcendence by drawing together two key themes within Burke's late
work: the relation of the symbolic and the non-symbolic and the drive toward "perfection."

It is widely acknowledged that a significant portion of Burke's later work
is devoted to unpacking the interrelationship of the symbolic and the non-
symbolic, of motion and action, within human experience. However, I call
attention to something often overlooked: the significance of transcendence
within these treatments of the subject. For example, in a comment on his
"Definition of Man," included in *Language as Symbolic Action*, Burke (1966)
underscores the "basic symbolic devices under which one should class man
as a being typically endowed with the powers of 'transcendence'" (p. 24). As
Burke makes clear throughout his later writings, these human "powers of

'transcendence'" are the direct result of our birth into symbolicity. Indeed, Burke consistently (and explicitly) characterizes the relationship between the symbolic and the non-symbolic as one of transcendence, stating that "action is possible only insofar as the rational agent transcends the realm of sheer motion" (p. 430). We might, then, read much of Burke's late work as a detailed examination of the *machinery* of transcendence.

These writings begin with the fundamental assumption that language is characterized by transcendence, that "the word 'transcends' the thing it names" (Burke, 1970, p. 16). According to Burke, this means that "A duality of realm is implicit in our definition of man as the symbol-using animal. Man's animality is in the realm of sheer matter, sheer motion. But his 'symbolicity' adds a dimension of action not reducible to the non-symbolic" (p. 16). For Burke, this "duality of realm," the division of word and thing, means that human life will necessarily be marked by a "fundamental principle," *duplication*, or "the split across the two realms of non-symbolic motion and symbolic action will necessarily manifest itself in endless variations on the theme of DUPLICATION" (Burke, 2003, p. 152).

This fundamental duplication, itself a symptom of our symbolic transcendence of the non-symbolic, naturally produces further complications: our words about the non-symbolic (transcending *duplications*) begin to produce a wealth of *discriminations* (Brock, Burke, Burgess, & Simons, 1985, p. 32) that themselves suggest profound and powerful *implications* (Burke, 2003, pp. 151–153). Thus, examinations of the symbolic impetus toward duplication, discrimination, implication, and imitation appear throughout many of Burke's later essays and chapters. Indeed, at one point, Burke identifies such efforts as "the very soul of logological inquiry" (Burke, 2003, p. 199; cf. Brock, et al., 1985, pp. 31–32; Burke, 2001b; Burke, 2003, pp. 181, 200, 206, 274).[11] Yet, these studies of the symbolic and the non-symbolic led Burke to another thematic exploration of transcendence—less the symbolic foundation of our efforts than our characteristic *love* of that "farther shore."

Burke (1978) is careful to note that the transcendence of the non-symbolic by the symbolic is not an abandonment or an overcoming of the material, since "though symbolism as such is a dimension that transcends the body, it is rooted in the body as a purely physiological organism" (p. 330). This caveat reflects the complexity of Burke's third conception of transcendence—the definition of it as a stretching toward, but not reaching, the beloved "beyond." In other words, the symbolic does not leave the non-symbolic behind; it *inspirits* it, it treats something "HERE" in light of something "THERE." This is why, for example, Burke tells us that "reference to the 'senses' must be examined for possible motivations not specifically 'sensory' at all. For, once 'the senses' begin operating in a given socio-semantic context, their sheer biological nature as 'senses' is by the same token already transcended" (Burke, 1966, p. 442).

As a result, many of Burke's writings from this period focus upon our love of the "beyond"—the "other shore" we reach toward and that infuses our view of the "here and now." *The Rhetoric of Religion*, for example, both explicates the practice of "logology" and trains its focus upon the "beyond." Early in the text, Burke (1970) explicitly grounds his analysis of theology within the symbolic machinations of transcendence:

> In all such cases, where symbolic operations can influence bodily processes, the realm of the natural (in the sense of the less-than-verbal) is seen to be pervaded, or *inspirited*, by the realm of the verbal, or symbolic. And in this sense, the realm of the symbolic corresponds (in our analogy) to the realm of the "supernatural." (p. 17)

Burke's logological reflections upon the non-empirical realms of the "supernatural" and the "natural" also lead him to emphasize transcendence as the link between symbolicity and the "perfect." As Burke argues, "One necessarily forms one's experience and expectations *in terms of* something or other, even if one is not working formally or deliberately with such structures of interrelated terms as is the case with philosophers, dramatists, and the like" (Burke, 1972, p. 42). However, Burke (1972) tells us, one of the most powerful and dangerous of temptations within human life is the *entelechial*, the drive to form one's experience in terms of its "perfect fulfillment" or culmination:

The dialectical design underlying the entelechial principle (in our strictly "logological" sense of the term) can be summed up thus:

(1) There is the *thing*, bread.

(2) There is the corresponding *word*, bread.

(3) Language being such as it is, with no trouble at all I can make up the expression, "perfect bread." (p. 59)

Now, however, the "perfect bread" of symbolicity transforms the empirical analogue into a subject for conflict and contestation (pp. 59–60). Burke argues that from this simple design emerges wranglings over the present, past, and future that characterize human social life. The transcending power of the word is responsible for the presence and power of perfection in human life; the perfected "beyond" of the symbolic, haunting our vision of the everyday, suggests the imperfect nature of the "here and now." This is why Burke describes human beings as "rotten with perfection"; or, otherwise said, as "moved by" the "principle of perfection implicit in the nature of symbol systems" (Burke, 1966, p. 17). A significant portion of Burke's later work calls us to carefully attend to this all-too-human love of that which lies "beyond" the "here and now" (e.g., Burke, 1972; 2003).

Indeed, one of the most prominent and recurring topics within Burke's late work involves the perfection of our technological prowess that was, even then, ensuring our perfecting/polluting of the earth (Burke, 2003, p. 82). As Burke notes, "'entelechy' may take on quasi-futuristic assumptions, by reason of the fact that the potentialities of a perfected symbol-system can be made to seem too 'clearly' like the proclaiming of a predestined era still to come" (Burke, 1972, p. 57). Burke identifies this entelechial form in the destructively "millenarian" discourses of technology and science. Burke's ironic (and perfectly so!) solution to this dilemma is "An ideal womb-heaven (I called it 'Helhaven') made possible by man's momentous advances in technology—hence, the Ultimate Culmination, Eden, and the Tower in one" (Burke, 1972, p. 54; cf. Burke, 2003, pp. 62–65, 82–88, 135). Further, he explicitly identifies the promptings of transcendence at work in this satirical solution—most notably in the "beyonding" language of Helhaven's slogan: "Onward, outward, and up!" (Burke, 1972, p. 55; Burke, 2003, pp. 65, 95). In its satirical representation of our drive for perfection and our love for the "beyond," Helhaven nicely encapsulates Burke's third conception of transcendence. What could be a more perfect reflection upon the tendencies natural to transcendence, themselves made possible by the transcending power of human symbolicity?

A CONCLUSION, BY WAY OF INTRODUCTION

Throughout the preceding discussion, I attempted to draw out three conceptions of transcendence within Burke's work while also demonstrating the power of this term to unite portions of Burke's distinguished career under its head. As is evident from this chapter, I believe that Burkean scholarship would be well-served by more explicit attention to this vital term. Although I have attempted to provide textual evidence to support this argument, there is additional evidence: the chapters that form the remainder of this volume. Each chapter demonstrates a specific way that Burkean notions of transcendence can illuminate dimensions of human social life, thereby addressing significant issues of conflict, disagreement, and change. Even though the authors wrote their chapters without the benefit (or obstacle!) of the argument presented above, I feel that each teaches us something significant about one or more of the three forms of Burkean transcendence I have identified in this introduction.

The text opens, appropriately enough, with the keynote speaker for the 2008 conference of the Kenneth Burke Society, John S. Wright. Wright's chapter, "Race Ritual, Then and Now: Bridging the Transcendental Dialectics of Kenneth Burke, Ralph Ellison, and Barack Obama," offers a detailed reading of American racial discourse, the comic corrective, and Barack Obama in light of exchanges about race between Burke and his long-time friend and "intellectual sparring partner," Ralph Ellison. Through his detailed examination of transcendence from Burke's work (in all three senses), and his systematic exploration of Ellison's work, Wright teases out the complexity of transcendence in relation to our enduring American "racial divide." He explores the hopes attending Obama's election, as well as the transcending possibilities attending this unique symbol-user and his attempts to create a "more perfect union"—drawing attention to the sufficiently comic, and logologically inclined, vocabulary necessary to grapple with the problem of evil in social life, and the ever-present temptations of order, sin, and punishment.

As James Klumpp's chapter, "Transcendence in the Barnyard: Thoughts on Strategic Approaches to the Political Art," demonstrates, Obama provides substantial material for analysis from a Burkean perspective. Less optimistic than Wright's, Klumpp's perspective on Obama, emerges from a transcendence-oriented discussion of Burkean politics. In Klumpp's view—drawing upon Burke's second conception of transcendence—politics is too often discussed in divisive terms, as a bitter struggle between competing voices. Within Burke's work, by contrast, Klumpp locates key resources for engaging politics as a *synthetic* art, one that aims to transform our communities and unite our perspectives, rather than to secure power over others. Klumpp's examination of Burke leads him to analyze both candidate and President Obama, and to search for signs of the transcending synthesis central to Burkean politics. However, Klumpp's detailed reading of Obama's rhetorical efforts leads him to express pessimism regarding Obama's ability to transform our politics and our communities through his leadership.

Our third chapter, by John Hatch—winner of the "top paper award" at the 2008 conference—returns to the subject of race in America. Unlike Wright and Klumpp, Hatch turns from the study of our current leader toward the struggle to secure reparations for black Americans. "Rounding (out) the Bases of Racial Reconciliation: (Dia)logology and Virginia's Apology for Slavery" examines the state of Virginia's apology for slavery in light of key Burkean terms and the burgeoning literature on reconciliation and forgiveness. Hatch's chapter draws Burkean transcendence and the work of Frye and Ricoeur, and ultimately argues that the Virginia apology, though significantly flawed, offers some measure of hope for progress regarding America's history of racial injustice and slavery. The chapter's aim is less to provide a criticism of this text than to carry out conceptual work. Hatch's essay outlines the Burkean argument for a complex and powerful conception of reconciliation, one rooted in the comic view of our common symbolic humanity and in our collective efforts to seek restorative justice.

Political struggle is also the subject of Theon Hill's chapter, "Triumph Over Tragedy: A Pentadic Analysis Contrasting Hillary Clinton's Health Care Reform Rhetoric from the 1993–1994 Campaign and 2008 Presidential Campaign." Hill takes as his point of departure the significant difference between Clinton's approach to health care as First Lady and as presidential candidate. How, Hill asks, might Burkean transcendence enable us to understand the difference between these two rhetorical endeavors? Hill argues that the success of Clinton's discourse on health care in the 2008 presidential campaign was due to a strategic shift in the pentadic terms featured in her speeches. According to Hill, we see a significant shift from Agency-Scene (in the 1990s) to Purpose (in 2008). The resulting shift, he argues, was accompanied by the deliberate adoption of a comic frame regarding Clinton's own leadership and advocacy of the issue. By rejecting the polarizing nature of the tragic in favor of a comic transcendence, Clinton was able to reframe her past rhetorical failure, and recast it as a preparatory step toward a truly universal health care plan for Americans.

With our fifth chapter, we shift somewhat from the "barnyard" of government to the no-less-political domain of self-help books. Cathryn Hill and Rick Coe's chapter, "The Good Wife (according to Dr. Phil, et al.): A Representative Anecdote of Burkean Analysis," provides a methodological innovation and a significant exploration of popular culture. Hill and Coe are interested in "manuals" about relationships that are marketed to women, and the books' attempts to transcend (in Burke's first sense) the conflicts besetting their readers. This leads Hill and Coe to engage a cluster-agon analysis of these texts, with an eye for the kinds of "medicine" that these books provide their readers. At the same time, concerned that these readers not be understood as simple pawns of these authors, Hill and Coe present the results of in-depth interviews and focus groups to provide a sense of how the meanings encoded within the books are altered by their readers. By drawing together these research techniques, Hill and Coe argue that women reading these books find a kind of comfort in them, a symbolically-generated feeling of success—a reassurance that they are doing the right thing in their relationships, despite their hardships. Of course, as Hill and Coe do not fail to point out, such comfort may come at a significant cost.

Abigail Selzer King, in her chapter, "Transcendence by Colonial Perspective: Bureaucratization, F. Max Müller, and the *Sacred Books of the East* (1879)," decisively shifts our attention as Burkeans and as readers of this volume. She calls for an extension of Burkean scholarship into the postcolonial, challenging us to harness Burkean concepts for the rhetorical analysis of colonialist texts and practices. As a result, she also represents a unique voice in this volume, given her focus upon the coopting of the Eastern world by the Western world. Drawing upon Burke's concept of the "bureaucratization of the imaginative," Selzer King demonstrates the symbolic, power-laden process whereby sacred oral practices are converted into religious doctrines—into *books*. She thereby traces the processes of transcendence engaged by Müller as he (re)constructs Eastern religious traditions for English readers. As Selzer King argues, the *Sacred Books of the East* thus functioned as an analogue and support to British colonialist practice. Its symbolic transcendence of Eastern religion was a necessary endeavor to ensure and facilitate economic and military domination. This, she argues, suggests the power of Burkean frameworks for the analysis of and engagement with colonialist rhetoric.

In chapter eight, Gregory Clark suggests the importance of Burke's third conception of transcendence. In "Transcendence After Dialogue," Clark asks a central question: How can we address our perspectival differences after reaching the limits of dialogue, or linguistic forms? Clark seeks in Burke's rhetorical writings a conception of transcendence that is not itself dependent upon dialogue, and he locates it precisely in the realm of the aesthetic. By tracing the connection between rhetoric and poetics, and between Burke and MacIntyre, Clark provides an argument for the rhetorical power of aesthetic experience. He draws heavily upon the importance of attitude, both in Burkean thought and in the aesthetic. Citing Burke's late essay on Emerson, Clark extends the discussion of transcendence to the realm of music and offers, as a case study, the "reluctant sextet." This anecdote demonstrates the transformative potential of one musical performance, an aesthetic transcendence that was possible despite the musicians' inability to reconcile their differences through dialogue. Although he recognizes the limitations attending such experiences, Clark sees in this example the potential for modes of mutual engagement and unity, even when language fails us.

If Clark's chapter suggests the power of reaching toward a "beyond," our final chapter, by Andrew King, underscores the dangers attending such practice. King's "Kenneth Burke and the Dark Side of Transcendence: Localism, Wendell Berry, and the New Southern Agrarians" echoes the entelechial critiques of industrialism and scientism that marked Burke's late work. King takes as his point of departure Burke's late essay on Emerson, but he reembeds this analysis within Emerson's original context, in arguments over the rising industrialization of England and New England. King ties these debates to those currently raging between industrial agriculture and the new agrarian movement, between capitalists and environmentalists. Through his

Burkean examination of Wendell Berry, King argues that we see in the new environmental movement a resurgence of the poetic, transcendence-filled insight of Burke and Emerson. King's call to join Berry offers us a final reflection that is also appropriate as an end to this chapter: "I would have people see humane farming practices, and I would have them experience the seeding and first emergence of a crop. That is, they need to experience the poetry of the earth. That would be an experience of transcendence worthy of our nature and responsibility as wordlings of this world, earthly bodies that learn language."

With that, I bid you happy reading.

NOTES

1. See, for example, his self-analysis of *Counter-Statement* in the preface to the second edition of the text: "one consideration fills me with unqualified delight. I refer to the fact that the book begins on the word 'perhaps' and ends on the word 'norm'" (Burke, 1968, p. xi).

2. As a result of my archival work in the Kenneth Burke Papers, I stumbled across Burke's early descriptions of the outline and content of *A Rhetoric of Motives*. At the time of the conference, I was developing an argument for reading this familiar book as a Platonic "Upward Way" (see Crable, 2009 for the published version of this argument).

3. For more on Burke's early years, including his aestheticist commitments and his work on the fractured and (at least somewhat) contradictory text, *Counter-Statement*, see Selzer (1996).

4. Here is where I differ somewhat from Zappen (2009), who does not distinguish between these two early works' treatment of transcendence (pp. 281–283). This is not to say that I believe that *Permanence and Change* and *Attitudes* are radically different; there is much that the two texts have in common. However, here I am simply pointing to the differences that make a difference—the features prompting Burke (1984), in later years, to call the two texts "companion volume[s]," and to also call *Attitudes Toward History* "not just a sequel, but in one respect an early revision of the first" (p. 377). Although my discussion of the differences between the texts differ from Burke's (at least in the Afterword, cited here), it is clear that he sees some significant differences of emphasis between these two early books.

5. Although this is not Burke's only mention of these terms, there are few points in the text where Burke discusses "upward" and "downward" transcendence. In two other places, Burke (1984a) specifically discusses these two variants of transcendence (pp. 106, 202) without invoking the comic frame—or the distinction between "true" and merely "verbal" transcendence. Finally, in his early discussion of the comic and the heroic, Burke contrasts the "upward" conversion, characteristic of the heroic, to the "downward" conversion of comedy (p. 43); but, he does not tie this discussion to questions of transcendence. Thus, although I would not overlook these other instances where Burke uses the term, I find that his discussion in the

"Dictionary of Pivotal Terms" signals the beginning of a transition toward a new conception of transcendence—one that is fully developed in *A Rhetoric of Motives*.

6. It is not exactly clear why Burke chooses to use the term "dialectical" for this order of terminology, especially since—at least in my reading—he clearly advocates for an ultimate vocabulary. Witness his clear caveat in discussing the difference between the second and third terministic orders: "The 'ultimate' order of terms would thus differ essentially from the 'dialectical' (as we use the term *in this particular connection*)" (Burke, 1969b, p. 187). He clearly makes a distinction between the Platonic-inspired, dialectical method of the text that includes all three orders of terminology and the dialectical order of terms.

7. For a compatible, but different, account of this discussion of transcendence, see Zappen (2009).

8. The design of this project underwent various permutations, and occupied Burke's attention for a number of years—yielding the manuscripts "Poetics, Dramatistically Considered" and "A Symbolic of Motives," as well as a number of essays collected elsewhere. Although a book-length version of this project has recently appeared (Burke, 2007), along with other portions of these manuscripts previously published (e.g., Burke, 2001a, 2001c), a unified volume of this material was not published during Burke's lifetime.

9. Elsewhere, Burke (1966) himself equates the terms transcendence and catharsis: "a Dramatistic approach to the analysis of language starts with the problems of terministic catharsis (which is another word for 'rebirth,' transcendence, transubstantiation, or simply for 'transformation' in the sense of the technically developmental . . .)" (p. 367). At other points, as in the essay on Emerson, Burke indicates that catharsis and transcendence are not synonymous: they indicate different dimensions of human symbol-use. It is not surprising, then, that he admits to indecision over the two terms in an extended "comment" written for *Language as Symbolic Action*:

> I must admit that the realms covered by the two terms considerably overlap. And both in previous works and later in essays included here, I have sometimes used one of the terms where I might as well have used the other. (p. 97)

Burke's inconsistency regarding these two concepts, I argue, reflects both his struggle to arrive at a satisfactory definition of the terms and his publication of (occasionally contradictory) portions of the unfinished *Symbolic* material.

10. This is not, of course, the only place in Burke's later writings where we find examples of earlier conceptions of transcendence. For instance, a version of his first definition of transcendence appears in this analysis of Henry Adams: "His ironic search for a new 'family' identity involved a figurative enrollment in a world of mechanisms that, though produced by persons, added up to a transcending of the personal (albeit by a kind of transcendence downward)" (Burke, 2003, p. 256). We also see citation of the Platonic dialectic—the production of transcendence through the Upward and Downward Ways—in many of Burke's later works (e.g., Burke, 1966, p. 96; 1967, pp. 63–64; 1970, pp. 8, 37, 254, 303; 2003, p. 244; 2007, pp.

23, 25–27). Some of this can be explained as the publication of material written at different points during Burke's decades-long work on *Symbolic*—thus reflecting the changes in Burke's understanding of transcendence. Yet, I would also suggest that Burke's third conception of the term does not so much reject these earlier versions as re-contextualize them within a more foundational account of the origin and nature of transcendence. On this view, there is no reason to eliminate these earlier versions of transcendence. Instead, one must simply ground them within a more holistic, more synoptic conception of the term.

11. We might even speculate that these transcendence-fueled meditations (i.e., the analyses of logology) began to consume a greater portion of Burke's attention in later years—leading to his difficulty in completing the project of the *Symbolic* (Williams, 2001, pp. 15–16).

References

Brock, B., Burke, K., Burgess, P. G., & Simons, H. W. (1985). Dramatism as ontology or epistemology: A symposium. *Communication Quarterly, 33*(1), 17–33.

Burke, K. (1966). *Language as symbolic action*. Berkeley, CA: University of California Press.

Burke, K. (1967). Rhetoric—old and new. In M. Steinmann, Jr. (Ed.), *New rhetorics* (pp. 59–76). New York, NY: Scribner's Sons.

Burke, K. (1968). *Counter-statement*. Berkeley, CA: University of California Press. (Original work published 1931)

Burke, K. (1969a). *A grammar of motives*. Berkeley, CA: University of California Press. (Original work published 1945)

Burke, K. (1969b). *A rhetoric of motives*. Berkeley, CA: University of California Press. (Original work published 1950)

Burke, K. (1970). *The rhetoric of religion: Studies in logology*. Berkeley, CA: University of California Press. (Original work published 1961)

Burke, K. (1972). *Dramatism and development*. Barre, MA: Clark University Press.

Burke, K. (1973). *The philosophy of literary form: Studies in symbolic action* (3rd ed.). Berkeley, CA: University of California Press. (Original work published 1941)

Burke, K. (1978). Questions and answers about the pentad. *College Composition and Communication, 19*, 330–335.

Burke, K. (1984a). *Attitudes toward history* (3rd ed.). Berkeley, CA: University of California Press. (Original work published 1937)

Burke, K. (1984b). *Permanence and change* (3rd ed.). Berkeley, CA: University of California Press. (Original work published 1935)

Burke, K. (2001a). "Glimpses into a labyrinth of interwoven motives": Selections from "A symbolic of motives." In G. Henderson & D. C. Williams (Eds.), *Unending conversations: New writings by and about Kenneth Burke* (pp. 81–98). Carbondale, IL: Southern Illinois University Press.

Burke, K. (2001b). Sensation, memory, imitation/and story. In G. Henderson & D. C. Williams (Eds.), *Unending conversations: New writings by and about Kenneth Burke* (pp. 202–205). Carbondale, IL: Southern Illinois University Press.

Burke, K. (2001c). "Watchful of hermetics to be strong in hermeneutics": Selections from "Poetics, dramatistically considered." In G. Henderson & D. C. Williams (Eds.), *Unending conversations: New writings by and about Kenneth Burke* (pp. 35–80). Carbondale, IL: Southern Illinois University Press.

Burke, K. (2003). *On human nature: A gathering while everything flows, 1967–1984.* W. H. Rueckert & A. Bonadonna (Eds.). Berkeley, CA: University of California Press.

Burke, K. (2007). *Essays toward a symbolic of motives, 1950–1955.* W. H. Rueckert (Ed.). West Lafayette, IN: Parlor Press.

Crable, B. (2000). Burke's perspective on perspectives: Grounding dramatism in the representative anecdote. *The Quarterly Journal of Speech, 86,* 318–333.

Crable, B. (2009). Distance as ultimate motive: A dialectical interpretation of *A Rhetoric of Motives. Rhetoric Society Quarterly, 39,* 213–239.

George, A., & Selzer, J. (2007). *Kenneth Burke in the 1930s.* Columbia, SC: University of South Carolina Press.

Rueckert, W. H. (1982). *Kenneth Burke and the drama of human relations* (2nd ed.). Berkeley, CA: University of California Press.

Rueckert, W. H. (2001). Kenneth Burke's "Symbolic of motives" and "Poetics, dramatistically considered." In G. Henderson & D C. Williams (Eds.), *Unending conversations: New writings by and about Kenneth Burke* (pp. 99–124). Carbondale, IL: Southern Illinois University Press.

Selzer, J. (1996). *Kenneth Burke in Greenwich Village: Conversing with the moderns, 1915–1931.* Madison, WI: University of Wisconsin Press.

Thames, R. H. (2007). The Gordian not: Untangling the *Motivorum. KB Journal, 3*(2). Retrieved from http://www.kbjournal.org/spring2007

Weiser, M. E. (2008). *Burke, war, words: Rhetoricizing dramatism.* Columbia, SC: University of South Carolina Press.

Wess, R. (2007). Looking for the figure in the carpet of the *Symbolic of Motives. KB Journal, 3*(2). Retrieved from http://www.kbjournal.org/spring2007

Williams, D. C. (2001). Toward rounding out the *Motivorum Trilogy*: A textual introduction. In G. Henderson & D. C. Williams (Eds.), *Unending conversations: New writings by and about Kenneth Burke* (pp. 3–34). Carbondale, IL: Southern Illinois University Press.

Zappen, J. P. (2009). Kenneth Burke on dialectical-rhetorical transcendence. *Philosophy & Rhetoric, 42,* 279–301.

1 RACE RITUAL, THEN AND NOW: BRIDGING THE TRANSCENDENTAL DIALECTICS OF KENNETH BURKE, RALPH ELLISON, AND BARACK OBAMA

John S. Wright

In a passage in his 1995 memoir, *Dreams from My Father: A Story of Race and Inheritance*, published a decade before announcing his campaign for the U.S. presidency, the then-little-known Illinois state senator, Barack Obama, presented a retrospective reading of his decision in 1983 to set graduate school at Harvard aside and instead become a community organizer in Chicago. Those few of his readers familiar by happenstance with Kenneth Burke's psychology of symbolic action would have recognized in that passage an uncanny, if unintentional, echo of Burke's trigonometric theory of literary expression as "dream, prayer, and chart."[1] Obama (1995, 2004) addressed an audience to whom he was presumably a stranger, but one with whom he sought more intimate identification; he confessed:

> At the time, I was operating mainly on impulse, like a salmon swimming blindly upstream toward the site of his own conception. In classes and seminars, I would dress up these impulses in the slogans and theories that I'd discovered in books, thinking—falsely—that the slogans meant something, that they somehow made what I felt more amenable to proof. But at night, lying in bed, I would let the slogans drift away, to be replaced with a series of images, romantic images, of a past I had never known.

They were of the civil rights movement, mostly, the grainy black-and-white footage that appears every February during Black History Month, the same images that my mother had offered me as a child. A pair of college students, hair short, backs straight, placing their orders at a lunch counter teetering on the edge of riot. SNCC workers standing on a porch in some Mississippi backwater trying to convince a family of sharecroppers to register to vote. A country jail bursting with children, their hands clasped together, singing freedom songs.

Such images became a form of prayer for me, bolstering my spirits, channeling my emotions in a way that words never could. They told me (although even this much understanding may have come later, is also a construct, containing its own falsehoods) that I wasn't alone in my particular struggles, and that communities had never been a given in this country, at least not for blacks. Communities had to be created, fought for, tended like gardens. They expanded or contracted with the dreams of men—and in the civil rights movement those dreams had been large. In the sit-ins, the marches, the jailhouse songs, I saw the African-American community becoming more than just the place where you'd been born or the house where you'd been raised. Through organizing, through shared sacrifice, membership had been earned. And because membership was earned—because this community I imagined was still in the making, built on the promise that the larger American community, black, white, and brown, could somehow redefine itself—I believed that it might, over time, admit the uniqueness of my own life.

That was my idea of organizing. It was a promise of redemption. (pp. 134–135)

That the rhetorical dream, prayer, and chart of Barack Obama's life as "construct" funnels into a "promise of redemption" makes the case for a Burkean approach to Obama's memoir even more compelling, inasmuch as sacrificial rituals of redemption through suffering and victimage provide a recurring motif in Burke's life-long preoccupation with the rhetorics of politics and religion. In Obama's autobiographical prose, the symbols of companionate suffering, of secular struggle converted to prayer, of utopian social dreams and consecrated song, and of a unifying community and order won through partisan sacrifice at the brink of chaos, all move toward consummation via what Burke has taught us is less a *promise* than a *process* of redemption. Such a process is keyed to the ritual unburdening of sin and evil, techniques of personal and social purification, the "perfecting" of a human vessel "worthy" of sacrifice, and—by perverse irony—the "Cult of the Kill."

Burke's (1961) text *The Rhetoric of Religion* uses the Bible's *Book of Genesis* (*Genesis*) and St. Augustine's *Confessions* to probe the uses of theological terminology. In the introduction, Burke provides a poetic capsule of his view of human history and the role of victimage within it:

> Here are the steps
> In the Iron Law of History
> That welds Order and Sacrifice:
> Order leads to Guilt
> (for who can keep commandments!)
> Guilt needs Redemption
> (for who would not be cleansed!)
> Redemption needs a Redeemer
> (which is to say, a Victim!).
> Order
> Through Guilt
> To Victimage
> (hence: Cult of the Kill) . . . (pp. 4–5)

"If we are right in what we take the Creation Myth in Genesis to be saying," Burke (1961) conjectured, "then the contemporary world must doubly fear the cyclical compulsions of Empire, as two mighty world orders, each homicidally armed to the point of suicide, confront each other" (p. 4). Writing these words at the height of Cold War machinations, he offered a clear diagnosis of relations between the U.S. and the U.S.S.R.: each is beset with anxiety, blames all its troubles on the other, and feels certain that if the other and its tendencies were but eliminated, all Disorder that goes with Order would be eliminated. In an explicit application of "transcendence by perspective," Burke proposes "to replace the present political stress upon men in rival international situations by a 'logological' reaffirmation of the foibles and quandaries that all men (in their role as 'symbol-using animals') have in common" (p. 5).

In elaborating this approach, Burke (1961) differentiates what he famously termed the "Upward Way," as opposed to the "Downward Way," of transcendence—a strategy of "mortification" or self-victimization, as opposed to a strategy of "scapegoating" through principles of externalizing sin and evil (p. 37). Part of what this chapter proposes is that, to the extent to which then-candidate and now-President Barack Obama has himself become a populist symbol of trans-racial "transcendence," he has done so by employing in autobiographical and campaign rhetoric a principle of "logological substitution." This principle is akin to Burke's extrapolations from Genesis: a "sacrificial" and "redemptive" substitution in which the compulsions of opposing black and white "races" replace those of two "world orders," and in which the "us versus them" antitheses of ritual scapegoating are instead introjected or internalized in the resolving, unifying "uniqueness" of Obama's trans-racial, transcontinental cosmology. In both Burke's and Obama's redemptive forays against binary politics and consciousness, though, the inevitable ambivalences entailed are mediated with "comic correctives" and "methodologies of debunking" that, on reflection, we see dramatized decades earlier—in the public and private dialogues Burke had engaged in, starting in the 1940s, with African American novelist and man-of-letters, Ralph Ellison. What is offered in this chapter is set of "bridging devices" or "symbolic mergers," in Burke's (1959) terms, that shift our angle of vision or "perspective," connect these objects of attention that are otherwise "not in line," and enable us to "transcend" dislocation (pp. 224–225).

THE REEMERGENCE OF TRANSCENDENCE

Given the perennial possibilities of the problem of the One-and-the-Many in American social and intellectual life, Burke's conceptual uses of "transcendence" and "perspective" in his long-strategic war against the tyranny of binary thinking, decision-making, and policy formulation should be happy allies in all our efforts—scholarly and otherwise—to create unity and community out of division. Transcendence and perspective are tools for conceptualizing alternative *points of view, worldviews,* and *visions* we need to confront in both the disconcertingly ephemeral and in the seemingly eternal antagonisms that bedevil our private and public lives. These are the same antagonisms that conspire to keep "us," and all the manifold "others" with whom we contend, in malingering states of active or immanent armed and unarmed conflict.

Academic concerns very rarely find themselves at the cusp or "cutting edge" of popular enthusiasm and public consciousness, or in the workaday lexicon of the proverbial man and woman on the street. The wonder of wonders, "transcendence," *is*, however, in the workaday air, on the airways, in newsprint, and on the Internet; it bubbles up in church pews, classrooms, talk radio, "reality TV," mass media punditry, street corner conversations, poetry slams, cartoons, and standup comedy routines. Probably not since the days of Ralph Emerson, Bronson Alcott, Margaret Fuller, and Henry Thoreau and company has "transcendence" spilled so profusely from American lips and tongues. Though the *Oxford English Dictionary* tracks the first appearance of "transcend" back to the early fourteenth century as a transitive verb meaning "to pass or go beyond (*physical* obstacles or limits)," "transcendence" seems to have surfaced at the outset of the sixteenth in the second act of *All's Well That Ends Well*, in lines concerning "a most weake-/And debile minister. [Of] great power, great/transcendence," whose *abilities* have enabled him to surmount or rise above his weakness and *debility* to a level of surpassing eminence and excellence (Shakespeare, trans. 2001, 2.3.34-36). In the hands of Immanuel Kant and the far-flung devotees of his brand of German Idealism, by the early nineteenth century, fine metaphysical distinctions are drawn between the *transcendent*, the *transcendental*, and the *immanent*—distinctions important to philosophers and theologians, but, since beyond the realm of human experience and cognition, are peripheral to ordinary discourse down below.

It is a wonder *beyond* wonders that this second coming of transcendence should be yoked so heavily to the *first* coming of an African American presidential candidate—a tall, lanky, close-cropped, black-white former professor of constitutional law. He is the abandoned son of an African immigrant and a contra-conventional, white Midwestern American anthropologist, an immigrant's son matured trans-continentally in Hawaii, Indonesia, and Chicago. Though never a Muslim, he was named first for what Sufi mystics call "grace" or "enlightenment," and second, for the most revered and storied of Muslim martyrs. After a rootless and unsurprisingly prodigal youth, he displayed a miraculous motivational turnabout, one that led ultimately to his becoming the first black president of the *Harvard Law Review* and a lucre-denying novitiate as a community organizer in a South-Side Chicago still haunted by the ghost of Bigger Thomas. Barack Hussein Obama next imbibed from Martin Luther King Jr.'s Christian call to action "the fierce urgency of now," and enlisted triumphantly, if serendipitously, in the bruising fray of Chicago machine politics. In the warp-speed space of four years, Obama beamed up from the obscurity of the Illinois state House to the U.S. Senate, moved on to a galvanizing speech at the 2004 Democratic National Convention, followed up with a historic presidential primary campaign that was witnessed by a rapt, global audience. As told by himself in his memoir—and re-fashioned now by legions of multimedia journalists—that framing story has become much too familiar in its details to bear repeating here. It is the less-plumbed *inner logic*—and its resonances across the humanities and social sciences, as well as its entanglement in the history of myth and ritual—that I want to ponder and wrestle somehow into a Burkean and Ellisonian perspective.

As Garrison Keillor (2008), "Lake Wobegon's" roving wordsmith, raptly notes in the Minneapolis/St. Paul newspaper, the *Start Tribune*, five months before Election Day, we "are all staring at Barack Obama, who is . . . a commanding presence," a Duke Ellington for modern times (p. OP5). Keillor had witnessed first-hand (along with twenty thousand others) the speech Obama gave in St. Paul, claiming victory in his protracted primary contest with Hillary Clinton for the Democratic nomination. If the *Prairie Home Companion*'s "Old Scout" speaks at all for so-called ordinary Americans, his awareness of the problem of how to frame a perspective on the Obama phenomenon is worth noting: "[T]he man can give a speech," he announces, adding that "Nobody else surfs on applause like Obama and drives his point home, and it all sounds as if he were telling you what he [actually] thinks and not reading off a Plexiglas reflector. . . . When you look closely at him he is a skinny young black guy . . . some will not get past what they see" (p. OP5). What, precisely, are we looking at? Disarmingly astute and wryly aware of our social history, but unschooled in the terminology of Burkean rhetorics and grammars, Keillor attempts to frame an answer this way:

> The year my father graduated from high school, Duke Ellington toured the country with his 15-piece orchestra, playing his hits "Mood Indigo" and "Don't Get Around Much Anymore" and "It Don't Mean a Thing (If It Ain't Got That Swing)" to ballrooms packed with fans; but things being what they were, they traveled in a private railroad car because you just never knew if you could get a hotel room *or* a meal in a restaurant or be turned away by some jerk in a suit and tie.
>
> They were all black, but Juan Tizol, the trombonist, was fairly light-skinned and had to wear blackface so nobody would think the band was integrated.
>
> Ellington didn't complain. He loved his work and he was cool and he didn't deign to address bigotry—he just played right through it.
>
> That era is not so distant. A culture doesn't turn on a dime. Race is a part of this race, even though nobody wants to think so. But Obama has gifts that transcend race and his own slim résumé. On the radio he is an orator resurrected from a distant time when people had higher standards for that sort of thing. He is graceful and quick and possessed of confidence, and if you like the English language you'll find a lot to admire in him. (p. OP5)

About the "Current Occupant," Keillor writes:

> whenever *he* steps up to the podium, public confidence drops like a rock. He's not a leader, he's just a regular feller. I know plenty of regular fellers, some smarter than others, and at the moment I am lean-

ing toward Obama. He has those gifts and when he launches forth against the dismal darkness of recent Republicanism, he is throwing nothing but strikes. (p. OP5)

Addressing the same Obama happening, a local African American newspaper laid out its front-page coverage with a huge, full-color photograph of the triumphant candidate onstage, microphone in one hand nestled beneath his chin, his the other hand raised in elegant gesticulation. Above the photograph, instead of a conventional, front-page feature title, ellipsis dots appeared, and were followed by a single, unmodified, decontextualized, bold-faced, floating signifier: TRANSCENDENCE. The black newspaper proceeded to flesh out this visible breach of the "who/what/when/why/where" "tagging" desideratum with a detailed, socio-historical elaboration for its readers of just why Obama's ascendancy represented a "moment of transformation" as well as a "moment of transcendence." Yet, Keillor's missive in the mainstream organ offered potentially deeper insights into the workings of the myth and ritual at hand, and of the trappings of "Obamamania" that had already configured this still largely opaque "trans-racial" man-of-words and politics into a contemporary, brown-skinned, heavenly, sky god and "solar hero"—one battling the underworld's dragons of darkness and division on behalf of a potentially "post-racial" New World Order, a revitalized American Dream, and "a more perfect union."

The processes—political, rhetorical, and mytho-poetic—by which human beings fabricate for ourselves images of such rising hero-leaders were objects of perhaps even greater fascination and analysis seven decades ago, in 1939. Then, in the depths of the Great Depression, the forty-year-old Burke—early in his on-and-off occupation as critic—and the twenty-four year old Ellison—an even more spottily employed aspiring writer-musician and recent Oklahoma migrant to New York City—first came into contact. They shared an investment in leftist political circles, where consternation over the Spanish Civil War and the rise of Nazi Germany mingled routinely with reverberations from the trial of the Scottsboro Boys and the grotesqueries of lynchings and race riots in the Jim Crow Southern *and* Northern precincts of the United States.

BRIDGING BURKE AND WRIGHT

From the outset, the encounters between Burke and Ellison pertaining to matters of transcendence and perspective pertained also to matters of race—and entailed the kind of collision of opposing points of view that Burke was then trying, *by definition*, to address. Two years after he had created a stir in Stalinist/Trotskyite circles at the 1935 First American

Writers' Congress in New York City, with the irreverently heterodox essay, "Revolutionary Symbolism in America," Burke (1937) published *Attitudes Toward History*, in which his "Dictionary of Pivotal Terms" included an entry on "Transcendence" that began in this now famous way:

> When approached from a certain point of view, A and B are "opposites." We mean by "transcendence" the adoption of another point of view from which they cease to be opposites. This is, at present, the nearest approach we can make to the process by verbal means. (p. 336)

Earlier in his dictionary, he had defined a particular kind of perspective, "perspective by incongruity," as "a method for gauging situations by verbal 'atom cracking.' That is, a word belongs to a certain category—and by rational planning you wrench it loose and metaphorically apply it to another category" (p. 308). This perspective by incongruity, or "planned incongruity," this "methodology of the *pun*," he said, enables one to interpret new situations by the "transcendence" of a "new start" that removes words from their "constitutional" settings.

If Burke's manner of applying his methodology had disconcerted the audience of "Revolutionary Symbolism," the 1939 audience for his lecture, "The Rhetoric of Hitler's 'Battle,'" found his methods no less problematic—save for listeners like young Ellison, who was introduced into this milieu by his new mentors: Richard Wright, a card-carrying Party member; Langston Hughes, a "fellow traveler." Burke's (1941b) approach to Hitler's newly translated autobiography, *Mein Kampf*, appealed to Ellison immediately. Several years before, in *Counter-Statement*, Burke had suggested, heretically, that changes of consciousness and the force of corollary aesthetics precede and ultimately determine political or economic outcomes—that symbols dictate actions. In 1939, when Burke's audience was inclined to simply dismiss Adolf Hitler's memoirs out of hand, Burke argued instead that a rigorous new kind of dissection was mandatory: "Our job is to find all available ways of making the Hitlerite distortions of religion apparent, in order that politicians of his kind in America be unable to perform a similar swindle" (p. 191).

By interpreting the symbolic patterns and actions in the Führer's anti-Semitic fantasies, Burke revealed how the Nazi cultural apparatus fused patriotic with religious symbolism to make ritual scapegoats of Jews, while at the same time submerging the economic forces driving the German nation fearfully toward wholesale panic. Drawing on recent Cambridge School studies of cult ritual and myth in primitive societies, Burke (1941b) demonstrates persuasively how Hitler manipulated *modern* anti-Jewish prejudice to promote Aryan national unification via "a fictitious devil function, gradually made convincing by the sloganizing repetitiousness of standard advertising techniques" (pp. 193–196). The seemingly opposed insights of Marx and Freud could be "transcended" via Burke's dislocating perspective, and he quotes extensively from Freud's *Totem and Taboo* to explain how Hitler, like a primitive or a paranoid, cast Jews in the form of an omnipotent, *economic* monster whose power over the political economy had to be crushed. As an example of "persecution mania," Hitler's life story functions rhetorically as a manifesto of race redemption and as the sacrificial dismemberment and expulsion of national enemies.

While hoboing his way to Tuskeegee College on railroad trains, Ellison himself came perilously close to the deadly "lynch law" predicament in which four black hoboes his own age had found themselves in nearby Scottsboro, Alabama a few years earlier. As a student, Ellison shared Tuskeegee's campus-wide outrage over the subsequent Scottsboro trial and the gruesome, public lynching in 1934 of a black man named Claude Neale. Underscoring this outrage was the active and passive complicity of state officials from Alabama and Florida in Neale's ritualistic torture, mutilation, and dismemberment. The suggested pertinence and potential power of mounting a Burkean analysis on home turf in America was incontrovertible to Ellison, as he later acknowledged. Of particular importance for his work on *Invisible Man* during the following decade, Ellison gleaned from "The Rhetoric of Hitler's 'Battle'" how heroic myth can mask pathological leadership in beams of sunlight and high-flung hopes. The Führer's book quickly became "the well of Nazi magic"; and the sky-god rhetoric of Hitler's dragon-battle for Aryan ascendancy revealed how a man of self-described "domineering apostolic nature" could insinuate the appealing logic and symbolic ritual of heroic "solar" biography into a quest for naked political power (Burke, 1941b, pp. 191–220).[2]

For all the explanatory power and experiential appeal of Burke's analytic modes of transcendence and perspective, Ellison's conceptual allegiance was pulled just as powerfully toward a competing point of view about the need for "transcendence by perspective" that Ricard Wright was busy formulating at almost precisely the same moment Burke's major statements on the matter had appeared. In the summer of 1937, a few weeks before *Attitudes Toward History* was published, Wright (1937) released, in the black radical journal *New Challenge*, a manifesto essay called "Blueprint for Negro Writing." The essay vaulted Wright into national notoriety to stake his own claim for intellectual leadership among African American writers and critics. A searing indictment of the "so-called Harlem School" of the 1920s for their alleged lack of intellectual discipline and political responsibility, Wright's "Blueprint" ratified the Sixth Communist International proposition of 1928 that "Negroes" in the United States constituted a nation within a nation, with a much misunderstood *revolutionary* imperative.

Though not explicitly hostile to Burke, Wright's conceptualization of the modes of transcendence and perspective most appropriate to black writers veered in alternative directions. Wright was a self-taught literary intellectual who was aggressively cosmopolitan and encyclopedic, despite his lack of formal schooling—not unlike Burke in that regard. As a result, Wright was similarly difficult to categorize: he was energetically modernist, a heterodox Marxist at best, and a defiant "Negro nationalist" who repudiated "specious and blatant nationalism." At the same time, he heretically toyed with the counter-conventional theory that an American class revolution could be successfully envisioned and carried out only with a black vanguard that had *transcended* the divisions between orthodox Marxist theories of class consciousness and Black nationalist prognostication. Wright (1978) insisted that

> the emotional expression of group-feeling which puzzles so many whites and leads them to deplore what they call "black chauvinism" is not a morbidly inherent trait of the Negro but rather the reflex expression of a life whose roots are imbedded deeply in Southern soil. . . . [Black writers] must *accept* the nationalist implications of their lives, not in order to encourage them, but in order to change and transcend them. They must *accept* the concept of nationalism because, in order to transcend it, they must possess and understand it. And a nationalist spirit in Negro writing means a nationalism carrying the highest pitch of social consciousness. (p. 42)

The possibilities and methodologies of transcendence, for Wright, lay not in the verbal "atom cracking" of Burkean "perspective by incongruity" (1959, pp. 308-311), but in the recovery and development of what Wright exalted as a "whole" sense of culture and tradition in an "organic," synthesizing, *transhistorical*, memory-bearing, potentially visionary power:

> What *vision* must Negro writers have before their eyes in order to feel the impelling necessity for an about face? What *angle* of vision can show them all the forces of modern society in process, all the lines of economic development converging toward a distant point of hope? (p. 45)

Rather than being framed as a linguistic procedure, analytical device, or method, "perspective," Wright (1978) insisted,

> is that part of a poem, novel, or play which a writer never puts directly upon paper. It is that fixed point in intellectual space where

a writer stands to view the struggles, hopes, and sufferings of his people. There are times when he may stand too close and the result is a blurred vision. Or he may stand too far away and the result is a neglect of important things. Of all the problems faced by writers who as a whole have never allied themselves with world movements, *perspective* is the most difficult of achievement. At its best, perspective is a *pre-conscious* assumption, something which a writer takes for granted, something which he wins through his *living.* (pp. 45–46)

Congenitally a rebel himself against literary formula and "programs," Wright (1978) was careful to emphasize that he did *not* mean that a black writer's sole concern must be with rendering the social scene, or that his or her choice of theme would be diminished: "In speaking of theme one must necessarily be general and abstract; the temperament of each writer molds and colors the world he sees, Negro life may be approached from a *thousand* angles, with *no limit* to technical and stylistic freedom" (pp. 46–47). Rather, what he did mean was that black

> writers spring from a family, a clan, a class, and a nation; and the social units in which they are bound have a story, a record. Sense of theme will emerge in Negro writing when Negro writers try to fix this story about some pole of meaning, remembering as they do so that in the creative process meaning proceeds equally as much from the contemplation of the subject matter as from the hopes and apprehensions that rage in the heart of the writer. (pp. 46–47)

Viewed in *this* perspective, for Negro writers, theme

> would rise from understanding the meaning of being transplanted from a "savage" to a "civilized" culture in all of its social, political, economic, and emotional implications. . . . [Black writers] must have in their consciousness the foreshortened picture of the *whole*, nourishing culture from which they were torn in Africa, and of the long, complex (and for the most part, unconscious) struggle to regain in some form and under alien conditions of life a *whole* culture again. (pp. 104-105)

As a direct extension of perspective, then, theme for black writers emerges "when they have begun to *feel* the meaning of the history of their race as though they in one life time had lived it themselves throughout all the long centuries" (Wright, 1978, p. 47).

Ultimately, Wright's approach to the problem of perspective was operationally *hermeneutic*, like Wilhelm Dilthey's mode of *recovery*, rather than *heuristic,* like Burke's mode of *discovery.* It was rooted in two of the three primary kinds of transforming perception that M. H. Abrams (1971) argues were bequeathed to twentieth century thinkers by nineteenth century Romantics. The first kind entailed seeing through revitalized eyes—the eyes of an oracle, a clairvoyant, a holy madman, or even a child (Abrams, 1971, pp. 375–377). Wright (1978) termed this "the complexity, the strangeness, the magic wonder of life that plays like a bright sheen" over both the familiar and the sordid, a kind of perception crystallized existentially in the world of black oral tradition and the vernacular (p. 50). Achieving the second kind of transformational perception means cultivating acts of trans-historical consciousness or epiphany, similar to William Wordsworth's "spots of time," in which otherwise ordinary human events and objects become charged with *extra*ordinary significance. Instead, Burke's way represented a modernized third mode of transformative romanticist perception: that of perceiving objects, beings, symbols, or situations as invested with values different from or opposed to those accorded by custom—values that were somehow reversible, as Burke's definition of transcendence made explicit. In "Blueprint for Negro Writing," however, only a brief appeal to verbal oxymoron (life's "complex simplicity") left visible traces of this modality on Wright's competing schema for transcendence by perspective.

The journey from here to the extraordinary, interlinking achievements of Burke and Ellison during the next decade must be greatly foreshortened to keep a focus on the Obama phenomenon from fading irrecoverably. To that end, I advance two questions about the cognitive dissonance "between a [philosophical] hard place and a rock" that Ralph Ellison found himself in while trying to choose between the enormously appealing but opposing perspectival possibilities that Kenneth Burke and Richard Wright set before him at the outset of his literary career. First, how might—or how *did*—he resolve this pull of allegiances (both personal and philosophical) to put himself on a unified and independent creative path over the course of the following decade, toward the creation of his masterwork, *Invisible Man*? Second, how does that (in Burke's words) "epoch-making" book, one that *Book Week* declared "the most distinguished novel since World War II" (Graham & Mack, 2004, p. 40), reflect the influence of two contending forms of "transcendence by perspective"?

ELLISON'S *INVISIBLE MAN* AS LEADER AND HERO

The weight of scholarly opinion, formulated over the course of half a century, views that Ellison chose to abandon his allegiances to radical racial chauvinism, ethnic nationalism, and his mentor, Wright, in favor of the aesthetically richer and more cosmopolitan and "universal" possibilities represented by Burke. Indeed, outside of Burke's own experiments in fiction, in the eyes of many (including Ellison himself) *Invisible Man* became what may well be the most "Burkean" American novel of all. As early as Irving Howe's (1963) famous essay, "Black Boys and Native Sons," Ellison and James Baldwin—putative "sons" of father-figure Wright—were accused of Oedipal disloyalties to, and precipitous defection from, Wright's generative naturalistic style and political outlook. In relegating Wright to the status of racial "relative" rather than literary "ancestor" in his famous rebuttal to Howe, "The World and the Jug," Ellison made the apparent apostasy more emphatic. "Wright influenced me *not* to be influenced," Ellison quipped on one public occasion caught on film.[3]

The entanglement is not so summarily resolved. Burke (1955) always counseled readers toward what he considered to be a healthy "intellectual mistrust" of easy solutions to entrenched dilemmas. In his poem "Dialectician's Prayer," and also in his doxology, Burke shows precisely how Ellison or any other worshiper of words might "pray" his or her way out of a perspectival quandary:

> Hail to Thee, Logos,
> Thou Vast Almighty Title,
> In whose name we conjure—
> May we compete with one another,
> To speak for Thy Creation with more justice—
> Coöperating in this competition
> Until our naming
> Gives voice correctly,
> And how things are,
> And how we say things are
> Are one. (pp. 39–40)

According to Burke's doxological prayer—public pronouncements and critical contentions not withstanding—Ellison did not abandon his allegiance to Richard Wright's modes of transcendence and trans-historical perspective. On the contrary, with the help of Burke's "perspective by incongruity," Ellison discovered a way *out* of "either/or" *to* "both/and" and to *antagonistic-cooperation*. When completed and published in 1952, *Invisible Man* abounded with evidence of *this* strategic and transcendent maneuvering.

Although Burke and Ellison would not meet until late 1942, Ellison had come to believe, with Burke, well *before* embarking on his novelistic experiment, that race relations and the "race war" Wright depicted so powerfully in *Uncle Tom's Children* (1938) and *Native Son* (1941) were captive to the trained incapacity of most Americans to see and imagine alternative ways of *sharing* social space and material resources. In *Permanence and Change*, Burke's (1935/1984) evolving "dramatistic" explorations of Order, Property, Guilt, Redemption, and Victimage led him (and subsequently, Ellison) to construe the "scapegoat mechanism" visited by Poor Whites upon Negroes as a function of such trained incapacity (p. 16). That incapacity could be remediated or reversed only through perspective by incongruity capable of shattering and reorienting the limiting visions and "methodical misnamings" of social possibility (Burke, 1935/1984, p. 69). In social praxis, perspective by incongruity functions as a magical but nonetheless utilitarian process that Burke associates with certain "kinds of hermeticism," with "logonomical purgatory," with the "realm of 'gargoyles,'" and with the rituals of exorcism (p. 69). Cultivating perspectives by incongruity in American society's then cross-racial tangle of psychosocial motives required a heightened receptiveness to jarringly new orientations and apprehensions. In the shifting landscapes of his projected ideas for a novel, Ellison struggled to balance the "purely rational or intellectualistic elements" against the "deep emotionality of the search for [such] new meanings" (Burke, 1935/1984, pp. 69–70).

Therefore, it made "logological" sense that what Ellison (1982) called the "psychogenesis" of *Invisible Man*, came through a World War II furlough's tonic state of "hyper-receptivity" (p. xiii). In the evolving social science of the era, it was a sociological truism that that African Americans' troubles sprang from their "high visibility" (p. xiii). Then at work on an ill-conceived war novel, Ellison, suddenly and intuitively, linked his war-weary shard of faith that somehow "war could, with art, be transformed into something more meaningful than its surface violence" (p. xiv), to an inner voice that brooded over the painful joke of black soldiers fighting for freedom in a war effort designed to return them home unfree. Echoing Burke's *heuristic* methodology of the pun and *counter*-statement, the voice proclaimed ecstatically, "I am an *invisible* man." Ellison's imaginative leap was an emphatic "logonomic rebuttal" that sprung out of Burke's creative heuristic—a punning perspective by *un*planned incongruity—that further spurred Ellison (1974) to abandon his *planned* war novel for a highly experimental, panoramic, and picaresque fictional "memoir" obsessed more broadly, as its author had become,

> with the nature of leadership, and thus with the nature of the hero . . . [and] with the question of just why our Negro leadership was never able to enforce its will. Just what was there about American society that kept Negroes from throwing up effective leaders? (pp. 185–186)

At the time, that despairing question was forced into the foreground of Ellison's consciousness at circumstances surrounding the famous March on Washington. This was *not* the March on Washington in 1963, at which Martin King, Jr. delivered his transfixing "I Have a Dream" speech at the foot of the Lincoln Memorial; it was the original, threatened-but-called-off March on Washington in 1941, organized by A. Philip Randolph and a fractious coalition of internally warring secular and religious leaders from the black Freedom Movement. The event was designed to put the heat of 100,000 black marchers on Franklin Delano Roosevelt unless he ended unfair labor practices, discrimination in the World War II industrial sector, and Jim Crow's rule in the U. S. military.

In other words, Ellison was not merely meditating on history, trans-historically or otherwise. He was conceptualizing against a backdrop of *real world* historical *action* and of *living* historical actors—some heroic, some not—while simultaneously dissecting Lord Raglan's (1956) path-breaking book, *The Hero: A Study in Tradition, Myth, and Drama*. With Raglan's guidance, Ellison explored the mythic and ritual substructure of American caste codes and political culture, focusing upon the conscious and unconscious "race ritual" that ranged across a spectrum of institutionalized behaviors—from the most violent and grotesque (lynching) to the most officially polite. His explorations yielded, as a narrative embryo and "representative anecdote," the barbaric high school graduation ritual undergone by a young, would-be orator and leader-of-his-people in the "Battle Royal" tale. Understanding Ellison's fictive and phenomenological imperatives, though, requires elucidating one of Ellison's own pivotal terms, "race ritual."

RACE RITUAL, THEN AND NOW

"Race ritual" remains a topic as yet neither indexed nor defined in standard reference books, bibliographies, or lexicons in the humanities or social sciences. Instead, it has housed itself in the vernacular process that Ellison theorized about as an unofficial fourth estate (Ellison, 1966, p. 99). Race ritual became a pivotal, extra-academic tool of cultural analysis for Ellison; his extrapolations drew upon the cross-cultural studies of myth and ritual by the "Cambridge Ritualists," Raglan's *The Hero*, and Burke's indigenous probes during his second phase of myth-ritual theorizing during the 1950s.[4] As Ellison read it, Raglan's myth-ritual theory proposed that a universal heroic "monomyth" contained, in narrative form, the birth, initiation, and death ritual of a prototypic royal personage.[5] Unlike Joseph Campbell, Raglan had little interest in the psychoanalytic or personal dimensions of hero myths, solar or otherwise. Raglan focused his energies on demonstrating similarities in the mythic biographies of heroes around the world, and he linked these myths to religious rituals that were first developed by the royal and priestly classes and then imitated by members of the working classes to understand the deeper meaning of the dramas they enacted. As a result, he argued that such rituals were the primary source of epic, legend, and narrative folklore.

With the concept of ritual drama, translated into Burkean terms and acting as an animating core, and with Lord Raglan's twenty-two part schematic of the myth of heroic biography guiding the ritual's understructure, Ellison (1966) carefully articulated a skeleton for the experimental narrative he famously encircled with a prologue and an epilogue:

> I began with a chart of the three-part division. It was a conceptual frame with most of the ideas and some incidents indicated. The three parts represent the narrator's movement from, using Kenneth Burke's terms, purpose to passion to perception. These three major sections are built up of smaller units, three of which mark the course of the action. . . . The maximum insight on the hero's part isn't reached until the final section. After all, it's a novel about innocence and human error, a struggle through illusion to reality. Each section begins with a sheet of paper; each piece of paper is exchanged for another and contains a definition of his identity, or the social role he is to play as defined for him by others. But all say essentially the same thing, "Keep this nigger boy running." Before he could have some voice in his own destiny he had to discard these old identities and illusions; his enlightenment couldn't come until then. (p. 177)

What has remained less decipherable to humanists and social scientists that grapple with Ellison's fiction and his cross-disciplinary critiques of culture are the modalities of race ritual that he discovered and deployed. Ellison was quite specific about his creative and critical application of broader theories concerning the relationship between myth, ritual, and folklore to the sphere of American race ritual. In a revealing interview on "The Art of Fiction," published in *Shadow & Act*, when asked to give the interviewer an example of the use of folklore in his work, Ellison (1966) responded:

> Well, there are certain themes, symbols and images which are based on folk material. For example, there is the old saying amongst Negroes: if you're black, stay back; if you're brown, stick around; if you're white, you're right. And there is the joke Negroes tell on themselves about their being so black they can be seen in the dark. In my book this sort of thing was merged with the meanings which blackness and light have long had in Western mythology: evil and

goodness, ignorance and knowledge, and so on. In my novel the narrator's development is one through blackness to light; that is, from ignorance to enlightenment: invisibility. . . . When I started writing, I knew that in both *The Waste Land* and *Ulysses* ancient myth and ritual were used to give form and significance to the material; but it took me a few years to realize that the myths and rites which we find functioning *in our everyday lives* could be used in the same way. . . . When I attempted to deal with the psychological strata—the images, symbols and emotional configurations—of the experience at hand, I discovered that the unities were simply cool points of stability on which one could suspend the narrative line—but beneath the surface of apparently rational human relationships there seethed a chaos before which I was helpless. People rationalize what they shun or are incapable of dealing with; these superstitions and their rationalizations *become ritual* as they *govern behavior.* The *rituals* become social *forms,* and it is one of the functions of the artist to recognize them and raise them to the level of [conscious] art.

I don't know whether I'm getting this over or not. Let's put it this way: Take the "Battle Royal" passage in my novel, where the boys are blindfolded and forced to fight each other for the amusement of the white observers. This is a vital part of behavior patterns in the South, which both Negroes and whites thoughtlessly accept. It is a ritual in preservation of caste lines, a keeping of taboo to appease the gods and ward off bad luck. It is also the initiation ritual to which all greenhorns are subjected. This passage, which states what Negroes will see, *I did not have to invent*; *the patterns were already there in society,* so that all I had to do was present them in a broader context of meaning. In any society there are many rituals of situation which, for the most part, go unquestioned. They can be simple or elaborate, but they are the connective tissue between the work of art and the audience. (p. 175)

To keep the connective tissue alive between the work of this chapter and its audience, I now want to point the way to a bridging conclusion that connects race rituals and to our transcendent, strike-throwing, hero-leader of a present historical moment with whom we began. If the route forward to the installation of President Barack Obama seems too murky from the point of origin, let me re-plot the course as follows.

Initially brought together by a shared sense of crisis in political leadership and modern letters during the years of the Great Depression and looming world war, Burke and Ellison became friends and allies in struggling for "transcendence by perspective"; their relationship lasted for more than four decades, and interpenetrated the published and unpublished work of both men. As Bryan Crable's (2003) scholarship has illuminated, at a time when Jim Crow laws and their *de facto* surrogates still had Supreme Court sanction, a Burke/Ellison dialogue on race, communicated in essays and correspondence, first crystallized at identifiable moments in the early 1940s. During this period, both thinkers were simultaneously absorbed with the dilemmas of public leadership and with competing concepts of transcendence and perspective among artist-intellectuals on the Stalinist/Trotskyite radical left. Left unresolved after the World War II decade, and in the wake of Burke's *Rhetoric of Motives* (1950) (where his attention to "race matters" was expressed more persistently than anywhere else) dialogue on race between the two men resumed directly and indirectly during the 1950s and 60s. Burke published *The Rhetoric of Religion* (1966) and *Language as Symbolic Action* (1966), and Ellison followed *Invisible Man* (1952) with the evolving drafts of a second, ultimately unfinished, novelistic trilogy. That manuscript trilogy reconfigured and transported Ellison's original concerns with the logonomical metaphor of invisibility and the dilemmas of public leadership into a new epoch of redemptive, interracial, civil rights social activism—both religious and secular. The initially sun-kissed "Camelot" presidency of John F. Kennedy, and the cloudier "Civil Rights/Vietnam War" presidency of Lyndon Johnson, transformed race relations and racial discourse and moved African Americans closer to the centers of political power than ever before in American life.

Two intriguing moments in Burke and Ellison's ongoing, private exchanges were marked, on the one hand, by Burke's heavily corrected, undated typescript draft essay from the early 1970s, "The Doing and the Saying." On the other hand, they were marked by an essay-letter to Ellison circa 1983, titled "Ralph Ellison's True-blooded *Bildungsroman*." In these texts, Burke advances a "logological" critique of what he terms "myth-men" and "perfectionist" theologies, parallel to his re-reading of Ellison's *Invisible Man*. Though no complete resolution of their early *differences* about race was at hand, Burke signaled a shift of emphasis about possible modes of transcendence and perspective. He creates a closer rapprochement with Ellison's still-evolving outlook (an outlook that, unfortunately, only became manifest *after* both men died in the 1990s) in *Juneteenth*, the posthumously edited extract from Ellison's uncompleted successor trilogy. *Juneteenth* is nominally a recursive fable that oscillates spatially and psychologically between Ellison's lovingly remembered Oklahoma past and a perennially corrupt government in the nation's seat, in Washington, D.C. The fable elaborates a Burkean, transcendental Rise/Fall/Redemption solar mythos. Its critique of a trans-racial solar hero—a critique that riffs heavily on James Joyce's "mythic method" and Daedalus/Icarus motifs—also prefigures, with sometimes startling power and clarity, pivotal aspects of the New Millenial ascendancy of Senator/President Barack Obama. Ellison casts Obama's fictional forerunner in mainstream and side-stream organs of popular imagination as a trans-racial solar *wunderkind* and evangelistic myth-man stumping for the revitalized American Dream of a more perfect union.

In our post-Obama context, we can appreciate the contemporary value of Burke and Ellison's decades-old drive to separate the history from the mythology of heroes and "Great Men or Women"—whether they are salvific or catastrophic—and to also separate the ritual from rational patterns of action, whether those actions be professedly insurrectionary or patriotic. That value lies, in part, in a kind of epistemological gyroscope that Burke and Ellison bequeathed us to help stabilize our grasp of those continuities in the human condition that endure in the face of social change that is accelerating, exhilarating, frightening, or unfathomable. We are not now, and never will be, free of myth or ritual—nor of charismatic men and women who wield them as apocalyptic fire or as heavenly, life-renewing light—not as long as we remain what Burke repeatedly calls "the symbol-making animal." Correlatively, Ellison's contention that in any society there are many "rituals of situation"— rituals "which, for the most part, go unquestioned," but nonetheless form "the connective tissue between the work of art and the audience" (Chester & Howard, 1995, p. 13)—that apply to leaders and also to the led. As such, a proper understanding of candidate Obama's globally televised March 18, 2008 speech on race, titled "Toward a More Perfect Union"—a speech compared to such hallmarks of American public oratory as the Gettysburg Address and Martin Luther King's "I Have A Dream" speech—requires closer acquaintance with at least one race ritual that Ellison dissected in the course of his early exchanges with Kenneth Burke and Richard Wright.

Crable (2003) has identified three crucial moments in Kenneth Burke's dialogue with Ralph Ellison between the mid-1940s and the publication of *A Rhetoric of Motives* in 1950 wherein, despite their warm analytical agreement on matters of myth, ritual, the modes of eloquence and power, and the philosophy of literary form, Burke and Ellison found themselves in unreconciled *dis*agreement over race matters, including: notions of identity, allegiance, organization, and transcendence. Crable points quite rightly to the exchange over Ellison's now-famous review of Richard Wright's *Black Boy* (1945), "Richard Wright's Blues," as a key to Ellison's refusal to surrender his racial allegiances to hypothetically non-racial political organizations, and to Burke's unyielding insistence that not doing so constitutes a chauvinistic failure to *transcend* a racial binary by denying its stalemated categories and opting, instead, for an identity beyond race.[6] Apparently, Burke was not fully aware that he was re-enacting—in his own terms, the "atom cracking" of "transcendence"—the entrenched rhetorical truisms of superordinate, white-black, liberal-progressive symbolic interrelations. He was also participating (inadvertently) in a long-standing race ritual that Ellison anatomized, even then, for another missive: "Beating That Boy," a 1945 review of Bucklin Moon's race relations anthology, *Primer for White Folks* that appeared in *The New Republic*. Ellison (1966) writes:

> During these post-military-phase-of-the-war days, when a Negro is asked what occurs when he visits with white friends, he is likely to chuckle and dryly reply, "Oh, we beat that boy," meaning to belabor in polite conversation what is commonly called the "Negro problem." Though Negroes laugh when the phrase is used, beneath its folksy surface there lies—like a booby trap in a music box of folk tunes—a disillusionment that only its attitude of detached participation saves from exploding into violent cynicism: its counterpart among those Negroes who know no whites as friends. (p. 105)

A kinetically alliterative metaphor for a social situation painfully familiar to black Americans, the phrase "beating that boy" gave ritual form to a recurring social situation that demanded strategic response under psychological pressure. Contending that "the racial situation has become like an irrational sea in which Americans flounder like convoyed ships in a gale," Ellison (1966) writes:

> The phrase rotates like a gyroscope of irony on which the Negro maintains a hazardous stability as the sea-tossed ship of his emotions whirls him willy-nilly along: lunging him toward the shoals of bitter rejection (of the ideology that makes him the sole sacrifice of America's tragedy; now away toward the mine-strewn shores of hopelessness (that despite the war, democracy is still discussed on an infantile level and himself in pre-adult terms); now smashing him flush against waves of anger that threaten to burst his seams in revolt . . . ; now teetering him clear on a brief, calm, sunlit swell of self-amusement . . . ; now knocking him erect, like a whale on its tail, before plunging again into the still dark night of the one lone "rational" thing—the pounding irrational sea. This is a nightmarishly "absurd" situation. (p. 105)

Six decades later, whether as candidate or as President, it has been only a little less so for Barack Obama, rotating now on a self-chosen "gyroscope of hope" rather than a "gyroscope of irony." In Ellison's (1966) time, and in terms of his deep, constitutional faith and democratic hope, the absurd qualities of the situation "need not be absolutely disadvantageous for the Negro"—nor, by extension, for the white American (p. 100). "It might, in a different culture, or a transformed culture, even be highly strategic," he speculated (p. 100); though, perhaps more so for the artist than the aspiring hero-leader—particularly a black or even "trans-racial" one. "For imprisoned in the deepest drives in human society," Ellison (1966) recognized, "it is practically impossible for the white American to think of sex, of economics, his children or womenfolk, or of sweeping socio-political changes, without summoning into consciousness fear-flecked images of black men" (p. 109). Accordingly, it is crucial for black Americans determined to "beat that boy" effectively to "detect the cracks in our most Liberty Bell voices" and understand the "new mood born in the hearts of Americans during the war" as "more precise in its fears (of racial bloodshed) than definite in its hopes (symbolized most concretely in the frantic efforts of interracial organizations and mayors' committees to discover a foolproof technique of riot control)" (p. 110).

OBAMA, BURKE, AND THE "PERFECT" UNION

In a hand-corrected typescript draft of "The Doing and the Saying," a draft that Burke sent to Ellison in 1970, the septuagenarian Burke continued toying with various concepts and definitions of (hu)man that he and countless others had postulated over the years: the "rational animal," the "featherless biped," the "naked ape," the "culture-bearing animal," and (the one he preferred, his own) the "symbol-using animal." Explaining the importance of symbolism, Burke postulates (using a hypothetical, primitive society that is possessed of material sources and the need to distribute them cooperatively) the necessity for members specialized in *doing* what is materially essential, and for those in *saying* that which is necessary for cooperation. Burke dubbed these latter prototypes "myth-men," those who exercise special symbolic skills "through a kind of formal completing, or perfecting" of transactions that, when ritually solemnized, generate a *"principle* of perfection," a mythic completion that becomes, in turn, the object of symbolic quest.[7]

However, in this Burkean model, once-candidate and now-President Barack Obama fits as myth-man and perfector of contracts *par excellence*. Obama's "Toward a More Perfect Union" speech self-consciously gestures toward mythic completion at the same time that it functions as Ellisonian race ritual. As a professorial specialist in Constitutional law, Obama (2008) crafted an opening allusion to the first sentence of that Constitution that is as carefully scripted and symbolic as are his reverberating uses of the case inflections of *"perfect," "perfect," "perfected," "unperfected," "perfection,"* "imperfect," and "imperfection." Similarly careful are the theological turns and tunings he worked in from the Wesleyan Methodist doctrines of Christian perfectionism that undergird eighteenth and nineteenth century reform movements and utopian experiments, as well as more modern doctrines of scientific secular progressivism. Obama's perfectionist rhetoric strategically counterpoints the darker side of "perfectioneering" that American media organs, as well as Obama's conservative opponents, identified in the religious apocalyptics of Louis Farrakhan's Nation of Islam and in the Black Liberation Theology of the dangerously erudite seminarian, James Cone and his incendiary disciple, the now very familiar and prophetically named, Reverend Jeremiah Wright.[8]

As Burke well understood, "perfect" and "perfection" derives etymologically from the Latin *per facere* or *per-factum*, meaning made through or thoroughly. They imply, as Burke also understood, a state of completion or totalization, as in that which is fulfilled or consummated. A perfect thing, then, suffers no lack or defect within the order of its perfectiveness. This concept of perfection is a transcendental one, in Kant's sense, realizable on various levels. In Burke's *The Rhetoric of Religion*, the "Epilogue, or Prologue in Heaven" dramatizes, as a formal paradox, a discourse between The Lord and Satan in which this "principle of perfection" and all pertinent definitions, axioms, propositions, demonstrations, corollaries, scolia, lemmas, and special cases are imagined to be at play.[9]

Burke (n.d.) offers a similar dissection of endings in "The Doing and the Saying," writing,

> a concern with "perfection" in this sense would be an instance of what I mean by an attempt to refurbish and re-adapt (at least for the study of mythic proclivities) the Aristotelian concept of the entelechy: the "aim" of an entity to fulfill the possibilities intrinsic to its nature, quite as a tree, a lion, a man, and a cockroach would each strive to develop in keeping with the laws of its kind, each set of such laws implying a different kind of completion or perfection; [so that] a cockroach should no more aim to fulfill himself as a lion than a lion should seek for perfection as a cockroach.

If Obama's "mythic proclivities" and perfectionist hopes for a revitalized American Dream and that "more perfect union" make him a possible target for comic or ontological correctives from Burke's late-life perspective, Ellison may have surreptitiously proven himself to be Burke's private accomplice in that "doing" and "saying." Tucked between the pages of Burke's rough draft in Ellison's files at the Library of Congress is a handwritten note in Ellison's unmistakable script: "Redd Foxx Joke: the most perfect hunchback / on the nature of perfection. / Preacher preaching on the Lord's having / made everything perfect—/ challenged by hunchback . . . / 'You're the most perfect H . . . '" (Ellison, n.d.).[10]

The tale might serve here, as well as a closing vernacular exemplum on the pluralities and puzzles of perspective and transcendence, a final "bridging device." The preacher and the hunchback joke serves as an ontological parable that recapitulates Plato's ancient arguments about the two kinds of perfection: "absolute versus relative" perfection on the one hand, and "substantial versus accidental" perfection on the other.[11] The hunchback's real problem, the joke implies, is that he suffers from a confusion of categories (between being a perfect hunchback rather than being an imperfect man), and not from the debilities of his actual physical condition. The preacher supplies an ontological, that is, *transcendental* "solution" to a material complaint. Burke's perspective in "The Doing and the Saying," however, pushes the implications of the same arguments, as reframed after Plato by Aristotle, into the moral and theological realm of "the problem of evil" and the Design Argument for God's existence, as dramatized in *The Rhetoric of Religion*'s "Prologue in Heaven." For Plato, all perfection resides in the Ideas, as they are said to be real, subsistent, hierarchically ordered. Aristotle rejected the Ideas of Plato as poetic metaphors, as abstract universals existing only in the mind—illusions that had to be stripped away. For Aristotle and his disciples, perfection lies only in "real" order, where it must be distinguished from a principle of *im*perfection. There, imperfection, to Aristotle, is potency, the capacity for being; perfection is the act of being itself. As Burke's wry logological analysis makes clear, however, there is no ongoing process of development in such a schema, and therefore no progress. Each being or thing attains its maximum perfection when all the potentialities with which its particular nature is endowed—whether that nature be as a tree or lion or man or cockroach—are released.

The presence of imperfection and evil in the world—in the Divine Works—is the underlying theological problem addressed by the tale of the preacher and the hunchback. The narrative voice is the voice of Enlightenment optimism and it's Design Argument: the Divine Blueprint inexorably works itself out, in all its detail. If we (the deformed and questioning hunchback) could but see world processes from God's perspective as Creator, all evil and imperfection would be only *apparently* evil and imperfect—a matter of our limited perspective, or of the Creator's design for some greater good. Ellison's deployment of Foxx's joke opens up the possibility of Burkean "identification" and shifts the narrative perspective from the preacher to the hunchback. He pulls the perspectival emphasis away from the ontological and epistemological toward the existential, treating the situation of the two principals as reversible. "What about me?" the hunchback asks, "What about me?" After all, who really is the butt of the ontological joke? Who, really, is confused about the nature of reality? Who do we, as listeners, identify with? Once we ask ourselves these questions—and hazard our own answers—the joke/tale becomes a potential vernacular prism and epistemological gyroscope. It is both ontological and logological in terms of Burke's corrective comic frame, as it envelops the whole ensemble of personae this chapter has juxtaposed, bridging along the way.

If we identify with the preacher, mesmerized by the unquestioned perfections of the Divine Works and their Creator, then, like Satan in Burke's "Prologue in Heaven," we become another of The Lord's Own Straight Men—perched alongside the Devil and striving hieratically not to be a holy fool. If we identify with the hunchback, seeing him as a kind of flawed but questing Everyman, then we join the congregation of God's "most perfect hunchbacks," those eternally grasping for perfection with the "audacity of hope," but bowed down with sin—original as well as self-inflicted—and praying for salvation.

Let us ask the hunchback's question of Obama, that audacious man-of-hope and trans-racial new First Citizen—he of the light and life-giving grace of the sun—who mirrors and projects our own conscious and unconscious visions of a possible "post-racial" New World Order. Though his inaugural one hundred days of political grace have passed, we might say that his is the staunchest candidacy, dramatistically though it appears, to stand as democracy's *most perfect* "myth-man," throwing the logological strikes Garrison Keillor finds so entrancing, and "beating that ever-present boy." Contrary inklings, however, might be discovered in a final exemplum from *Dreams from My Father* that flourishes a bit of Burkean word magic in the course of framing an attitude toward history and the possibilities of perfecting a New World Order—magic that is much darker metaphysically than most of Obama's appraisers have reckoned him to possess. In the closing section of his triptych memoir, "Kenya", having finally journeyed to his estranged and now dead father's African country of origin, Obama confronts the puzzling fragments of the senior Obama's bitter life in an ancient homeland that is ravaged by pandemic poverty and tribal conflict. While on safari to the Great Rift Valley, and like a foreign *wazungu*—or white man, as his Kenyan sister tells him—narrator Obama (1995, 2004) pauses his personal story of race and inheritance to ground it in a primeval past. On the site of what physical anthropologists and DNA tracings tell us may be the origins of the human species, he re-orchestrates a portion of the biblical Creation of the Divine Works in a passage that crafts what are perhaps his memoir's most stunningly pictorial lines:

Dawn. To the east, the sky lightens above a black grove of trees, deep blue, then orange, then creamy yellow. The clouds lose their purple tint slowly, then dissipate, leaving behind a single star. As we pull out of camp, we see a caravan of giraffe, their long necks at a common slant, seemingly black before the rising red sun, strange markings against an ancient sky.

It was like that for the rest of the day, as if I were seeing as a child once again, the world a pop-up book, a fable, a painting by Rousseau. A pride of lions, yawning in the broken grass. Buffalo in the marshes, their horns like cheap wigs, tick birds scavenging off their mud-crusted backs. Hippos in the shallow riverbeds, pink eyes and nostrils like marbles bobbing on the water's surface. Elephants fanning their vegetable ears.

And most of all the stillness, a silence to match the elements. At twilight, not far from our camp, we came upon a tribe of hyenas feeding on the carcass of a wildebeest. In the dying orange light they looked like demon dogs, their eyes like clumps of black coal, their chins dripping with blood. Beside them, a row of vultures waited with stern, patient gazes, hopping away like hunchbacks whenever one of the hyenas got too close. It was a savage scene, and we stayed there for a long time, watching life feed on itself, the silence interrupted only by the crack of bone or the rush of wind, or the hard thump of a vulture's wings as it strained to lift itself into the current, until it finally found the higher air and those long and graceful wings became motionless and still like the rest. And I thought to myself: This is what Creation looked like. The same stillness, the same crunching of bone. There in the dusk, over that hill, I imagined the first man stepping forward, naked and rough-skinned, grasping a chunk of flint in his clumsy hand, no words yet for the fear, the anticipation, the awe he feels at the sky, the glimmering knowledge of his own death. If only we could remember that first common step, that first common word—that time before Babel. (pp. 356–357)

In *The Rhetoric of Religion*, as noted at this chapter's outset, Burke's (1961) exegesis of the first three chapters of Genesis demonstrates his dramatistic method of probing "associational clusters," or "equations" (e.g., Burke, 1941a, p. 20). At the same time, it links the biblical Creation Myth to the idea of Order and Dominion and the Iron Law of History that demands Sacrifice, breeds Guilt that, in turn, needs Redemption and that ultimately requires a Redeemer who, again, consummates the Cult of the Kill. Obama's dreamlike account of his private African epiphany publicly divulges a macabre, revisionary cosmogony that rearticulates the tensions between two, quite different, primeval myths of Creation propounded successively in Genesis. Though both relate the origination of the physical world, its animal creatures, and humanity, the first "priestly" account was a poem or hymn that was optimistic and expansive, and begins with God's establishing a sublimely "good" created order, with human beings as its crown, and culminates with the establishment of a legitimate cult ritual at Mount Sinai. The second "Yahwistic" account portrays a relentlessly dark and pessimistic pattern of human error that stretches from the Original Sin of the First Man and Woman to the shattering hubris of tower-building at Babel and the Lord's global, prophylactic dispersion of corrupt humanity and the accompanying confusion of tongues.

Biblical scholars agree that this second, dismal mythic account of Sin, Guilt, and Punishment is the older source, and that it was originally developed as a folktale that reflected the concerns of a peasant society. Its God is anthropomorphic, its human creatures are part of the mundane natural order of the animate and inanimate over which they hold Dominion and the power of naming. Though Death, as a specific consequence of Sin, enters the mortal situation of the human as a judgment from God, *Genesis* does not develop a theology of Death. The associative cluster of Obama's cosmogonic images adheres to this darker, more pessimistic perspective on the phases of primeval history. Its binary tensions deftly pit heavenly theophany against earthly purgatory, collective carnage against individual restraint, and demonic passion against unimpassioned forbearance.

Likened to the polychromatic intensities of Henri Rousseau's proto-surrealistic tableaus of savage, jungle, dream-worlds, the landscape of Obama's creation fable in the memoir focuses upon a decisively anthropomorphized death scene that recalls the world of medieval bestiaries; it is perhaps more than painterly modernism. Obama's primary dramatis personae, the "tribe" of hyenas—as human analogues, and not a "herd" or a "pack" who are feeding on a dead wildebeest, recalls the supernatural hellhounds of Greco-Roman Hades, whose bloody spittle, in dropping to earth, mark the point of entry to, and departure from, the realm of the dead. Nocturnal creatures in collusion with sinister forces, Obama's hyenas are night-visioned, spirit beings on an evil errand in a twilight realm, a realm where human perception falters. In traditional African folk tales, as in Obama's transcultural imagination, the hyena vies for supremacy with the vulture, who, unlike its mythological European counterpart, is less a symbol of death than a regenerative messenger of the sky gods, a winged initiate or sorcerer that has been cleansed and scorched by the ordeals of earthly carnage and who ensures the cycle of regeneration by transforming carrion and filth into new life.

In Obama's capsule cosmogony, the vultures are also anthropomorphized; they wait "with stern, patient gazes" and hop away "like hunchbacks" in the face of encroachment by thhe hyenas. As metaphors for the soul and symbols of escape, safety, or forbearance, these great carrion birds, though deemed unclean and outcast in most Christian bestiaries, are also identified with the "conquest of fear" and the "song of confidence" of the temple fugitive in *Psalm* 27.[12] Even more pertinent for our consideration is Obama's second anthropomorphizing phrase, as it is rooted in an age-old observation that vultures look ugly and hunchbacked on the ground, but fly with more grace than almost any other bird. In African and African American traditions, the hunchbacked, grounded vulture often takes the part of a clown or that of a child that lurches or hops awkwardly on the earth. The vulture is like Pulchinello or Harlequin in *commedia del arte*. It is also like Victor Hugo's Quasimodo, the tragicomic hero with a hunched back who is neither animal nor human, normal nor ideal, and who may also be a Prince of Fools; Quasimodo's enduring appeal lies in the compelling intuition that, in the human form, God created an imperfect image of himself, one hobbled and bent by society, a recalcitrant body, and temptation—but is a body that, ultimately, has the power to transcend its constraints and achieve wholeness and freedom.

In Obama's image of the hunchbacked vulture straining "to lift itself into the current" of the higher air, where it's "long and graceful wings became motionless and still" like the elemental silence, a subtle balance of "transcendence by perspective" is established between his Bible's competing versions of Creation and human perfectibility. The word magic of Obama's cosmogonic fable operates explicitly through modes of trans-temporal clairvoyance—"seeing as a child once again," as Wright and Ellison affirmed—rather than through Burke's verbal atom-cracking of perspective by incongruity. Obama's First Man has no word for his primeval fear and awe of the sky gods, or for death as a spiritual and not merely natural event. Recovering the "first common word" for that primeval experience ("the time before Babel") becomes, for Obama, the transcendent goal of human history. It is a return to the beginning, a time when the creator's Original Intention, aborted by human sin and rebellion, is fulfilled, and the vision of a New Creation—imperfect by measure of the Bible's first imagining, but capable of being *perfected* in its second one—can become the catalyst for human salvific and redemptive action. In other words, Barack Obama's sacred blueprint for "a more perfect union" is grounded logologically in these dialectics of symbolic action, as are the more secular dialectics of his fervent constitutionalism and public sphere engagements that are apparently fated to continue "beating that boy." The hunchbacked vultures in his African version of Genesis and the Cult of the Kill cease being ugly eaters of carrion during flights of spirit that "transcend" the earthbound carnage and grotesqueries for the solar freedoms above. Like the hunched backs of the doomed souls in Dante's *Purgatorio*, the contorted spine may conceal an attitude of prayer; and, as with the church-going but doubtful hunchback of Ellison, Foxx, and the Laughing Philosophers, President Obama's "upward way" to redemption, like ours, may ultimately lie in how deftly he can navigate the chasms between existential realities and ontological jokes.

Cynics, both ancient and modern, have always declared that the dreams of a perfect society and of a perfect man and woman—a New Adam and Eve—are illusions that, like those of Ellison's *Invisible Man* or Burke's "Prologue in Heaven," must be stripped away in the face of human limitation and incontrovertible fact—just as Jack-the-Bear's illusions are stripped in the closing, hallucinatory dream sequence of Ellison's chiaroscuro tale of American darkness and light, blindness, and insight. There, the Burkean mythman dreams that his testicles have been cut away, his tethers to a reality he cannot change but also cannot put aside. They have, he concludes, "balled the Jack"—*de-balled* him that is—fusing the imagery of black popular street dancing with the surrender of his illusions. Mutilated spiritually and deformed by brutal experience, he seeks redemption by rising up from solitary hibernation to act responsibly, seek communion and reciprocity, and ask his auditors, "Who knows but that, on the lower frequencies, I speak for you?" (Ellison, 1982, p. 581). His last word and testament ritualizes what Burke and Ellison agreed is a "situational substitution" for the perfect hunchback's transcendental question, a logological equation that rides high on irony, supplies a comic corrective for human frailty, gratifies the tribe of Laughing Philosophers, and keeps balling all the jacks.

NOTES

1. Counterpointing Sigmund Freud's libidinally oriented psychoanalytic interpretations decades earlier, Burke (1941a) proposed, in *The Philosophy of Literary Form*, a rhetorical framework for understanding such texts. First, a "dream" dimension deciphered the conscious or unconscious symbolization of the speaker's attitude. Second, a "prayer" dimension located the public content of the speaker's audience-regarding stratagems. The third "chart" dimension stressed a reality-oriented "naming" of the particular rhetorical situation that the speaker of the text faced.

2. Concomitantly, Richard Wright (1991), who, four years later, divined in the Nazi phenomenon as an analogue to Bigger Thomas's inner void, admitted that despite his fervent anti-fascism, he was fascinated by Hitler's rhetoric and was

> reminded of the Negro preacher in the South telling of a life beyond this world, a life in which the color of men's skins would not matter, a life in which each man would know what was deep down in the hearts of his fellow man. (p. 865)

The will to solidarity and certainty, central to the oratorical traditions of black leadership and liberation—now visible in Obama's shining Constitutionalist dialectics and in the Reverend Jeremiah Wright's apocalyptic jeremiads—are mirrored darkly (if obversely) in the Führer's autobiographical rhetoric and its sense of redemptive mission. Joining them are other psychic forces more delusive or dangerous: the evocation of a God-given kingdom to be won from a unchanging tyrant who appears in many guises, and is an enemy to all; the total, unspoken identification of the aspiring leader with the people, and the joining of his rebirth and revitalization with theirs; the assumption of specious group unity and the obsession with enemy spies and dis-unifiers; the sexualization of political conflict and the hyper-masculine verbal imagery spun by the ascending leader-lover of the people who would keep *his* nation "pure" and woo "her" from external and internal seducer-rivals; the vaunted readiness to deploy armed violence in the name of reason, humility, peace, and love; the enticing design of personal religious conversion and self-sacrifice grafted onto the processes of secularly sanctioned empowerment; the satisfactions of ceremonial ritual itself, detached from moral ends; and the soothing, studied presentation of the leader's political activities as the creative extension of his *artistic* and literary ambitions (Wright, 2006, pp. 97–98).

3. To see this candid moment, see Kirkland (2004).

4. By the "Cambridge Ritualists," I refer primarily to the work of Jane Harrison (1850–1928), Gilbert Murray (1866–1957), Francis Macdonald Cornford (1874–1943), and Arthur Bernard Cook (1868–1952), in tandem with the academically unaligned Lord Raglan. The whole "myth-ritual" enterprise had begun under the influence of the Scottish historian of religion, William Robertson Smith (1846–1894) and his disciple, Sir James George Frazer, author of *The Golden Bough* (1890), whose evolutionary schema of human culture development through successive stages of magic, science, and religion Burke turned to his own purposes. Smith's primary work, *Religion of the Semites* (1890), insisted that what mattered most to the ancient worshipping community was *action* rather than belief, the correct *performance* of *ritual* rather than mere intellectual *acceptance* of explanatory myth or doctrine. The Cambridge Ritualists who came after Smith and Frazer tried mainly to uncover the primitive, preliterate ritual forms or patterns underlying classical and modern works of literature. Though fascinated with the evolutionary question of whether action (ritual) or explanation (myth) came first, almost none of them investigated actual living cultures or performed anthropological or folkloric fieldwork; instead, they simply speculated about the relation between myth and ritual based on their readings of classical texts. For more on these thinkers, see Gras (1994).

5. Usually this royal personage was a king or son of a royal virgin, who was also considered the incarnation of a god. Often, this involved reference to a solar or lunar deity or demiurge, reflecting the elaborate (and heavily institutionalized) solar worship characteristic of the religions of Nilotic Africa, Greco-Roman Europe, and the Indian subcontinent.

6. Although Burke did not recognize this, the issue was one that Wright (1978) had broached in his 1937 "Blueprint for Negro Writing," where he argued that

> the emotional expression of group-feeling which puzzles so many whites and leads them to deplore what they call "black chauvinism" is not a morbidly inherent trait of the Negro but rather the reflex expression of a life whose roots are imbedded deeply in Southern soil. (p. 42)

7. Carrying the process one definitional step further, a characteristically Burkean list of such "myth-men" included witch doctors, medicine men, shaman, oracles, poets, dancers, musicians, painters, actors, dramatists, artists-in-general, and (above all) priests and prophets. Modern ad-writers, publicity men, and the like Burke considered *not* proper instances of the myth-man, since so much of their symbolizing did not aim at the kind of summarizing utterance that characterizes mythic completion and the principle of perfection.

8. Interestingly, Ellison's (1999) *Juneteenth* foreshadows Reverend Wright's fatherly tutelage of the Obama before his candidacy, in the novel's adoption by the Reverend "Daddy" Hickman of the fatherless youth. This youth, born of a white woman and a wandering black apostate, literally passes from childhood "Bliss" through to initiatory whiteness, on his route to becoming the Promethean "First Man" of a vaunted New World Order: "Adam Sunraider." Sunraider's senatorial career carries him skyward, like Daedalus's unwary son, Icarus, to the mythical sunlight of "perfected" but precarious political power—power over which the shadow of political assassination hangs and will fall.

9. For those unfamiliar with the text, Burke's "The Lord" is described in the stage directions as "a Blakean bearded patriarch," and Satan is described as an "agile youth, wear[ing] fool's cap with devil's horns, and a harlequin costume of two colors, dividing him down the middle" (Burke, 1961, p. 276). The two figures are on "quite friendly terms" with The Lord "affectionately amused by his young companion, while Satan, over-hasty, mercurial, is an intense admirer of the older man" (Burke, 1961, p. 276). These stage directions, Burke (1961) suggests, are logologically convertible to those of a minstrel show or a vaudevillian "Gag Man and Straight Man" comedy routine (pp. 273–276). As Satan and The Lord discuss the Earth-People the Lord has created, the principle of perfection enters when, after having invented the most ingenious symbol system of all—money—the Earth people discover that money introduces the principle of redemption by payment, and with it a guilt so powerful that only a perfect, sacrificial substitute for themselves—The Lord's Only Begotten Son—will expiate it. An inescapable *cycle* of guilt, redemption, and scapegoat sacrifice fuels a logic of perfection that is both theological and "logological," so that the very idea that a perfect being is possible establishes the actual world as

the "best possible world": Burke's echo of the Leibnizian endgame lampooned in Voltaire's *Candide*.

10. Most readers of this essay will remember Redd Foxx as the irascible but endearing old junk dealer from the 1970s television sitcom, *Sanford & Son*, the long-running black-cast makeover of a British working class original that remained a Hollywood Top Ten first-run attraction for years and a syndication staple ever after. *Sanford & Son* had not yet been conceived when Ellison inserted his abbreviated version of Foxx's joke as a gloss on Burke's essay about myth-men and the perils of "perfection." The Redd Foxx that Ellison alluded to bore dim relation to the blustering, bumbling old codger with whom mainstream American viewers became so comfortable. Born John Leroy Sanford in St. Louis, Missouri in 1922, he had migrated north to Chicago as a boy, ran away from home to New York City as a young man, and tried his hand at playing music, odd jobs, and chitlin' circuit vaudeville before discovering his true calling as a pioneering, solo stand-up club comedian. John Elroy Sanford literally invented the market for XXX-rated "blue" humor "party albums" in the 1950s and 60s, starring on more than fifty under-the-counter albums that sold more than ten million copies. John Elroy landed in Harlem in 1939, not long after Ellison had come to the Big Apple from Oklahoma. As a "Chicago Red," Sanford worked alongside street hustler Malcolm Little (*"Detroit* Red") before Little's jailhouse conversion to the Nation of Islam and his new baptism as "Malcolm X" (Gates & Higginbotham, 2008, pp. 350–351). Elroy later dropped his own street monicker, *"Chicago* Red," for "Redd Foxx" in double homage to one of his baseball heroes *and* to the bushy-tailed, four-legged, randy folk trickster-figure who stalked black oral traditions of a cunning predator and wily prey:

> But, I *could* have been a preacher. Comedy is like preaching. . . . It's like the story about the crippled man who had so much faith that he threw away his crutches . . . and there he was crawling around trying to get them back. . . . Religion is strange. . . . Everybody wants to go to heaven; then when you die, they lower you into the ground and some bastard comes along and builds a condominium over your ass. (Foxx & Miller, 1977, p. 250)

11. The preacher tale that Ellison cribbed from a Redd Foxx performance is one that Foxx himself cribbed from an unlikely preliminary source, one traceable most probably to an early nineteenth century edition of *The Laughing Philosopher* (Bull, 1825). Though its origins in vernacular lore are obscure and the variations numberless, the prototype of the joke as printed in *The Laughing Philosopher* proceeds as follows: A clergyman once delivered a discourse on the Divine Works. In the course of his remarks, he said that everything God had made was perfect in its kind. As the preacher descended from the pulpit, he was accosted at the door by an ugly, ill-formed hunchback of a man, who, looking him in the face with a malicious grin, pointed to his hump and asked the antithetical question, "What, sir, do you think of my form; what about me? Do you think me to be perfect?" "Why yes," replied the preacher, hesitating a moment before grinning back at him, "You are the most perfect hunchback I have ever seen!" *The Laughing Philosopher* glossed the tale by announcing: "Here is genuine Wit. It consists, as everyone will perceive, in

assuming the idea of a hunchback as a conception of the perfect, and then classing the individual present under it as an embodied realization of that idea" (Bull, 1825, p. 204).

12. Generations of African American preachers have subsequently transformed this Psalm into sermonic anecdotes, on the one hand, about Brother Buzzard (the vulture's American cousin) who either faithfully *or* lazily "waits on the Lord" (Vs. 14) for salvation. On the other hand, preacherly traditions proliferated about the Psalm's temple fugitive summoning courage in the face of the enemies who "eat up his flesh" ("utter slanders against me," Vs. 2) like a pack of wild beasts.

REFERENCES

Abrams, M. H. (1971). *Natural supernaturalism: Tradition and revolution in romantic literature.* New York, NY: W. W. Norton & Company, Inc.

Bull, J. (Ed.). (1825). *The laughing philosopher: Being the entire works of Momus, jester of Olympus, Democritus, the merry philosopher of Greece, and their illustrious disciples, Ben Johnson, Butler, Swift, Gay, Joseph Miller, esq., Churchill, Voltaire, Foote, Steevens, Wolcot, Sheridan, Curran, Colman, and others.* London: Sherwood, Jones.

Burke, K. (1935/1984). *Permanence and change: An anatomy of purpose.* Berkeley, CA: University of California Press.

Burke, K. (1937). *Attitudes toward history.* Berkeley, CA: University of California Press.

Burke, K. (1941a). *The philosophy of literary form: Studies in symbolic form.* Baton Rouge, LA: Louisiana State University Press.

Burke, Kenneth (1941b). The rhetoric of Hitler's "Battle." In K. Burke, *The philosophy of literary form: Studies in symbolic action* (pp.191–220). New York, NY: Vintage.

Burke, K. (1955). *Book of moments: Poems 1915–1954.* Los Altos, CA: Hermes.

Burke, K. (1959). *Attitudes toward history.* Los Altos, CA: Hermes.

Burke, K. (1961). *The rhetoric of religion: Studies in logology.* Boston, MA: Beacon.

Burke, K., (n.d.). The doing and the saying. Kenneth Burke Letter File, Ralph Ellison Papers. (Unpublished typescript.). Washington, D.C.: Library of Congress.

Chester, A., & Howard, V. (1995). The art of fiction: An interview. In M. Graham & A. Singh (Eds.), *Conversations with Ralph Ellison* (pp. 6-19). Jackson, MS: University of Mississippi Press.

Crable, B. (2003). Race and *A Rhetoric of Motives*: Kenneth Burke's dialogue with Ralph Ellison. *Rhetoric Society Quarterly, 33*(3), 5–25.

Ellison, R. (1966). *Shadow & act.* New York, NY: New American Library.

Ellison, R. (1974). On initiation rites and power: Ralph Ellison speaks at West Point. *Contemporary Literature, 15*(4), 165–186.

Ellison, R. (1982). *Invisible man.* New York, NY: Random House.

Ellison, R. (1999). *Juneteenth: A novel.* John Callahan (Ed.). New York, NY: Random House.

Ellison, R., (n.d.). Redd Foxx joke. Kenneth Burke Letter File, Ralph Ellison Papers. (Manuscript longhand insert.). Washington, D.C.: Library of Congress.

Foxx, R., & Miller, N. (1977). *The Redd Foxx encyclopedia of black humor.* Pasadena, CA: W. Ritchie Press.

Gates, H. L., Jr., & Higginbotham, E. B. (Eds). (2008). *African American national biography.* (Vol. 3). New York, NY: Oxford University Press.

Graham, M., & Mack, J. D. (2004). Ralph Ellison, 1913-1994: A brief biography. In S. C. Tracy (Ed.), *A historical guide to Ralph Ellison* (pp. 19-55). New York, NY: Oxford University Press.

Gras, V. (1994). Cambridge ritualists. In M. Groden, & M. Kreiswirth (Eds.), *The Johns Hopkins guide to literary theory & criticism* (pp. 128–131). Baltimore, MD: Johns Hopkins University Press.

Howe, I. (October 1963). Black boys and native sons. *Dissent,* 20–25.

Keillor, G. (2008, June 15). What, precisely, are you looking at? *Star Tribune,* p. OP5.

Kirkland, A. (Producer). (2004). *Ralph Ellison: An American journey* [Motion picture]. United States: California Newsreel.

Lord Raglan, FitzRoy Richard Somerset. (1956). *The hero: A study in tradition, myth, and drama.* Westport, CN: Vintage.

Obama, B. (1995, 2004). *Dreams from my father: A story of race and inheritance.* New York, NY: Three Rivers Press.

Obama, B. (2008, March 18). Toward a more perfect Union. *New York Times.* Retrieved from http://www.nytimes.com/2008/03/18/world/americas/18iht-18obama

Shakespeare, W. (2001). *All's Well That Ends Well* (B. A. Mowat & P. Werstine, Eds.). New York, NY: Washington Square Press.

Transcendence. *Insight News,* June 15–19, 2008, 5.

Wright, R. (1991). *"How Bigger was born," afterword to* Native Son. New York, NY: Library of America.

Wright, R. (1978). "Blueprint for Negro writing." In E. Wright, & M. Fabre (Eds.), *Richard Wright reader* (pp. 36–50). New York, NY: Harper & Row.

Wright, J. S. (2006). *Shadowing Ralph Ellison.* Jackson, MS: University Press of Mississippi.

2 Transcendence in the Barnyard: Thoughts on Strategic Approaches to the Political Art

James F. Klumpp

There is a long history of Burkean approaches to politics. Burke himself, while making his reputation in literature and music, turned to criticism of politics in the 1930s, first in "Revolutionary Symbolism in America" (1935), and then in "The Rhetoric of Hitler's 'Battle'" (1939).* The former, delivered at the First American Writers' Congress, advised the burgeoning Communist movement on connecting their appeals with American experience. The latter, one of Burke's most powerful criticisms, explored the cathartic connection between Hitler and the German *Volk*. Murray Edelman (1964, 1971, 1977, 1988) and later, Dan Nimmo (1974), developed fully-appointed political theories based in Burkean insights. They were not alone in this effort. Hugh Dalziel Duncan (1968) provided a Burkean treatment of politics as one of his eleven offices of social order. Bernard Brock (1966) wrote an important treatise that used Burkean terminology and perspective to understand strategic responses to political situations. Similarly, Burkean criticism of political leadership flowed through political communication literature, including key essays by Ling (1970) and Birdsell (1987) that fleshed out the importance of definitions of situation in political maneuvering. Most recently, Bernard Brock, Mark Huglen, Sharon Howell, and I (2005) followed up on earlier work by Brock (1965) to suggest ways to understand the general, political ideological landscape using Burke's *Attitudes Toward History* (*Attitudes*) and *Grammar of Motives* (*Grammar*).

Despite all this activity, there remains potential for greater insight into political rhetoric through Burke's philosophy of linguistic realism. Rather than building on previous Burkean political theories and criticism, I want to go inside Burke's perspective on politics and tease out an alternative emphasis. Curiously, Burkeans in political communication have paid the least attention to *Rhetoric of Motives* (*Rhetoric*) as a source for Burke's thinking on politics.[1] I want to go there in order to see the images of politics that he presents, as these lead us back to *Grammar* and to dialectic—now read as necessarily present in politics.

THE TWO BURKEAN IMAGES OF POLITICS

Two metaphors provide images of politics in the pages of Burke. The first is the metaphor of the human barnyard. Near the end of the *Grammar of Motives* (1945/1969), where Burke was transitioning into *Rhetoric*, he writes:

> The *Rhetoric*, which would study the "competitive use of the cooperative," would be designed to help us take delight in the Human Barnyard, with its addiction to the Scramble, an area that would cause us great unhappiness could we not transcend it by appreciation, classifying and tracing back to their beginnings in Edenic simplicity those linguistic modes of suasion that often seem little better than malice and the lie. (p. 442)

There are an incredible number of cues here that say much about politics. Beginning at the end, politics is "malice and the lie." Certainly, this image has controlled our perspective on political rhetoric for the last third of the twentieth century. Burke warns, though, that these only "seem" to be the character of politics. He promises an Eden beyond the "great unhappiness" of this construction, one in which we can actually "take delight." The key is to "transcend [the barnyard] by appreciation"—probably in both senses of that word—and find the simplicity of suasion. This is *not* "persuasion"; although *Rhetoric* is elsewhere called a handbook of rhetorical devices (Burke 1945/1969, pp. xvii-xviii), immediately, the introduction to *Rhetoric* reveals the irony that while "moving in on" the shared identity of a community, an individual rhetor may, in fact, play both games: the rhetoric may seek self-interest but see that self-interest as doing good for the community. Indeed, the reference to Eden reminds us that the original sin of humanity was the conceit of individual judgment. As *Rhetoric of Religion* (1961/1970) assures, the compensation for the estrangement born in the garden, Babel after the Fall, is the gift of naming, of language.

Rhetoric of Motives (1950/1969) begins in killing and emerges with "identification" as its key term, leading to the second key metaphor for politics: courtship. Courtship is charged through with estrangement. Burke writes, "By the 'principle of courtship' in rhetoric we mean the use of suasive devices for the transcending of social estrangement" (p. 208). This is the realm of mystery in which estrangement becomes identification, and identification becomes consubstantiality. Where else in human relations do we take such delight and revel in the emotions that transcend the "great unhappiness" of the barnyard's messiness? Burke describes courtship in terms that emphasize bridging sexual difference and social standing. The individuality of those who are estranged does not disappear in courtship, but the mystery transforms the difference into the joint oneness of identification. Surely the cathartic power of this mystery is at the heart of the courtship metaphor. Politics pervades this section of *Rhetoric of Motives*, but nowhere more evidently than in Burke's conclusion that "A ruler who would put people at their ease would do so at his cost, unless he could still somehow manage to glow in the light of his office, being at once both a 'good fellow' and 'standoffish'" (p. 209).

DIALECTIC AND POLITICS

The offish, detestable filth of the "human barnyard" is read against the beautiful dance of courtship. Working with these two images of politics requires that we understand the character of dialectic. "By dialectics in the most general sense we mean the employment of the possibilities of linguistic transformation," Burke (1945/1969) writes in *Grammar* (1945/1969, p. 402). I focus on the importance of "linguistic transformation." Burke's development of dialectic acknowledges a debt to Aristotle and Kant, but the emphasis here is clearly on Kant. Burke's dialectic is not a philosophical dialectic (like Plato's and Aristotle's reasoning to certainty), and not a historical dialectical (like Hegel and Marx's belief in a material dialectic with determined telos), but is instead a *linguistic* dialectic (Klumpp 1993, p. 157).

This linguistic dialectic displays fundamental contextualist and organic assumptions about the human power to organize life with the facility of language. There are three keys to working with linguistic dialectic. The first key to grasping Burke's dialectic is *symbolic action*. In differentiating dialectical terms from positive terms, Burke (1951/1969) identifies the dialectic as "words that belong, not in the order of *motion and perception*, but rather in the order of *action and idea*" (p. 184). Thus, the dialectic is not rooted in the referential construction of language—that words refer to things that are manipulated verbally, and that the manipulations are expressed in discourse— but in a view that language is an essential tool with which humans do things.

Words do not mean in and of themselves; rather, they are the substance of a constructive process in which their potential to coordinate action is played by those engaged in discourse.

Second, Burke's dialectic demonstrates *synthetic power*. Burke sorts terminology into positive, dialectical, and ultimate terms. Positive terms are referential; they point to physical things. They are the heart of what he calls "semantic meaning" (Burke 1941/1973, pp. 138–140) and what others have called the pointing function of words. Dialectical terms, Burke (1951/1969) writes, do not point in the same way. Our referring them semantically to internal states is a metaphoric use, one that creates trouble with referential theories of language. Dialectical terms are interpretive devices through which we relate understanding to valuing and to the coordination of action (p. 184). With dialectical terms, we conduct the drama of human action, aligning our social constructs with our interpretations of the world around us to steer social action. As we work with dialectical terms, we array them with strategies that invoke ultimate terms:

> The "dialectical" order would leave the competing voices in a jangling relation with one another . . . ; but the "ultimate" order would place these competing voices themselves in a *hierarchy*, or *sequence*, or *evaluative series*, so that, in some way, we went by a fixed and reasoned progression from one of these [terms] to another, the members of the entire group being arranged *developmentally* with relation to one another. (p. 187)

For Burke, the power of linguistic dialectic lies in the way that dialectical terms pull from positive and ultimate terms. Weaving positive terms into the dialectic texture provides the grounding of our language in the material world; the ordering performed by ultimate terms provides the motivation that shapes actions in response to that world.

The third key to Burke's linguistic dialectic is the interrelation of *social estrangement and identification*. The power of language is not in a causal power to induce changes in attitudes or beliefs, or even to induce behavior. Rather, the power of language lies in its ability to meld differences and estrangement into a dance of coordinated action. Burke (1951/1969) expresses this notion most famously in his statement that the word for the old rhetoric—a rhetoric of the causal power of words—is "persuasion," and the word for the new rhetoric is "identification" (p. xiv). The counterpart to the dialectic of language is the figure Burke (1945/1969) uses to describe the working of the pentad:

> Distinctions, we might say, arise out of a great central moltenness, where all is merged. They have been thrown from a liquid center

to the surface, where they have congealed. Let one of these crusted distinctions return to its source, and in this alchemic center it may be remade, again becoming molten liquid, and may enter into new combinations, whereat it may be again thrown forth as a new crust, a different distinction. (p. xix)

Of course, this is a positive metaphor for the dialectical, in which distinctions merge in the ambiguity of language—it is the essence of the dialectical. Moreover, this image follows the principles of Hegelian logic, that: no dialectical concept is meaningful in its pure form; when taken to an extreme, dialectical substance turns into its opposite; and, finally, dialectical contrasts exist even following their merger in a transcendent term. Thus, dialectic urges us to see the contrasting indicators whose symbolic merger makes our active world. There are many such dialectics central to constructing action, but let me name a few of the more important in politics:

- Positive and ultimate terms. Burke calls his viewpoint "linguistic realism," and it is the merger of dialectical terms with the positive that employs the material in the service of realism. Yet, the processes of priority, sequencing, narrative, and motivation, lie in the merger of this nexus with the power of ultimate terms to negotiate an ordering that is active response. We can say that linguistic dialectic reaches down to the concrete realism of the positive and up to the ordering potential of ultimate terms.
- Identification and division. This dialectic emphasizes the social nature of human action. Burke (1951/1969) labels the terms "compensatory" (p. 22). If we were totally divided from others, there would be no basis for communication; if we were totally identified, there would be no need. So, it is the fact of our relations with others that gives rise to communication. Note also that identification does not obliterate division; we are both joined and separated from others (p. 21).
- Merger and division. In this pair, ambiguity works to achieve generalization and identification. Burke (1945/1969) recalls Plato's praise in the *Phaedrus* for those who can work with these two to trace and manipulate plurality and unity in nature (p. 403).
- Consubstantiality and identity. This pair is a counterpart of identification and division. It manages the substance of our symbolic action to give pattern to our experience.
- Permanence and change. A primary function of the dialectic is to provide the sense of continuity that marks our experience. Permanence stresses our constructing of experiences in familiar patterns; change

stresses that the originality of every moment requires our adapting those familiar patterns to new circumstances.

All of these, and similar dialectical terms elsewhere in Burke, define the forces that we negotiate with our language.

Strategically, this reading of Burke views politics as a human activity that orients our public experiences toward public action. Those who participate in the political art are users of language in the process of cajoling others toward meaningful life in the polis. The two images of politics interact in this view: The human barnyard represents that struggle for advantage carried out within the dialectic, and courtship represents the effort to array the dialectical, to transcend its disputes with appeals to the ultimate.

BARACK OBAMA

Certainly, the public face of politics in the United States for the last four decades has been characterized more by the barnyard than by courtship. The attack mode, its stridency, and the emphasis on building contrasting bases have been primary factors in the failures induced by the barnyard, and we are left with an inert government that is unable to employ the subtleties of courtship to achieve effective action on public problems. The phenomenon that is Barack Obama has played—and been played—against this background.

Even as a physical presence, of course, Obama represents courtship. Not only does he stand astride American racial estrangement, but part of his symbolic relation to it is the courtship that bore him as a son: a Kenyan father and a mother from Kansas. That biography was played prominently in establishing his public persona. Most evidently, as the 2008 presidential season evolved, the responsiveness of voters to the entreaties of an African American became a major media theme. In addition, the primary campaign for the Democratic nomination presented him in relationship to the estrangement of sex. Indeed, many of the roughest moments in a generally well-danced campaign were the awkward moments of gendering in relationship to fellow candidate, Hillary Clinton.

To a greater degree than most, Obama's messages were subtly and strategically crafted—the rhetoric of courtship seemed to dominate the raw harshness of the barnyard. Consider the title of his campaign book: *The Audacity of Hope: Thoughts on Reclaiming the American Dream*. Titles, Burke (1951/1969) writes, are terms of the dialectic (p. 184). The vocabulary of Obama's title is clearly drawn from the cluster of courtship more than the cluster of the barnyard. It is gentle. The main title works on the subtle tension of dialectic: audacity is insistent, but not aggressive; hope is an optimism of spirit that does not threaten. The subtitle contains a shadow drama—someone has been blocking the American dream—that transforms the tension into a renewal of hope. We can, he says, reclaim the dream. Indeed, the action ends with thought that is appropriate for dreams as a context. The strategy is best described as invitational (Foss & Griffin, 1995).

To examine Obama's message more closely, consider a passage from *The Audacity of Hope*. This passage features faith and abortion, issues that have been played, alternatively, by Democratic candidates as ways to "fire up the base" or as the third rail of politics. Obama (2006) addresses them forthrightly with a style that is typical of his political rhetoric. I quote at length:

> TWO DAYS AFTER I won the Democratic nomination in my U.S. Senate race, I received an email from a doctor at the University of Chicago Medical School.
>
> "Congratulations on your overwhelming and inspiring primary win," the doctor wrote. "I was happy to vote for you, and I will tell you that I am seriously considering voting for you in the general election. I write to express my concerns that may, in the end, prevent me from supporting you."
>
> The doctor described himself as a Christian who understood his commitments to be comprehensive and "totalizing." His faith led him to strongly oppose abortion and gay marriage, but he said his faith also led him to question the idolatry of the free market and the quick resort to militarism that seemed to characterize much of President Bush's foreign policy.
>
> The reason the doctor was considering voting for my opponent was not my position on abortion as such. Rather, he had read an entry that my campaign had posted on my website, suggesting that I would fight "right-wing ideologues who want to take away a woman's right to choose." He went on to write:
>
>> I sense that you have a strong sense of justice and of the precarious position of justice in any polity, and I know that you have championed the plight of the voiceless. I also sense that you are a fair-minded person with a high regard for reason. . . . Whatever your convictions, if you truly believe that those who oppose abortion are all ideologues driven by perverse desires to inflict suffering on women, then you, in my judgment, are not fair-minded. . . . You know that we enter times that are fraught with possibilities for good and for harm, times when we are struggling to make sense of a common polity in the context of plurality, when we are unsure of what grounds we have for making any claims that involve others. . . . I do not ask at this

point that you oppose abortion, only that you speak about this issue in fair-minded words.

I checked my website and found the offending words. They were not my own; my staff had posted them to summarize my prochoice position during the Democratic primary, at a time when some of my opponents were questioning my commitment to protect Roe v. Wade. Within the bubble of Democratic Party politics, this was standard boilerplate, designed to fire up the base. The notion of engaging the other side on the issue was pointless, the argument went; any ambiguity on the issue implied weakness, and faced with the single-minded, give-no-quarter approach of antiabortion forces, we simply could not afford weakness.

Rereading the doctor's letter, though, I felt a pang of shame. Yes, I thought, there were those in the antiabortion movement for whom I had no sympathy, those who jostled or blocked women who were entering clinics, shoving photographs of mangled fetuses in the women's faces and screaming at the top of their lungs; those who bullied and intimidated and occasionally resorted to violence.

But those antiabortion protesters weren't the ones who occasionally appeared at my campaign rallies. The ones I encountered usually showed up in the smaller, downstate communities that we visited, their expressions weary but determined as they stood in silent vigil outside whatever building in which the rally was taking place, their handmade signs or banners held before them like shields. They didn't yell or try to disrupt our events, although they still made my staff jumpy. The first time a group of protesters showed up, my advance team went on red alert; five minutes before my arrival at the meeting hail, they called the car I was in and suggested that I slip in through the rear entrance to avoid a confrontation.

"I don't want to go through the back," I told the staffer driving me. "Tell them we're coming through the front."

We turned into the library parking lot and saw seven or eight protesters gathered along a fence: several older women and what looked to be a family—a man and woman with two young children. I got out of the car, walked up to the group, and introduced myself. The man shook my hand hesitantly and told me his name. He looked to be about my age, in jeans, a plaid shirt, and a St. Louis Cardinals cap. His wife shook my hand as well, but the older women kept their distance. The children, maybe nine or ten years old, stared at me with undisguised curiosity.

"You folks want to come inside?" I asked.

"No, thank you," the man said. He handed me a pamphlet. "Mr. Obama, I want you to know that I agree with a lot of what you have to say."

"I appreciate that."

"And I know you're a Christian, with a family of your own."

"That's true."

"So how can you support murdering babies?"

I told him I understood his position but had to disagree with it. I explained my belief that few women made the decision to terminate a pregnancy casually; that any pregnant woman felt the full force of the moral issues involved and wrestled with her conscience when making that heart-wrenching decision; that I feared a ban on abortion would force women to seek unsafe abortions, as they had once done in this country and as they continued to do in countries that prosecute abortion doctors and the women who seek their services. I suggested that perhaps we could agree on ways to reduce the number of women who felt the need to have abortions in the first place.

The man listened politely and then pointed to statistics on the pamphlet listing the number of unborn children that, according to him, were sacrificed every year. After a few minutes, I said I had to go inside to greet my supporters and asked again if the group wanted to come in. Again the man declined. As I turned to go, his wife called out to me.

"I will pray for you," she said. "I pray that you have a change of heart."

Neither my mind nor my heart changed that day, nor did they in the days to come. But I did have that family in mind as I wrote back to the doctor and thanked him for his email. The next day, I circulated the email to my staff and had the language on my website changed to state in clear but simple terms my prochoice position. And that night, before I went to bed, I said a prayer of my own— that I might extend the same presumption of good faith to others that the doctor had extended to me. (pp. 195–198)

The passage is structured around two narratives, both placed within the context of his political campaign for the Senate. In the first, a doctor emails Obama with the gentle criticism characteristic of the coy pursuer in a courtship. The doctor expresses admiration and even acknowledges joy in his primary vote, but warns of a rhetorical awkwardness that threatens a failed courtship. The reason for the estrangement is not, however, their disagreement over abortion; it is the style of the charge that opposition to abortion emerges from "right-wing ideologues." The form of the email echoes Obama's own favored form—rich recitation of shared commitments—but ends with a charge of betrayal: in this case, betrayal of "fair-mindedness," a trait that the doctor begs to share with Obama.

Obama interrupts this narrative with a second one that takes place at a campaign rally in down-state Illinois—a place of intense courtship for every Chicago politician seeking a state office in Illinois. Obama is met by right-to-life demonstrators picketing outside the site of one of his rallies. He sets up the characters in this narrative—himself and the demonstrators—against counterparts haunting their courtship. An argument by dissociation contrasts these peaceful supplicants with "antiabortion" protestors who confront, deny rights, and even perpetrate violence. The story sets *his* actions against the background of our familiar ur-narrative of campaigns: handlers who "go on red alert" in fear of losing control of the situation, and who demand that he slip in a backdoor. Obama resists their entreaties.

As he arrives at the rally, he sets the narrative into motion. His telling begins by describing his interlocutors with dimensions of shared American values: a family with children; he in jeans, a plaid shirt, and a St. Louis Cardinals hat. They carry "homemade" signs. After a handshake, Obama invites them inside. They decline politely. The husband speaks first, reciting his admiration for Obama, but asserting his disbelief that someone with these qualities can support "murdering babies." Obama's response displaces the dialectical exchange into the morality of abortion and the women who seek abortions. He reassures the interlocutor that all understand the moral pain. The interlocutor offers positive evidence—statistics—but these are deflected into a strategy that emphasizes the ultimate ordering of a joint pursuit of ways to decrease the frequency of abortion. The encounter concludes with Obama repeating his invitation for them to come into his world, the rally. Again they refuse, but with a consummate embracing of Obama from the wife: she will pray that Obama experiences a change of heart.

Obama then returns to his initial narrative of the doctor's letter. Now, though, the letter appears in the context of that remembered family. The offending passages on the website—passages, we are assured, that were the work of an anonymous handler—are changed. Obama ends his day, like the protestor with shared values, praying that he may follow the way of reconciliation. The passage illustrates many of the strengths of Obama's appeal: The dialectical realm is ordered through the ultimate structure of shared American values. Disagreements are acknowledged, but transcended. Narratives are constructed with multiple signals of identification, and many are grounded in a romantic picture of the American middle class: the sincerity of the homemade signs, the jeans and baseball cap, polite decency, and the role of prayer. Even a projection of the post-political dialectical realm is here. Of course, "post-political" is not the correct term; "post-barnyard" may be a more accurate characterization. This world leaves behind handlers of all stripes, and leaves democratic citizens interacting with each other in a ritual of courtship.

Yet, Obama's weaknesses may be on display here as well. In the thematic call for an end to hyper-partisanship that characterized the discourse of the 2008 campaign, he succeeded in contrasting the barnyard and courtship as political styles, but perhaps with an "either/or" assertive force rather than a "both/and" dialectic. Within the dominance of the political narrative of the barnyard, "either/or" potentially transforms the necessary wrangle of politics into hypocrisy. As the campaign evolved, Obama's *theme* chained into the broader political arena—including the media—but his *style* did not. Nor has the increasing politicization of electronic media or the party discipline of Congress yielded to his entreaties since.

Furthermore, "the audacity of hope" is not cathartic. A number of years ago, while researching in a library, I came across the diary of James Iredell, the first Senator from North Carolina. The diary is divided in two distinct parts, separated by many years of inattention. The first part is written by a young James Iredell. Intertwined through these pages are ambition, a desire to make a mark on the world, and an intense pining for the beautiful Hannah Johnson. Iredell's descriptions of his yearning for Hannah are every bit a part of the forming character expressed in those pages. The second part is written by a confident and accomplished man who is grateful for achieving his youthful dreams. This part opens with a brief narrative that fills in the intervening years. Iredell tells the diary that he had successfully courted Hannah, and that, together, they had reached the fullness of life that completed his sense of accomplishment. Obama seems stuck somehow in the first part of this diary. Hope is not an accomplishment; it is anticipation. The denouement is not catharsis, but separation. Division on the issue continues, and the smooth dialectic of taking up specific actions into a cathartic vision is still not fully developed.

THE TRANSITION TO PRESIDENT

I presented these ideas publically at the triennial Kenneth Burke Conference at Villanova University in the summer of 2008, after Obama was identified as the presidential candidate of the Democratic Party, but before his election as president. Obviously, the question that followed the presentation was: Would the characteristics I described continue into his presidency? How would he play the dialectic of the barnyard and courtship?

There have been moments of courtship. On election night in Grant Park, Chicago, Obama (2008) opens his speech to the large crowd and to the citizens beyond:

> If there is anyone out there who still doubts that America is a place where all things are possible; who still wonders if the dream of our founders is alive in our time; who still questions the power of our democracy, tonight is your answer. It's the answer told by lines that stretched around schools and churches in numbers this nation has never seen; by people who waited three hours and four hours, many for the very first time in their lives, because they believed that this time must be different; that their voice could be that difference. It's the answer spoken by young and old, rich and poor, Democrat and Republican, black, white, Latino, Asian, Native American, gay, straight, disabled and not disabled—Americans who sent a message to the world that we have never been a collection of red states and blue states: We are, and always will be, the United States of America. It's the answer that led those who have been told for so long by so many to be cynical, and fearful, and doubtful of what we can achieve to put their hands on the arc of history and bend it once more toward the hope of a better day. It's been a long time coming, but tonight, because of what we did on this day, in this election, at this defining moment, change has come to America.

Here is a voice that transformed the moment into historical significance. That significance is not simply in terms of transcending the moment, but of tying the night into dreams and visions that define the American experience. It was also positively grounded: the lines of voters, the waits, the rich diversity of people, and the expressions of difference and hope in those lines. The speech is not simply an interpretation of a result, but an account of an experience shared by those who listened. The speech's account transforms the barnyard experience of an election campaign at its climax into a national achievement. The celebration is symbolic action; the speech is symbolic action. The speech provided a sort of catharsis that orders the divisiveness of the election into the achievement of a goal historically located at the creation of national meaning. A journey had transformed the nation. In the days that followed the speech, public discussion echoes the sense of national accomplishment—the barrier of race that, for so long, defined possibilities was punctured through the actions of citizens who identified through this man.

Somehow, the implied courtship in "We, the people" seemed more whole, more meaningful to many.

Perhaps this is too optimistic a reading. Perhaps the speech terminates the barnyard, orders it to the decision that was the election, but leaves the dialectic of politics behind and opts for the strategies of courtship. To be sure, it offers a vision of national purpose and achievement, but perhaps it does not so much transform the difference of the politics played out in the dialectic as it suppresses those differences to the symbolic unity—a unity built on the public's relationship to its new president's race. In so doing, perhaps it only performs the typical ritualistic process between the election and the inauguration: the celebration of national unity exemplified in the patriotic acceptance of election results and the peaceful transfer of power.

Obama's (2009a) inaugural address, as is characteristic of the genre, celebrates this standard ritual in its opening paragraphs. The inaugural address is, in fact, heavy on strategies that define the identity of national purpose with the symbolic meaning of the first ascendance of an African American to the presidency. The ancestral narrative of the pioneer experience is expanded to include those who "toiled in the sweatshops" and "endured the lash of the whip." This expanded notion of "we" is then celebrated in traditional ways: the dedication of the present moment, founded in the sacrifices of earlier generations. It presents action framed in commitments of policy; for example, Obama declares that "We will build the roads and bridges, the electric grids and digital lines that feed our commerce and bind us together." Again, commonalities are celebrated in the speech, abstract enough in character to safely suppress differences. That, Burke would tell us, is the language of courtship.

Of course, this standard transition has its ritualistic time, and that time ends after the inauguration. As of this writing, the dialectical struggle of politics has been renewed. Health care reform is preoccupying his administration and his discourse. Opposition is affirming the reality of the barnyard metaphor. Town Hall meetings are raucous and rude. Efforts for "bipartisanship" are met with Congressional votes nearly along party lines. Half-truths and falsehoods fill the public domain. For a master of the synthesis of courtship and the barnyard, this is the time for dialectic, for transforming the disputes of politics through language's potential for synthesis. This is the moment to see if Obama has mastered Burkean possibilities.

Alas, there is much potential yet unfulfilled. On June 11, 2009, in the midst of the wrangle over health care policy, Obama (2009b) conducted a town hall meeting at Southwest High School in Green Bay, Wisconsin. Certainly, the choice of venue and format forecasts dialectic within the synthetic power of courtship and the wrangle of politics. The president was among the people, encouraging them to participate in a dialogue—one whereby the dialectic of the barnyard could be transformed through an exchange of democratic discourse. Of course, as town halls have evolved, barriers remain. If the possibilities of courtship point to the "transcending of social estrangement" (Burke, 1951/1969, p. 208), the clear status difference between a president and a school teacher or nurse must be overcome. When the speakers "conducting" these town hall meetings begin with a lengthy statement, the estrangement of power is reinforced. Anger often results when the promise of dialogue meets the reality of opening statements, and when a speaker seeks to retain control of the town hall meeting that he or she sponsored. Estrangement of status clashes with the promise of communion, yielding a whiff of hypocrisy that intensifies the wrangle. Our focus should be on the possibilities of strategy within the exchange. We should assess the speaker's response to a challenge that differentiates status presents. Without the estrangement of status, the need for courtship vanishes.

The strategic choices made within the hour-long discussion in Green Bay demonstrate the weaknesses of Obama's (2009b) attempt to dialectically synthesize the potential of courtship and the actuality of the political barnyard. Even at a basic level, that of producing identification with the audience, Obama's strategies are surprisingly crude. There is the "it is great to be back in Green Bay" and a reference to the Packers, Green Bay's most central civic icon—its professional football team. There was even a rather direct appeal: "Come on, we can bring everybody together." In fact, this identification strategy itself suggests that this was not the work of a transformative politician; the strategy is so standard that it stands as a sign of the typical discourse of the barnyard. Identification by geography defines commonality at the circumference of the empirical audience for the event; it does not transcend the event—celebrating the principles, commitments, history, or even commonalities of the national public. Rather, it isolates the moment from the national dialectic toward which the town hall meeting is to contribute.

The moment featured in the media's diffusion of the event was, in fact, also an attempt at identification. A citizen introduced himself and his daughter to President Obama, noting that his ten-year-old daughter was missing a day of school to be at the town hall meeting. The President offered to write a note to the teacher asking that the daughter be excused. Of course, here was the chief executive of the United States engaging a simple act of civic truancy, a flattening of status in reaching out to the simple transgression of a ten-year old. At the same time, here was the cop celebrating his power by canceling a traffic ticket. The act of identification became a symbolic expression of status estrangement.

At a deeper, substantive level that effective political identification achieves, Obama's (2009b) strategy forsook the transformative power of courtship for the raw wrangle of identification through division. The following paragraph from the President's introduction illustrates the giving of an account of the political moment:

> So don't let people scare you. If you like what you've got, we're not going to make you change. But in order to preserve what's best about our health care system, we have to fix what doesn't work. For we've reached the point where doing nothing about the cost of health care is no longer an option. The status quo is unsustainable. If we don't act, and act soon to bring down costs, it will jeopardize everybody's health care. If we don't act, every American will feel the consequences in higher premiums—which, by the way, means lower take-home pay, because it's not as if those costs are all borne by your employer; that's money that could have gone to giving you a raise—in lost jobs and shuttered businesses, in a rising number of uninsured and a rising debt that our children and their children will be paying off for decades. If we do nothing, within a decade we will be spending one out of every five dollars we earn on health care. And in thirty years, we'll be spending one out of every three dollars we earn on health care. And that's untenable. It's unacceptable. I will not allow it as President of the United States.

Here is the language of the barnyard. We do not have the comic frame: those who would scare you are not simply mistaken, they are ill-motivated. There is no attempt to transcend this division. The audience is warned of the interlocutor. Here, the President is a protector, warning of the dangers in this wrangle. As protector, the President postulates himself not as an expression of public will, but as a policy manipulator with the cathartic power to promise, "we're not going to make you change." Here is the emphasis on differentials of power and points of policy action that places citizens into a matrix of power that differentiates the powerful and the powerless, the political world of the wrangle.

The paragraph rests its description of the health care system in a positive vocabulary. There is statistical evidence to accompany the discussion of employers, raises, and other economic facts. Clearly, these facts are marshaled in a dialectical effort—to make the case for reform, but that case does not draw *both* from the ultimate *and* the positive in conducting the dialectic. The ultimate—the promise of good health, or even the desire to provide for a family and a better world for one's children—is not drawn into the account. In fact, the unsustainability of the status quo is a threat as scary as what those "other people" will offer. Obama fails to construct a framework that realigns the failures into a cathartic promise of change. Thus, the alignments of the paragraph quoted above are divisions and threats, they lack the transcendent powers contributed by the potentiality of ultimate terms. In fact, the analytic resources of division are much more powerful in this account than the resources of merger. The issues predominate—costs, the number of uninsured, the impact on national debt—with only a vague "what's best in our health care system" as counterweight.

The compensatory possibilities that would counter the fear that is the theme of this paragraph are introduced in the next:

> Health care reform is not something I just cooked up when I took office. Sometimes I hear people say, he's taking on too much, why is he—I'm not doing this because I don't have enough to do. (Laughter.) We need health care reform because it's central to our economic future. It's central to our long-term prosperity as a nation. In past years and decades there may have been some disagreement on this point, but not anymore. Today, we've already built an unprecedented coalition of people who are ready to reform our health care system: physicians and health insurers; businesses and workers; Democrats and Republicans. (Obama, 2009b)

The merger here is "agreement." This merger is not, however, so much with the resources of ultimate terms as with the arrangement of the political landscape. "You" is the persona of the paragraph quoted earlier; "I" is the persona of the paragraph quoted above. "We" slips from a generalized, corporate civic reference to the building of a political coalition, and that coalition-building is based in categories of status, not a broad public identification. The pointing function in the vocabulary of this paragraph—the resources of positive terms—is comparatively weak. Terms such as "economic future" and "long-term prosperity as a nation" are also more reports on effects than they are the defined ultimate terms of national public courtship.

These paragraphs do not work with the resources of permanence and change to frame the political moment—nor, indeed, does Obama's entire statement. The value of commitments, history, and principles in a rhetoric of permanence and change lies in their ability to expand the circumference of the political moment into a substantive identification—one that connects the wrangle of the barnyard to the identity of civic courtship. Since these strategies fail to transcend the current dispute by assimilating it into a broader narrative, they also fail to call upon Obama's full resources in the dialectical dispute.

Not even transitioning to a question-and-answer format could displace these tendencies to emphasize the barnyard. Of course, one difficulty of the overt exchange of question-and-answer is that the speaker must respond to the question asked, or risk the charge that he or she is not truly in exchange with the questioner. As a consequence, the trick is to respond to the sub-stance of the question, but to strategically array rhetorical resources to fur-ther the political goal. In town hall meetings, questions are often devoid of the rhetorical sophistication that I am demanding of Obama. For example, the father whose daughter accompanied him to the town hall meeting began by reciting his personal story of involvement in managing health care re-sources. He then asked a non-sequitur question: "What is the timeline that we have set up for this? . . . for the uninsured being able to get . . . something . . . ?" This is a performance that begins with "I" and ends in a technical, positive inquiry. Obama (2009b) responded by saying:

> Well, look, we're not going to be able—whatever reforms we set up, it will probably take a couple of years to get it in place . . . . There are some things that I think we should be able to do fairly quickly. For example, the pre-existing condition issue, some of the insurance reform issues I think we should be able to get in place more rapidly. The thing that I think we're going to have to spend the most time thinking about and really get right—and you probably know more about this than I do, because you're working with a lot of these em-ployers and insurers and so forth—is how do we change the medi-cal delivery systems that can either drive costs way up and decrease quality or drive cost down and improve quality? Let me describe to you what's happening, part of the reason that Green Bay is doing a better job than some other parts of the country. There are places where doctors typically work together as teams. And they start off asking themselves, "How can we provide the best possible care for this patient?" And because they're coordinating, they don't order a bunch of duplicative tests. And the primary care physician who ini-tially sees the patient is in contact with all the specialists so that in one meeting they can consult with each other and make a series of decisions. And then they don't over-prescribe, and they make deci-sions about how quickly you can get somebody out of a hospital, be-cause oftentimes being in a hospital actually increases the incidence of infection, for example. So there's a whole series of decisions that can be made that improve quality, increase coordination, but actu-ally lower costs.

The question was indeed transformed into something broader than tim-ing, but the transformation was not a rich synthesis that draws upon ultimate terms to achieve a catharsis with health care reform. The resources of the positive are emphasized, but are hardly even drawn into generalization, and they are certainly not made meaningful with the resources of ultimate terms. Merger is the cooperation of physicians, not the actions of a unified people achieving their common commitments and identifying goals. In fact, a cold division of analysis controls this answer. The vocabulary that adds scope is not of transcendence, but a "spreading" through the health care system.

Of course, the failures here do not necessarily predict failure for the Obama administration's health care reform efforts; politicians do succeed, despite dwelling in the political barnyard. My purpose is not to predict success at policy, but rather to point to the partiality of our politics and to assess Obama's promise as a departure from that partiality. Kenneth Burke provides us a glance at a richer and more fulsome image of democratic politics. Against this measure, Obama remains short of bringing the full range of his political resources into the dialectic of politics. The moments of courtship remain separated from the moments of political wrangling, and the synthetic power to merge these two moments into a leadership that brings true change—a change that permeates the culture—remains elusive.

CONCLUSION

In the beginning of this chapter, I teased out an alternative to traditional conceptions of politics, one rooted in Burke's symbolic perspective. This alternative posits politics as a mode for transforming communities and emphasizes the synthetic powers of language—but not because synthesis is the essence of politics, but because our politics and our analysis of politics have lopsidedly featured the divisiveness of the political art. Through his invocation of the wrangle of the barnyard and of courtship, Burke describes a rich, functional politics through which a society can adjust to its evolving character and context. As a consequence, the vision I have deployed invokes a politics that operates at the dialectical level of dispute and disagreement, while also productively permitting the evolution of society's motivations and orientations.

Over the last half century, the divisive voice of politics in the United States has been louder than the inspirational. With the exception of John Kennedy and Ronald Reagan, the discourses of politics have seemed harsh and characteristic of the Burkean barnyard. Burke's political vision, however, was not to re-balance harshness and inspiration. Rather, it was to create a dialectic of politics that would meet the exigencies of the time, calling upon the many resources of language to bring a public together in pursuit of a just and prosperous society. In this difficult endeavor, the synthetic power of language is key. The many synthetic opposites, the pairs of terms tracked by Burke—such as positive and ultimate terms, identification and division, merger and division, consubstantiality and identity, and permanence and change—represent the resources that symbolic action employs to unleash the creative power of social estrangement and identification.

During the 2008 presidential election season, Barack Obama inspired many people. He seemed to be a master of the dimensions of courtship in politics. His admirers were not only numerous, but were also dedicated. He inspired involvement in a new generation of citizens. In his rhetoric, he not only performed the courtship of the citizenry, but he also wrangled with opponents on the style of their politics. He offered a new voice worthy of attention. So, in considering the crafting of this chapter, shining this Burkean scheme upon Obama's discourse seemed a way to explore its intricacies.

Comparing Barack Obama to Martin Luther King Jr. is perhaps unfair. King was, after all, a favorite for the title of greatest rhetor of the twentieth century. King never entered electoral politics, but the ultimate power of his rhetoric has no greater symbol than Barack Obama's election as President of the United States. King may be a paradigmatic case of the successful synthesis of the two metaphors of politics. He was able to point clearly to the injustices of his society, but did so in a way that their injustice emerged from their violation of the identity of the culture that sustained them. Further, in this effort, he called upon the ultimates of his culture to motivate commitments to redress the violations of that identity. His rhetoric established a motivational momentum that carried the culture in a definable direction in that half century.

Obama shares King's power to order the dialectic through the ultimate, but has yet to achieve King's skill in giving the dialectic the realism of the positive. Obama provides moments of political courtship that are unmatched, perhaps, since King. His ability to debate the intricacies of policy and to defend his mandate within the arena of the barnyard remains uncertain. However, the political voices typical of these two metaphors have not yet given way to a synthetic voice: the voice of leadership that accepts the division of the wrangle and reorients them through hierarchies of values lying at the heart of the political culture. Sometimes his gestures toward identification have the tin sound of a lapel pin rather than the dialectical tension of consubstantiality and identity. Sometimes he chooses among the ultimate terms that shape courtship, or among the positive terms of the policy wonk with which political battle is performed, rather than calling upon the resources of each kind of term in transforming public understanding of social problems. Thus, this Burkean way of seeing the political art defines a political challenge, to Obama and to all Americans. The politics it describes—including the power to transform the culture it serves—represents a possibility not yet realized, but perhaps envisioned in and for our time.

NOTES

1. To this point, most work on Burke and politics has called upon *Permanence and Change* (1935/1984) and *Attitudes Toward History* (1937/1984). These two books were written during Burke's most active political period (the 1930s) while *A Rhetoric of Motives* was written after Burke's interests had turned more toward the philosophical task of creating a system for understanding language and action. My goal is to draw upon later texts, when Burke looks back upon his active political period and learns about how politics works from it.

REFERENCES

Birdsell, D. S. (1987). Ronald Reagan on Lebanon and Grenada: Flexibility and interpretation in the application of Kenneth Burke's pentad. *Quarterly Journal of Speech, 732*, 67–79.

Brock, B. L. (1965). *A definition of four political positions and a description of their rhetorical characteristics.* (Unpublished doctoral dissertation). Northwestern University, Evanston, IL.

Brock, B. L. (1966). Political speaking: A Burkeian approach. In W. H. Rueckert (Ed.), *Critical responses to Kenneth Burke, 1924–1966* (pp. 444–456). Minneapolis, MN: University of Minnesota Press.

Brock, B. L., Huglen, M. E., Klumpp, J. F., & Howell, S. (2005). *Making sense of political ideology.* Lanham, MD: Rowman and Littlefield.

Burke, K. (1935, 27 April). Revolutionary symbolism in America. Speech at the American Writers' Congress, New York. In H. S. Simons, & T. Melia (Eds.), *The legacy of Kenneth Burke* (pp. 267–273). Madison, WI: University of Wisconsin Press, 1989.

Burke, K. (1935/1984). *Permanence and change: An anatomy of purpose* (3rd ed.). Berkeley, CA: University of California Press. (Original work published 1935)

Burke, K. (1937/1984). *Attitudes toward history* (3rd ed.). Berkeley, CA: University of California Press. (Original work published 1937)

Burke, K. (1939). The rhetoric of Hitler's 'Battle.' *Southern Review, 5*, 1–21. Repr. in *The philosophy of literary form* (pp. 191–220). Berkley, CA: University of California Press.

Burke, K. (1941/1973). *The philosophy of literary form: Studies in symbolic action* (3rd ed.). Berkeley, CA: University of California Press. (Original work published 1941)

Burke, K. (1945/1969). *A grammar of motives.* Berkeley, CA: University of California Press. (Original work published 1945)

Burke, K. (1951/1969). *A rhetoric of motives.* Berkeley, CA: University of California Press. (Original work published 1951)

Burke, K. (1961/1970). *The rhetoric of religion: Studies in logology.* Berkeley, CA: University of California Press. (Original work published 1961)

Duncan, H. D. (1968). *Symbols in society.* New York, NY: Oxford University Press.

Edelman, M. J. (1964). *Symbolic uses of politics*. Urbana, IL: University of Illinois Press.

Edelman, M. J. (1971). *Politics as symbolic action: Mass arousal and quiescience*. Chicago, IL: Markham Press.

Edelman, M. J. (1977). *Political language: Words that succeed and policies that fail*. New York, NY: Academic Press.

Edelman, M. J. (1988). *Constructing the political spectacle*. Chicago, IL: University of Chicago Press.

Foss, S. K., & Griffin, C. L. (1995). Beyond persuasion: A proposal for an invitational rhetoric. *Communication Monographs, 62*, 2–18.

Klumpp, J. F. (1993). A rapprochement between dramatism and argumentation. *Argumentation and Advocacy, 29*, 148–63.

Ling, D. A. (1970). A pentadic analysis of senator Edward Kennedy's address to the people of Massachusetts, July 25, 1969. *Central States Speech Journal, 21*, 81–86.

Nimmo, D. (1974). *Popular images of politics*. Englewood Cliffs, NJ: Prentice Hall.

Obama, B. (2006). *The audacity of hope: Thoughts on reclaiming the American dream*. New York, NY: Three Rivers Press.

Obama, B. (2008). *Barack Obama's election night remarks*. Retrieved from http://www.politico.com/news/stories/1108/15294.html

Obama, B. (2009a). *First inaugural address*. Retrieved from http://www.bartleby.com/124/pres68.html

Obama, B. (2009b). *Remarks by the President in town hall meeting on health care, Southwest High School, Green Bay, WI*. Retrieved from http://www.whitehouse.gov/the_press_office/Remarks-by-the-President-in-Town-Hall-Meeting-on-Health-Care-in-Green-Bay-Wisconsin/

Pepper, S. (1942). *World hypotheses: A study in evidence*. Berkeley, CA: University of California Press.

3 Rounding (Out) the Bases of Racial Reconciliation: (Dia)Logology and Virginia's Apology or Slavery

John B. Hatch

As Germany and other interests that profited owed reparations to Jews following the holocaust of Nazi persecution, America and other interests that profited owe reparations to blacks following the holocaust of African slavery which has carried forward from slavery's inception for 350-odd years to the end of U.S. government-embraced racial discrimination—an end that arrived, it would seem, only just yesterday.

— Randall Robinson

Redressing slavery should be about honor, not alms. It should be about black pride and dignity, and, last but not least, it should be about commemorating and memorializing the slaves.

— Roy L. Brooks

The shift in orientation from the first quote to the second illustrates the motive power of reconciliation as trope and terminology to reshape responses to collective injustice. Both Robinson (2001) and Brooks (2004) unapologetically advocate slavery reparations, and both construct an urgent, moral exigence for addressing the racialized legacy of slavery. Nonetheless, their divergent framings of that exigence exemplify the difference made by the choice of reconciliation discourse. What might seem, on the surface, to connote a simple matter of healing divisions or reuniting alienated parties, "reconciliation" proves instead to be a painful and profound discursive process of ethical transcendence (and transformation) by perspective in rhetorical dialogue. Far from glossing over justice, reconciliation reframes *redress* (understood as ordered compensation) into a voluntary and creative *re-dressing* of unhealed wounds; it transforms atonement (as victimage) into *at-one*-ment (reuniting offenders and the offended in a moral community of shared values and mutual benefits). Thus, in Brooks's (2004) model of reparations, racial reconciliation is the chief goal of slave redress and is a federal apology for slavery is the *sine qua non* for reaching this objective. In turn, full atonement—including reparations in the form of a national slavery museum and an atonement trust fund—facilitates black forgiveness (pp. 138–163).

What of Robinson's (2001) very pointed concern: the *debt* that America owes blacks in terms of uncompensated labor, lives and cultures lost, and rights and freedoms suppressed? When we speak of forgiveness, is justice not on the verge of being dissolved in a sea of forgetfulness? This question presupposes a semantic ideal of strict justice (exacted in terms of monetary calculations), whereas reconciliation aims at what Kenneth Burke (1941/1973) refers to as the "poetic ideal," the attainment of "a full moral act" motivated by a wholeness of ethical perspective (p. 148). In a sense, reconciliation aims at *poetic justice*, not as a solely symbolic rectification (i.e., a "merely rhetorical" invention), but rather as an inventive approach to justice that *reorients and reconstitutes the terms* of a just society in the process of substantively rebalancing moral scales.

This essay explores elements and operations of that process, both in terms of key Burkean concepts and in texts of the first state apology for slavery. Just as Brooks places apology at the heart of redress, so will a fuller understanding and a fairer assessment of this lately emerging phenomenon—the slavery apology—be central to appreciating how racial reconciliation may rhetorically recast the coinage of redress into something fuller and more ethically satisfying than strict material compensation. This exploration promises rich payoffs in terms of re-tooled Burkean instruments of analysis, enriched understandings of a social phenomenon that are relatively new to the arenas of politics and academia, and potentially expanded political options for dealing with the persistent legacy of racism.

Indeed, the transcendence and enlargement of perspective produced by a decade (and more) of vigorous reconciliation discourse on global and local stages has significantly transformed the terms of America's national "conversation on race," at least at some levels. Perhaps the change is best exemplified by the fact that President Bill Clinton who, despite his initiation of an unprecedented National Conversation on Race, declined to apologize for slavery out of fear that it might open a floodgate of reparations demands. More recently, Florida's Republican governor Charlie Crist not only affirmed the legislature's passage of a thorough apology for slavery and racial discrimination, but also suggested that the state consider *offering reparations* to African Americans (Hafenbrack & Kennedy, 2008).

As a result, in this chapter, I present a distillation of Burkean insights that have emerged in an ongoing investigation of racial reconciliation (Doxtader & Villa-Vicencio, 2003; Hatch, 2003; Hatch, 2006a; Hatch, 2006b: Hatch, 2008), followed by an illustrative analysis of Virginia's ground-breaking slavery apology of 2007. I begin by explicating reconciliation as a form of epideictic discourse that seeks to shore up, repair, or reconstruct the ethical foundation (*ethos*) of a society cleft by a legacy of violence and injustice. I then address how it does this work, taking key aspects of Burkean thought (framing, grammar of motives, and logology) in new directions. In light of popular and scholarly reconciliation discourse, my reworking of these concepts converges in a framework of constitutive values that also serve as rhetorical frames on the project of reconciliation. Using this framework, I then examine Virginia's trailblazing slavery apology to illustrate how reconciliation transforms the terms of racial justice and healing in productive, if somewhat problematic, ways.

RECONCILIATION: REDEMPTION REFRAMED IN DIALOGUE, OR ACCEPTANCE IN THE MAKING

In his pioneering studies of reconciliation in South Africa and beyond, Doxtader (2003) shows that the concept constitutes "a call for rhetoric and a form of rhetorical activity. In both, individuals locked in conflict employ speech to turn historical justifications for violence toward mutual oppositions that set the stage for civil (dis)agreement and common understanding" (p. 268). As a result, Doxtader characterizes reconciliation as "a rhetorical performance and norm of rhetorical practice that productively opposes the definitional logic that sustains identitarian thinking and some forms of identity-based politics" (p. 269). Elsewhere, I have suggested that reconciliation is a *dialogic* rhetoric (Hatch, 2003) that (re)shapes the collective self, the Other, and their relationship in language, while also knitting the torn ethical fabric of society. Although reconciliation addressed to recent, violent conflict may be a matter of *realpolitik* that enables political transition,[1] Brooks (2004) insists that the legacy of slavery and Jim Crow is an exigence for "moral reflection rather than political confrontation," leading to moral *action* in accord with what he calls the "post-Holocaust spirit of heightened morality, identity, egalitarianism, and restorative justice" (pp. xii, 141). As a performance of public reflection on the past, then, reconciliation is fundamentally *epideictic*, as I have contended elsewhere (Hatch, 2008).[2] Through representative apologies and related acts, reconciliation displays historical actions and agents against a backdrop of enlarged social values, it seeks to reconstitute alienated parties' identities *in relation* to one another, it enacts a kind of healing and redemption for (and among) them, and it (re)establishes their mutual and common good as the ground for political action. The question is: How does it accomplish this epideictic work? The answer, I believe, lies at the nexus between Burke's notions of *framing*, the motive power of *terms* of human action, and logology.

In *Attitudes Toward History*, Burke (1984) shows that humans inevitably construct, and choose among, construals of the universe or history that suggest how one should act in the face of evil or suffering. Through these terminological systems or frames, we "name the friendly or unfriendly functions and relationships in such a way that we are able to do something about them," and in so doing, "we form our characters, since the names embody attitudes" (p. 4). Frames, then, are inherently ethical orientations. Although all such framing entails accepting certain elements and rejecting others, Burke refers to the more well-rounded and enduring naming-systems that enable one to find a meaningful place within one's historical situation as "frames of acceptance."

Reconciliation, I argue, involves *acceptance in the making*—a process of reframing the historical situation (and of "trying on" different frames) in order both to *accept* it and *make it more acceptable* (redeeming it). As a process of negotiation *between* parties, reconciliation entails productive interplay among disparate frames of reference on the situation, leading to greater depth perception and coordination of action for the shared good of parties whom historical actions have set each other at odds. Thus, *reconciliation is a form of transcendence by perspective*. Indeed, previous work in the field has characterized the nature of that transcendence. Doxtader's (2003, 2007) analysis implicitly locates reconciliation between the comic and the tragic, claiming that it stands, as Burke (1984) writes, in "a deeply ambiguous relation to the law of non-contradiction," such that it "both opposes exclusivity and puts the exclusive into play" (pp. 274–275). Elsewhere, I have applied Burkean frames for such analysis, arguing that reconciliation seriously addresses injustices between parties (in a tragic frame) *and* re(dis)covers their inherent relations (in a comic frame) as grounds for peace (Hatch, 2008).

Characterizing reconciliation as tragic-comic creates a temptation to resolve its contradiction in a tidy Hegelian synthesis; however, Doxtader (2007) warns against dissolving reconciliation's contingency into a matrix of mutually compensatory concepts (p. 137). On the contrary, reconciliation is better understood as "the inauguration of a dialectic with more than two sides" (Doxtader, 2003, p. 59). In a study of reconciliation discourse across disciplines (Hatch, 2008), I found that many of its recurring debates revolve around key value-terms that are bound up in multiple dialectical relationships with one another, including:

- peace (or, "reconciliation" as peace-making) vs. truth (in history, memory, etc.);
- justice vs. truth;
- agency (especially forgiveness, granting amnesty, or "grace,") vs. truth;
- justice vs. peace;
- justice (often as repentance/restitution) vs. agency (in the form of forgiveness or amnesty); and
- peace (or "reconciliation") vs. agency (of victims).

From such debates, one can distill four broad, polysemic values (or value-constellations) that recur as terms in tension, controversy, and conversation (Hatch, 2008). These are: Truth (factuality, historicity, sincerity, and so on), Agency (that is, *agent*-cy: responsibility, freedom, grace, etc.), Justice (fairness, right, law), and Peace (unity, harmony, civility, and the like). Each of these constellations of terms may work not only as a focal point of attention, but also as a point of view in reconciliation. In other words, they function both as value-terms in focus and as *terministic screens* (Burke, 1966).

Northrop Frye's (1957) literary theory of myths suggests the possibility of treating this "tetrad"—Justice, Peace, Truth, and Agency—as a deep structure of values across many cultures and ages. Out of the diversity of literary genres, Frye distills four fundamental mythic forms: comedy, tragedy, irony, and romance. As a result, we can profitably approach Frye through Burke's (1941) own terministic screen of dramatism, viewing literature as a stock of orientations to life or "equipment for living" (pp. 293–304). If we do so, we may then reasonably suppose that, along with the comic and tragic frames so thoroughly explored and explicated by Burke, the ironic and romantic frames represent definitive and significant orientations to human existence and public discourse. If the tragic frame aligns with a law/justice orientation, and if the comic frame aligns with a peace/harmony orientation, then the romantic and ironic, I argue, correspond with orientations dominated by agency and truth, respectively. As characterized by Frye (in partial contrast with Camille K. Lewis's (2008) recent proposal[3]), romance hinges on unfolding triumphant heroism; its driving principle is a revelation of powerful and/or virtuous agen(t)cy through adventures and trials that test the hero. Ironic literature, on the other hand, embodies a kind of cynical realism. In other words, irony exposes the baser motives and fundamental realities/truths underlying human pretensions of (romantic) virtue, (comic) peacefulness, and (tragic) justice.

While he does not speak of a "romantic frame" *per se,* in *Attitudes Toward History* Burke (1984) does identify a related form—the epic—as a typical frame of acceptance for people living "under primitive, non-commercial conditions" of perpetual struggle with the natural elements and tribal enemies (p. 34). To "make men 'at home' in those conditions," the epic "magnif[ies] the role of the warlike hero . . . 'advertising' courage and individual sacrifice for group advantage" (pp. 35–36). Because Burke relegates the epic to a pre-commercial era, he does not treat it as a viable orientation to the present. Similarly, Burke's treatment of romanticism as a characteristic "rejection philosophy" of the nineteenth century obscures the potential value of a romantic frame (p. 29).

In contrast with Burke's historical approach, Frye (1957) presents romance as a perennial mythic form and, by implication, as a frame of potentially significant applicability to the present world. For Frye, the defining element of the romance is the heroic quest—a thread that ties romantic literature of the nineteenth century back to the epic itself through tales of adventure and heroism in the intervening ages. Romance "is nearest of all literary forms to the wish-fulfillment dream," and has a "perennially childlike quality" (p. 186). In one sense, it is *ego*-centric in that it is centered on an *agent* whose strength of character transcends or overpowers adverse circumstances. In contrast irony "attempts to give form to the shifting ambiguities and complexities of unidealized existence" (p. 223). Its core value, I argue, is naked truth: debunking myths, deflating heroes, and showing things as they really are. Thus, if the follower of Burke is to translate Frye's mythic form of irony into a frame, the term "realistic frame" may be more serviceable than "ironic frame," especially given the much broader and fuller sense with which Burke has imbued the term "irony." Nonetheless, in at least one place, Burke (1984) counterposes "irony" to romanticism, just as he locates "the 'debunking' school of biography" in opposition to hero-worship within the epic frame (p. 36).[4] Thus, a Burkean take on Frye's mythic forms (as frames) might well support Frye's claim that the pairs *comedy/tragedy* and *irony/romance* are opposites.

Similarly, among the dialectics posed in reconciliation literature, the strongest oppositions appear between peace(making) and justice, and between truth (as disclosing or remembering wrongs, facing material realities, etc.) and agency (in forgetting/transcending the past, or relying upon mere words of apology, forgiving, or symbols of reconciliation to inaugurate a new future). I take the parallel between these two sets of oppositions as indirect support for my argument that comedy, tragedy, irony (*a la* Frye), and romance *as frames* correspond with peace, justice, truth, and agen(t)cy *as terministic screens*. Furthermore, both as terms and as frames, Agency, Justice, Peace, and Truth are constitutive values—an ethical grammar of reconciliation—that, *together*, must motivate reconciliation (while informing and reforming each other) if it is ultimately to be satisfactory.

While Burke's pentad (Scene, Act, Agent, Agency, Purpose) is an ontological grammar of human motivation centered in the notion of *action*, I propose this tetrad of value-terms as a parallel and complementary *axiological* grammar of motivation grounded in the notion of *purpose*, particularly in a sense of the *good* toward which human action *should aim*. The term Agency, shared by both grammars, brings the difference into clear focus. In the pentad, Agency is a construed means by which action is taken toward whatever purpose the discourse has constructed. In the tetrad I propose, by contrast, Agency connotes the parties' capacity for action as subjects: Agen(t)cy as an ethical good that encompasses such values as freedom, self-determination, responsibility, accountability, and dignity—all values that reconciliation purportedly should enhance or recover.[5] As such, it is one measure of the goodness or rightness of the purpose constructed in reconciliation discourse. Reconciliation *imposed* on victims of oppression does not truly reconcile because it does not facilitate a restoration of agency—of choice and voice—for those who have been deprived of it; as such, it sustains the injustice that goes hand-in-hand with conflict and enmity between groups. On the other hand, reconciliation that does not aim, at least obliquely, toward forgiveness may represent a denial of victims' freedom (and perhaps responsibility) to transcend the past at some point.[6]

RECONCILIATION, RELIGION, AND (DIA)LOGOLOGY

Taking agency and forgiveness seriously in relation to sociopolitical realities may raise eyebrows. Indeed, Christian Lundberg and Joshua Gunn (2005) specifically critique liberal faith in "an evangelical subject enthusiastically wedded to a humanist gospel that has elevated agency to the status of the godly, lording over the material and spiritual universe" (p. 84). They also emphasize that the existence of agency in human affairs does not, in itself, demonstrate the existence of some irreducible *agent* (subject) as its source. Rather, using the Ouija board as a metaphor, Lundberg and Gunn contend that agency may arise from "language, ideology, perhaps even a spirit" (p. 88). This analysis gives rise to a serious concern, however: Absent any given or inalienable agency inherent in their selves as subjects, upon what *ethos* (place) might victims of oppression stand against the unjust language, ideology, and spirit of a regime?

A different spiritual metaphor for agency suggests an answer to this problem, in both theory and practice. In the African American worship experience, rhetorical agency is jointly enacted and co-produced in a dynamic, communal interplay of personal and collective voices of members possessing (and being possessed by) the Spirit (Asante, 1998, pp. 103–107). Agency flows among congregants in the improvisation of song, testimony, preaching, and congregational response, is inspirited by biblical narratives and tropes, and is hermeneutically appropriated through black oral traditions. This moving of the spirit in black congregations has been a lifeline of agency in a hostile sea of whiteness (in contrast to the spidery threads of morbid fascination emanating from the Ouija board). It has also sustained a subjectivity their oppressors could not deconstruct, subjugate, or subvert.[7] As such, the black church has, more often than not, nourished a capacity for forgiveness hand-in-hand with resistance against injustice.

The concept of forgiveness, like reconciliation and atonement, bears strong religious overtones. It is not surprising, then, that writers and activists operating self-consciously out of faith traditions have made a disproportionate contribution to thinking and acting for social reconciliation during the past two decades. Reconciliation's epideictic focus on the ethical terms under which a good society may be (re)constructed, together with its frequent grounding in religious traditions, points toward logology as a resource for understanding and critiquing its discourse. In *The Rhetoric of Religion*, Burke (1961) introduces logology as an epistemological framework for understanding language as symbolic action, and makes his case for modeling logology after the verbal *form* of theological assertions (while bracketing its content). Burke reasons that theology "almost necessarily becomes an example of words used with thoroughness. Since words-about-God would be as far-reaching as words can be, the 'rhetoric of religion' furnishes a good instance of terministic enterprise in general" (p. vi). As epistemology logology provides a conceptual forum where the religious and the secular may meet without reducing one to the other.

Among the analogies Burke sees between logology and Christian theology, the formal similarity between the linguistic situation and the Trinity is particularly relevant. Burke suggests that the relation between a thing and its name is like that between the Father and Son, or God and the Word (*Logos*). In each case, the former can be said to "generate" the latter, while the latter embodies/governs knowledge of the former. Thus, these "opposites" (Father-Son, thing-name) are properly understood as interdependent *counterparts* that are characterized by a relation of "correspondence" or, in personal terms, "communion" (theologically identified as a third "person"—the Holy Spirit). However, Burke's emphasis on "correspondence" (language as representation) over "communion" (language as dialogue), renders his logology less helpful than it could be in understanding reconciliation. Indeed, his comic frame (and his critical motto, *ad bellum purificandum*) notwithstanding, Burke offers little hope or direction for promoting harmony in (inter) action. Perhaps that is because, as some critics point out, he tends to over-emphasize the symbol as the essence of language, the negative as its defining characteristic, and hierarchy-building as its compulsion.[8]

However, language itself need not be seen primarily through the lens of its negativity.[9] In this light, logology might reasonably be rendered as dia-logology, treating terms not merely as mechanistically interconnected, but as *inter-acting* with one another in the dialogic dynamism of discourse. This notion is certainly not absent from Burke's (1969) work; it leaps from his de-scription of irony as that which

> arises when one tries, by the interaction of terms upon one another, to produce a *development* which uses all of the terms. Hence, from the standpoint of this total form (this "perspective of perspectives"), none of the participating "sub-perspectives" can be treated as either precisely right or precisely wrong. They are all voices, or personali-ties, or positions, integrally affecting one another. (p. 512)

I argue that an ironic logology, or (dia)logology, better accounts for the dy-namic and (inter)personal process of coming to terms in reconciliation.

One confronts another problem when attempting to apply Burkean lo-gology to reconciliation discourse, with its frequently religious terminolo-gy or grounding narratives. Burke's understandable obsession with negative and hierarchical impulses in language led him to focus on these elements in Christian religious texts to the detriment of other, equally important el-ements. For instance, Burke's logological analysis of the Judeo-Christian scriptures yields a cluster (or "cycle") of terms implicit in the idea of *Order* (both as prohibitive command and as hierarchy), despite his acknowledge-ment of the prevalence of *covenant* language in biblical texts.[10] If Order (as prohibition and hierarchy) is one side of the Covenant coin, surely a term such as Communion or Relation constitutes the other. Here, the positive commands to love God and one's neighbor as oneself are implied. Agency is opened up and pervaded by what Paul Ricoeur (1995) refers to as "solicitude" for others, with the suffering that compassion entails (pp. 180–194). Sacrifice is less a matter of victimage or scapegoating, and more a matter of loving self-limitation and self-giving—all for the benefit of the Other with whom one is in covenant and through whom one's identity is (re)defined. It is precisely such notions that the rhetoric of reconciliation calls humans to grapple with, in tandem with concerns for a just order.

Significantly, recent Christian models of reconciliation have shifted away from the legalistic, hierarchical redemption model that dominated Western theology for centuries, and moved toward a re-discovery of the relational emphasis in gospel teachings (Battle, 1997; Cartwright, 1997; De Gruchy, 2003; De Young, 1997; Helmick & Peterson, 2001; Hines & De Young, 2000; Tutu, 2000). Some theologians even insist that both the juridical and the relational aspects of alienation and reconciliation are equally pivotal, and must be addressed together (Harakas, 2001). Paul Ricoeur's philosophical treatment of ethics parallels this theological reintegration of the juridical and relational, providing a basis for correcting the imbalance in Burkean logology *vis-à-vis* reconciliation. In *Oneself as Another*, Ricoeur (1995) sums up the ethical intention as *"aiming at the 'good life' with and for others, in just institutions"* (p. 172). The "good life" has do with making meaningful connections—between oneself and others, community, and tradition, and among the multiple roles and aims by which one's self is already constituted—and developing a narrative unity of a life fulfilled in meaningful projects in the world. Ricoeur does not view language primarily as an instrument of human agency that separates us from our "natural" condition and imposes order(s), but as the medium in which we creatively (re)construct our lives as stories "with and for others."

Nonetheless, the dangerous potential for instrumentalizing others within one's narrative project, and thereby doing them violence, is not lost on Ricoeur. The phrase "in just institutions" supplies what he sees as an essential, if secondary, corrective to this proclivity in pursuing a narrative unity of life, one that is complicated and conflicted by the competing interests and narratives of others (Ricoeur, 1995, 2000). The task of these institutions is to ensure a modicum of *respect* for each person, *reciprocity* between persons, and to mediate disputes among them impartially while regarding each equally as a subject of justice (i.e., that they are held to the same standard).[11] Here Burke's recognition of the inescapable, moral(izing) negativity of human agency in language is confirmed, but with a crucial difference: For Ricoeur, the positive desire to live well with and for others is clearly the prior impulse, and the negative is its dialectical shadow that tests whether the institutional order or hierarchy humans inevitably build in pursuit of narrative unity and social good is a *just* order, upholding the *rights* of each Other. Thus, the ethico-moral life cannot be reduced to either the good or the right alone; rather, it aims at the *critical good*, or what John Wall (2002) characterizes as "the creative, poetic mediation of genuinely other and conflicting goods into new areas of now *critically shared moral meaning*" (p. 56).

Like Burke's logology, Ricoeur's ethical theory reflects a willingness to treat religious tradition as a vital resource for understanding human motivation. The latter additionally moves beyond understanding to *evaluating* motives and actions in terms of the kinds of human values that are worked out with particular thoroughness in religious traditions. His treatment of ethics supports an understanding of reconciliation as a work of limited and accountable rhetorical agency in dialogue, chastened by the painful truth that one or more of the parties have exercised their agency unethically by subverting or suppressing the agency of the different Other, perpetrating injustice and violating the human connection that binds them to that Other, and the reality that the damage caused by such injustice is not entirely reparable. For this reason, reconciliation's tragi-comic redemption can never yield total absolution or perfect social harmony; it requires what Ricoeur calls *critical phronesis*, a work of judgment that yields a modicum of justice and a common good that is never complete.

The Tetrad as a Critical Tool in the Burkean Tradition

If the work of Ricoeur offers a grounded and well-rounded, ethical approach to evaluating reconciliation practices, Burkean dramatism and logology suggest a way of doing rhetorical criticism of reconciliation discourse. My derivation of the tetrad Agency-Peace-Justice-Truth from studies on reconciliation in public theology, political philosophy, and other fields, reflects the Burkean focus on terms and terministic screens (or frames). At the same time, it suggests the possibility of enlarging logology (as dia-logology) by placing Relation (the locus of Peace or harmony) opposite Order (the locus of Justice or law) as a second center from which to play out the terms of the human covenant, thus counterbalancing redemption as victimage (as in the sacrificial cult of the Mosaic Law) with the common, biblical sense of redemption as ransoming, releasing, or buying someone out of debt or slavery because of kinship or kindness (Wall, 2002). Within this matrix, *forgiveness* emerges as an act that both *remembers* an injurious act and *releases* its agent from resentment or blame. This costly exercise of agency acknowledges the claims of justice in the very act of freeing both offending and offended parties from the "the Iron Law of History / That welds Order and Sacrifice" (Burke, 1961, pp. 4–5). *Repentance* emerges as *metanoia*, a change of mindset from slavish obedience to (or a rebellious violation of) a tragic system of law to a fuller moral act. This fuller act acknowledges responsibility for injury and trustingly embraces the grace of (potential) forgiveness so as to live freely and justly for the good "with and for others." Reconciliation, then, becomes more than a momentary lull in an endless war engendered by the conflicting demands of hierarchy or empire; it signifies a restoration of covenantal *relation* as an intrinsic good (as captured in the South African concept of *ubuntu*).[12]

Given situational conflicts among goods, and the pull of ethnocentrism, reconciliation must attend to, and be shaped by, the terms of Just Order as well as Peaceful Relation if it is to stand the test of time; it must be tragic-comic (and realistic-romantic). Burke's depiction of irony in the relations among dramatistic terms applies, then, not only to his pentad, but also to the tetrad I propose. Just as Burke recognized a "central moltenness" at the heart of the pentad, so the project of reconciliation (captured in a wealth of public and published discourse that has grappled with its meaning, means, and measures over the past decade) discloses the interdependence of value-terms and gives rise to hybrid terms, such as *restorative justice* and *restorative truth*, reflecting a process of *transcendence by perspectives-in-dialogue* that grasps at the fullness of its ultimate ethical aim. The language-game of reconciliation not only presents four ethical "bases" to be rounded by reconciling parties, but it also widens the paths from base to base and favors those able to establish standpoints between bases.

The tetrad differs from the pentad not only in its focus on ethical terms of social existence, but also in its intrinsic ethical orientation. Burke's dramatistic pentad is a device for *description*, disclosing how motives are construed in discourse; as such, any ethical judgments that the critic renders on such constructions of motive must be imported from some external value-structure. The tetrad, however, is meant as a parallel and complementary framework for evaluation (as well as description); it is a distillation of popular and scholarly efforts to clarify the values that reconciliation must (re)establish or reintegrate, and how.

Analyzing reconciliation discourse through the tetrad allows the observer/critic to examine how (and how much) it attends to, and is oriented by, each of these four terms in relation to one another and to the rhetorical situation. Beyond this, the explanatory-critical power of the tetrad lies in the claim that *each term potentially serves as a rhetorical frame for each of the other terms*. Thus, when analyzing a piece of reconciliation discourse, the critic looks not only for traces of each ethical value in the words and images of the text, but also considers which term (or combination of terms) may frame or color those traces (Hatch, 2008). The latter is more subtle, and requires careful observation. It is akin to pentadic analysis, in which the critic assumes that one of the five elements (Scene, Act, Agent, Agency, Purpose) controls the rhetor's construction of motive for an action, dominating or framing the other elements. In the tetradic conception of reconciliation, I assume that traces of the four ethical terms will be present in different proportions (as *foci*) within in any given reconciliation text. Further, I assume that one of the terms—justice, agency, peace, or truth—may have constrained how the others appear.

Let us consider how this rhetorical dynamic might typically manifest it-self. As I noted, the strongest ethical polarizations in reconciliation tend to emerge between truth and agency, on the one hand, and between justice and peace or unity on the other. Thus, in the wake of historical atrocities, one possibility is that a kind of realism—a compulsion to face truth—would treat agency/grace as a matter of little weight or value. Conversely, romanticism (i.e., a perspective dominated by the value of agency) would make light of realities, such as the economic deprivations still suffered by victims of past atrocities, while valorizing efforts to transcend such limitations. Along the peace-justice dialectic, another possibility is that a comic (or a communal unity/harmony) orientation would highlight the importance of commonalities and connections between victims and victimizers while also softening the lines between justice and injustice and euphemizing evil acts. Conversely, a tragic (justice-oriented) frame would etch the divisions between offenders and the offended more deeply, possibly reducing the colors of their humanity to a black-and-white contrast between good and evil.

At the same time, the dominant (framing) value would tend to shade or shape how traces of other values appear in the discourse. For instance, a comic framing privileges historical truths that suggest a more shared ethical ground than moral disparity among perpetrators and victims. Such discourse might claim the importance of history and truth, and thus present many historical facts. Yet, it would select those facts according to the valorization of fundamental unity/peace that controls the rhetor's constructed vision of reconciliation's exigence and its fitting response. Similarly, reconciliation in the comic frame would valorize agency for promoting harmony, while down-playing agency aimed at fighting and rectifying injustice.

Parties to past injuries and conflicts approach the possibility of recon-ciliation with somewhat predictably disparate orientations. Former victim-izers often find comic correctives (an apprehension of an underlying oneness and the realization of common humanity, such as racial color-blindness) far more attractive or compelling than the tragic discourse of justice. The latter separates them from the victims, weighs them on the scales of morality, and requires sacrifice on their part (e.g., acceptance of guilt and shame, humble acknowledgment and regret, or material reparation) if the scales are to be rebalanced. For victims who have suffered much and feel the enduring ef-fects of violation, a comic invocation of shared humanity and the common good may seem too light a sentence on the tongue of a former victimizer. They might rather believe that the offending party should be weighed down by tragic guilt and by the Other's unspeakable suffering and, as such, feel bound to speak heavy (yet inevitably inadequate) words of repentance and regret. As such, the truth of the past and its effects upon the present chasten any romantic notions of mere transcendence and quick forgiveness. For parties that have benefited from past oppression, on the other hand, their power (and their desire to forget a past that might fuel retribution) conditions them to make much of human agency to fashion a new future.

The crux of reconciliation, then, is the hard rhetorical-ethical work of *reframing* the rhetorical situation such that unjust and divisive social arrangements can be re-made *collaboratively* with the well-rounded perspective and depth perception that comes from seeing through multiple lenses together. For the party that bears the wounds of oppression, forgiveness may both prepare the way for receiving an apology and follow from it (Lazare, 2004; Schreiter, 1998). In either case, the psychological literature on forgiveness indicates that the key transformation lies in what Robert D. Enright calls the "work" phase: *reframing* the offending party as fellow-human, as more than merely "evil-doer" or "enemy," but as a person with whom the offended party shares the capacity for both good and evil (Enright, Freedman, & Rique, 1998). In preparation for this difficult, comic apprehension of commonality and concomitant development of empathy, the victim must also face the romantic challenge of agency: The victim must choose a new attitude toward the offender (after having realistically faced the violation and the harm it caused) and believe that this choice can overcome the harm.

APPLYING THE TETRAD TO APOLOGIES (FOR SLAVERY)

For the party that perpetrates oppression, reframing typically means casting off rose-colored, romantic-comic glasses and facing the exigence for reconciliation through stark, black-and-white realism and the deep reds of tragic sacrifice—sacrifices already forced upon the victims, and sacrifices that must now be made by the beneficiaries if any sense of justice is to be restored and if peace is to stand on some semblance of solid ground. Thus, if an apology for a real and egregious offense is to contribute to ethical reconciliation, it must demonstrate such reframing by the party that committed the offense. It requires thoroughly and truthfully acknowledging what that party did, including the harmful effects of the misdeeds on the victims, and judging those deeds in stark terms as flagrant and inexcusable violations of moral principle, human dignity, relational mutuality, and the like (e.g., Edwards, 2005; Hearit, 2006; Koesten & Rowland, 2004; Lazare, 2004). A satisfactory reconciliation apology for such a grievous phenomenon as slavery, in other words, would frame it realistically and tragically while also keeping in view the common humanity of perpetrator-beneficiaries and victim-survivors, and would express faith in their capacity to *act* together for a different future. An ethically coherent apology would not *presume* on the victim-survivors' agency to transcend past horrors and present pain, but would *honor* whatever measure of forgiveness or transcendence they have already exhibited—thereby doing them symbolic justice through moral recognition and respect of their agency (an agency that was formerly denied or destroyed).

I have argued that reconciliation, especially regarding historical atrocities like slavery, is fundamentally epideictic discourse. Apologies such as the recent state resolutions of regret for slavery and racism exemplify this *epideixis*—"showing forth" history in a new light of self-criticism, displaying appropriate attitudes toward immoral (and moral) actions in the state's past, and performing a ritual (re)commitment to the rights and well-being of wronged parties as full members in society with claims to its founding principles and values. In Ricoeurian terms, epideictic allows participants to appropriate and enact the moral order of a utopia (a "no-place") to narratively refigure their lives or relations according to that order, and also to prefigure a wider community restored to its highest ideals in practice (Ritivoi, 2006). The tetrad is a grammar of such utopian visions, an underlying order that is implicit in, yet obscured by, what Burke (1969b) memorably refers to as "the Scramble, the Wrangle of the Market Place, the flurries and flare-ups of the Human Barnyard"—including the competing rhetorics of peace, justice, truth, or agency (p. 23).

When the tetrad comes to bear on society in a compelling narrative, epideictic address, or ritualistic performance, the barnyard scramble may become a more ordered, cooperative endeavor in which parties round these four ethical bases and follow shared ground rules, even as they contend together. The baseball metaphor breaks down, of course, in that the tetrad (logologically understood) allows for different temporal out-workings of truth, agency/grace, peace/harmony, and justice in reconciliation. These values may come in focus (or come to bear as frames) in any order, yet each of them always already implicates the others. Each value in the tetrad pertains especially to one of four ethico-rhetorical thrusts in an historical apology: *truthfully* acknowledging history, recognizing victims' *agency* by commemorating their ancestors and including their voices, offering *just* atonement by regretting and correcting old wrongs, and engendering substantive *peace* through meaningful reconciliation.[13]

The recent state apologies primarily embody the first two thrusts: acknowledging a historical pattern of heinous actions toward African Americans and (in most cases) recognizing their sufferings, struggles, survival, and triumph in the face of that history (Hatch, 2008).[14] The apologies also express regret and mention racial reconciliation as a desirable horizon. Their deficiency lies in largely ignoring (or disclaiming) the possibility of atonement through some form of reparation. Instead, they offer symbolic justice in the process of putting truth on record by denigrating the wrong-doing of states and honoring the virtuous agency of those who persevered and graciously contributed to the good of the state that wronged them. Virginia's trailblazing resolution sets the pattern and provides a valuable test case for the tetrad as a critical tool, especially because the resolution richly exemplifies reconciliation as a messy process of negotiated reframing. Unlike later state apologies, Virginia's resolution achieved passage only after the original, tragic-realistic version offered by its African-American sponsor in the Senate underwent a substantial, romantic reframing by the House, and after a conference committee produced a compromised version in which romantic self-commemoration and tragic-realistic self-judgment coexisted in painful tension, culminating in an expression of "profound regret" (S. Res 332, 2007). Below, I offer a summary tetradic analysis of this apology as it evolved.

Tragic Regret Packaged in Romantic Commemoration: Virginia's Apology

Virginia's resolution was a significant breakthrough after a decade of U.S. resistance to apologizing for slavery, beginning with U.S. Representative Tony Hall's failed resolution in 1997 (Hatch, 2008; H.R. 96, 1997). Senator Henry Marsh introduced the resolution into the majority-Republican legislature in early January of 2007, while Donald McEachin sponsored an identical version (HJR 728) in the House. After Marsh changed "atone" (implying reparation) to "acknowledge with contrition," the Senate unanimously approved the resolution, and it was sent to the House (Jarvie, 2007). The House Committee on Rules, however, did not accept its wording, and offered a substantially revised substitute (Jarvie, 2007). Conceding that the new version at least preserved the spirit of the original, Marsh and McEachin submitted it to a conference committee comprising members of both houses of Congress. This committee evidently achieved a highly satisfactory compromise: its version won unanimous approval in both houses on February 24, 2007 (Whitley, 2007). As Virginia prepared to celebrate the four hundredth anniversary of the nation's first permanent English settlement at Jamestown, its General Assembly issued the nation's first legislative apology for slavery. Let us examine the negotiated reframings through which the apology emerged as a public statement.

Marsh's original resolution is dominated by the value of truth. The first "Whereas" clause states that the institution of slavery has existed since antiquity, thus establishing a realistic frame for the lengthy litany of abuses that follows. At the same time, the language of this unfolding history lesson is frequently tragic: blacks were "brutalized, humiliated, dehumanized," suffered "the worst holocaust of humankind," and were subjected to "virulent and rabid racism, lynchings, disenfranchisement," and the "legally sanctioned deprivation of . . . their endowed rights" (S. 332, 2007).[15] Overall, the original version's focus on historical facts rather than human agents eclipses judgment in terms of choice, virtue, and vice. Blacks' agency is buried in a history that tramples them at every step; for example: "in spite of their loyalty, dedication, and service to the country" and "the political, social, and economic gains they made during Reconstruction" (S. 332, 2007). As a result, Virginia and the United States enter into the picture more as a scene or even as tools of slavery than they do as perpetrators. Perhaps out of fear that a tone of blame would doom the resolution, Marsh's version resorts to acknowledging factual truth framed by a somewhat detached, if not tragically inflected, realism.

By contrast, later versions of the resolution bring the romantic frame to bear on the past as well, adding clauses that praise human agency directed to good ends. Much of this shift in framing and emphasis occurred in the writing of the amended House version by Republican John M. O'Bannon, III. O'Bannon's revision is almost a complete rewrite. Among other changes, it reduces Marsh's litany of the evils of slavery to a briefer overview; it eliminates several strong references to the *present* symptoms of slavery's legacy; it omits Marsh's reference to "the broken promise of '40 acres and a mule'" (i.e., reparations) (S. 332, 2007); it eliminates Marsh's claim that "the perpetual pain, distrust, and bitterness of many African Americans could be assuaged" by an apology (S. 332, 2007); and O'Bannon tacitly locks the door on reparations by claiming that "even the most abject apology for past wrongs cannot right them, nor can it justly impute fault or responsibility to succeeding generations or justify the imposition of new benefits or burdens" (S. 332 [H1], 2007). Not content with this protective clause, O'Bannon further softened Marsh's already-revised phrase, "acknowledge with contrition," to "express . . . profound regret" (S. 332 [H1], 2007).

One might conclude, then, that the House version ignores the claims of justice. That conclusion would be incomplete, since O'Bannon also *added* clauses highlighting how seriously Virginia had transgressed its own principles. For example, the amended version characterizes slavery as

> an institution directly antithetical to and irreconcilable with the fundamental principle of human equality and freedom, and which, having been sanctioned and perpetuated through the laws of Virginia and the United States, ranks as the most horrendous of all

depredations of human rights and violations of our founding ideals in our nation's history. (S. 332 [H1], 2007)

It also notes that "the abolition of slavery was not followed by prompt fulfillment of those founding ideals, but rather by systematic discrimination, enforced segregation, and other insidious institutions and practices toward Americans of African descent" (S. 332 [H1], 2007).[16]

Still, O'Bannon's House-amended version strongly counters the tragic, self-deprecating tone of the original by celebrating the state's recent contributions to the advancement of civil rights by offering a romantic treatment of the state's history of diversity. The impact of this larger framing is to constrain the condemnations found in the middle portion of O'Bannon's version: Its praise of harmonious diversity and heroic agency paints over the dirty details of historical truth and lingering injustice. Virginia, a seedbed of American diversity, is an agent of good; slavery and racism are removable (if noxious) weeds. The only place in which the amended version comes close to denigrating Virginia as an *agent* of evil is the second "Resolved" clause that expresses "profound regret for the Commonwealth's role in sanctioning the immoral institution of human slavery, in the historic wrongs visited upon native peoples, and in all other forms of discrimination and injustice" (S. 332 [H1], 2007). Yet, the clause comically qualifies those misdeeds as "rooted in racial and cultural bias and misunderstanding" (S. 332 [H1], 2007).

The final version, submitted by the conference committee, combines material from both earlier drafts and achieves stronger acknowledgment by omitting most of the romantic-comic elements from its portrayal of Virginia. Yet, it also deflects attention from many African Americans' tragic perspective on past oppression, instead offering a romantic portrayal of them as victorious survivors.[17] Perhaps that is because Virginia's resolution won adequate support only by linking its statement of acknowledgment and regret to the celebration of Jamestown, a reference that appears front and center in the final version. Indeed, the final version of the resolution addresses Native Americans (who helped the Jamestown settlers, yet suffered at the hands of Virginians) along with African Americans. The second clause states:

> [T]he legacies of the Jamestown settlement and the Virginia colony include ideas, institutions, and a history distinctive to the American experiment in democracy, and a constellation of liberties enshrined in the Virginia Declaration of Rights and the Virginia and United States Constitutions. (S. Res 332, 2007)

By implication, Virginia's ethos is that of a basically *good* agent, a leader in propagating fundamental American values. Turning the commemorative clock to more contemporary events, the seventeenth clause completes the circle of collective self-regard that frames Virginia's history in reflection romantically:

> [I]n recent decades, Virginia's affirmation of the founding ideals of liberty and equality have been made evident by providing some of the nation's foremost trailblazers for civil rights and electing a grandson of slaves [former governor Douglas Wilder] to the Commonwealth's highest elective office. (S. Res 332, 2007)

In this resolution, Virginia appears as a heroic agent of liberty and equality by first propagating these ideals, and then by affirming them in practice. If Virginia is guilty of crimes against African Americans, those crimes are a departure from its true, better self: a leading agent of liberty and equality.

Nonetheless, the fourth "Whereas" clause acknowledges that, "despite the 'self-evident' character of these fundamental principles, the moral standards of liberty and equality have been transgressed during much of Virginia's and America's history" (S. Res 332, 2007). The next clause names "the maltreatment and exploitation of Native Americans and the immoral institution of human slavery" as "directly antithetical to and irreconcilable with the fundamental principles of human equality and freedom" (S. Res 332, 2007). The body of the resolution now expresses romantic esteem for these two minorities, and pronounces tragic judgment on Virginia. It presents Native Americans first as *agents* of good—both in terms of the Jamestown settlers and with their own cultural self-preservation—and then as victims of oppression in various forms. It recounts abuses against Americans of African descent brought to North America as "involuntary immigrants," starting in Virginia(S. Res 332, 2007). It acknowledges the peculiar cruelty of American slavery and the violations and cultural destruction it wrought. The fifteenth "Whereas" clause closes the frame of tragic judgment around America's and Virginia's legally sanctioned practices of slavery, squarely declaring them "the most horrendous of all depredations of human rights and violations of our founding ideals in our nation's history" (S. Res 332, 2007). The clause does not bring closure to Virginia's self-judgment at the point where slavery ends; rather, it notes that "the abolition of slavery was followed by systematic discrimination, enforced segregation, and other insidious institutions and practices toward Americans of African descent" (S. Res 332, 2007).

The resolution now turns to the possibility of redemption for a state whose abuses were "rooted in racism, racial bias, and racial misunderstanding" (S. Res 332, 2007). Its sixteenth clause expresses the need to promote reconciliation and "avert the repetition of past wrongs" through "the spirit of true repentance" (S. Res 332, 2007). After citing Virginia's recent contributions to civil rights, the resolution issues a grammatically conflicted call to commemoration:

> WHEREAS, the story of Virginia's Native Americans and the enslavement of Africans and their descendants, the human carnage, and the dehumanizing atrocities committed during colonization and slavery, and, moreover, the faith, perseverance, hope, and endless triumphs of Native Americans and African Americans and their significant contributions to this Commonwealth and the nation should be embraced, celebrated, and retold for generations to come. (S. Res 332, 2007)

The convoluted structure of this clause is such that a romantic celebration of these oppressed minorities' agency overshadows tragic judgment on the atrocities perpetrated through Virginia's democratic tyranny of the majority.

If Virginia (with its minorities) is a basically heroic and honorable agent, the climactic action through which its moral resolve triumphs over the demons of the past is a bittersweet, tragic-comic performance in the present: The members of the General Assembly "hereby acknowledge with profound regret the involuntary servitude of Africans and the exploitation of Native Americans, and call for reconciliation among all Virginians" (S. Res 332, 2007). Citing Jamestown's four hundredth anniversary, they also "call upon the people of the Commonwealth to express acknowledgment and thanksgiving for the contributions of Native Americans and African Americans to the Commonwealth and this nation, and to the propagation of the ideals of liberty, justice, and democracy" (S. Res 332, 2007). Here, tragic self-judgment and comic reconnection, as well as realistic acknowledgment and romantic valorization, converge in a complex and unstable rhetorical compound.

CONCLUSION: A ROUNDABOUT ROUTE TO SUBSTANTIAL REPAIR

Virginia's apology thoroughly illustrates the sort of imperfect, contextualized, and contingent transcendence by perspective that typifies reconciliation. Like South Africa's truth and reconciliation process (Doxtader, 2001), Virginia's resolution is the product of a political compromise; it reflects a dialogue among *victim*, *victimizer*, and *Virginia* perspectives, and illustrates the interactions among Justice, Peace, Truth, and Agency as terministic screens. Settling neither for a comic vision of unity nor tragic division by race, and neither romantic celebration nor realistic remembrance, Virginia's apology tries all these lenses on for size, seeking to see the rhetorical situation whole and round while straining for an ethical vision large enough to unify diverse Virginians in a project of acknowledgment and reconciliation. The resolution's negotiated character rounds out its acknowledgment, and does a kind of verbal justice to Virginia's victims, that approaches Burke's poetic ideal. Yet, its roundness also blunts the incisiveness of Virginia's self-critique. The original version clearly implies a need for reconstructive surgery in the body politic (i.e., reparation); that implication is virtually absent from the accepted version.

Thus, we confront again the question raised at the beginning of this essay: What of the material disparities between races in the present; what of the debt that America owes blacks? Is Virginia's apology ethically null and void because it deflects such questions? Taking it in context (as rhetoric and reconciliation should be), I believe the answer is no. Despite its shortcomings, the Virginia resolution constitutes a significant step forward from the simplistic division between comic-romantic and tragic-realistic perspectives on race that characterize the responses to Tony Hall's proposed U.S. slavery apology in 1997 (Hatch, 2008). A decade of global and local public discourse regarding reconciliation has helped bring about a dia-logos of ethical terms, a transcendence by perspective that enables political leaders to envision new ways of making good on the promise of a just society. Virginia's apology, in turn, has blazed a trail for other apologies to make much clearer, unqualified statements of apology.[18]

While Florida's 2008 slavery resolution disclaimed any basis for litigation, its governor found it possible to wonder aloud about offering reparations to African Americans. This contradiction suggests that one may read the flight from reparations warrants, in part, as an effort to escape from the potentially enormous and unremitting sacrifices demanded by the Iron Law of (court) Order—justice in a purely tragic frame. Reconciliation opens up the possibility of voluntary sacrifices and creative, negotiated reparations in which agency bends its force toward justice as a *virtue* rather than capitulating to the machinery of the justice *system*. Reconciliation's ironic dia-logos among Agency, Truth, Justice, and Peace gives rise to conceptions of *restorative justice*, replacing a fixation on *offenders'* status, legal defense, and just deserts with a focus on *victims'* needs for acknowledgment, recognition, and negotiated restitution.[19] At the same time, reconciliation does not lose sight of their potential to survive, thrive, and forgive; it refuses to place victims' agency solely in the service of justice, but tempers the tragic call to justice with a comic recognition of shared humanity. Thus, as Brooks (2004) proposes, reparation truly contributes to the good of victims and society when it substantiates an apology and facilitates forgiveness—when atonement becomes at-one-ment, or reconciliation.

Notes

1. In such situations, the cessation of violence, the restoration of order, the reconstitution of national identity, and/or the reconstruction of political systems tends to dominate the exigence for reconciliation (Crocker, 2006; Doxtader, 2001; Salazar, 2002).

2. As most readers of this chapter are aware, Aristotle (1991) conceived of epideictic as the genre of rhetoric that aims to praise the honorable and blame the shameful in human affairs.

3. Lewis (2008) acknowledges the importance of Burke's comic and tragic frames, but proposes a third frame of acceptance—romance—as a more fitting characterization of the attitude found in evangelistic sectarian discourse. Lewis explains:

> When "cornered," as Burke described, the sectarian *separates* from the dominant culture, and that separation forces an entirely new rhetoric . . . . Neither tragically purifying nor comically correcting, the sectarian unequivocally and unalterably woos its Other. When tragedy kills and comedy critiques, the suitor charms. The evil enemy, which the comic transforms into a mistaken adversary, becomes a Beloved in the romantic's sight.

I would suggest that Lewis's romance as *self-differentiating* and *wooing* is one very common variant within a larger umbrella orientation that highlights the protagonist (agent) on a quest or mission to *distinguish* him or herself by *winning* (e.g., *triumphing over* circumstances and antagonists or *winning the affections of* a beloved).

4. Of nineteenth-century romanticism, Burke (1984) writes, "A kind of 'two-world' scheme arose, the antithetical worlds of the practical and the esthetic, with a few writers like Mann trying, by mixture of irony and melancholy, to mediate between them" (p. 30).

5. For an introduction to the vigorous debates regarding rhetorical agency, see Geisler (2004) and Lundberg and Gunn (2005).

6. For example, Brooks (2004) suggests that black Americans have a "civic duty," though not a "moral duty," to forgive America once the government has atoned for slavery and Jim Crow through an apology and meaningful reparations (pp. 164–169).

7. For an account of how congregants in the early black church jointly constructed a sense of free agency and subjectivity (as the chosen people of God), see Lincoln (1984, pp. 63, 70).

8. As a result, I contend that the study of reconciliation also provides occasion to enrich and sharpen logology as a critical tool. For two influential critiques of Burke, see Chesebro (1992) and Condit (1992).

9. For example, in a theory of "rhetoric as coherence," Mark L. McPhail (2002) emphasizes the metaphoric, connection-building capacity of language to re(dis)cover an underlying unity. On another front, John Stewart (1995) argues for moving

beyond the atomizing *symbol* model to an understanding of language as *articulate contact*; in this light, the bridging/connecting capacity of language, and the possibility of peaceful coherence, become more evident. Mikhail Bakhtin (1986) shows that language is intrinsically dialogic, whether communicators seek to communicate dialogically or not. Contrary the structuralism of modern linguistics (*a la* Ferdinand de Saussure), Bakhtin regards living responsive utterances (whether a single-word interjection or a lengthy formal address) as the paradigmatic element of language. As such, the structures of language bear the marks and meanings of the innumerable prior interpersonal and public conversations. Viewed in these terms, rhetorical genres are dialogized (Bakhtin, 1986), and languages reflect the *heteroglossia* of intercultural exchange (Bakhtin, 1981).

10. Burke's rationale for basing his cluster of interrelated terms on Order rather than Covenant is that the former, unlike the latter, "clearly reveals its dialectical or polar nature, on its face" (i.e., "Order implies disorder, and vice versa"); as such, it allows him to show that "guilt and vicarious sacrifice are intrinsic to the idea of Covenant" (Burke, 1961, p. 181). Yet, Burke's resultant cluster of terms fails to include other terms that are equally intrinsic to the idea of Covenant, and are highlighted especially in the prophets and the Christian testament: love, care, community, faithfulness, even friendship.

11. John Wall (2002) reads respect or reciprocity in Ricoeur as

> a predominantly *negative* concept, the negative side, if you will, of the positive aim of the narrative unity of a life. It demands that one *not* instrumentalize others, that one acknowledge in others a certain "genuine otherness" to which one must not do violence. (p. 54)

12. Desmond Tutu (1999) explains his sense of this African anthropological concept:

> It is to say, "My humanity is caught up, inextricably bound up, in yours." We belong to a bundle of life. We say, "A person is a person through other persons." It is not, "I think therefore I am." It says rather: "I am human because I belong. I participate. I share." (p. 31)

13. In reconciliation discourse, the notion of peace becomes enriched, connoting a sense of well-being in community that depends in part on truth, justice, and inclusive agency (like the Hebrew notion of *shalom*).

14. The states that have apologized for slavery include Virginia, Maryland, North Carolina, and Alabama (in 2007), New Jersey and Florida (in 2008), and Connecticut (in 2009).

15. To see O'Bannon's impact on the resolution, compare the enacted version, Senate Resolution 332 (2007), to Senate Bill 332 (2007).

16. See also Gibson (2007).

17. The original version notes that, for many blacks, "the scars left behind are unbearable, haunting their psyches and clouding their vision of the future and of America's many attributes" (S. 332, 2007).

18. The resolutions by North Carolina, Alabama, and New Jersey do just that. See Senate Bill 1557 (2007); House Bill 321 (2007); House Bill 270 (2007).

19. Restorative justice has been the subject of extensive theorizing (Zehr, 1990, 1997), and was the foundation for the work of South Africa's Truth and Reconciliation Commission (Kiss, 2000).

References

A Concurrent Resolution Apologizing for the Wrongs of Slavery and Expressing New Jersey's Profound Regret for Its Role in Slavery, H.R. 270, 212th New Jersey Legislature. (2007). Retrieved from http://www.njleg.state.nj.us/2006/Bills/ACR/270_I1.HTM

A Joint Resolution Expressing the Profound Regret of the North Carolina General Assembly for the History of Wrongs Inflicted Upon Black Citizens, S. 1557, North Carolina General Assembly. (2007). Retrieved from http://www.ncleg.net/Sessions/2007/Bills/Senate/HTML/S1557v3.html

Acknowledging the Contributions of Varied Races and Cultures to the Character of the Commonwealth of Virginia, and Expressing Profound Regret for Slavery and Other Historic Wrongs, S. 332 [H1]: Amendment in the nature of a substitute, Virginia General Assembly. (2007). Retrieved from http://leg1.state.va.us/cgi-bin/legp504.exe?071+ful+SJ332H1

Apologizing for Those Who Suffered as Slaves under the Constitution and Laws of the United States until 1865, H.R. 96, 105th Cong. (1997).

Apologizing for the Wrongs of Slavery; Expressing Profound Regret for Alabama's Role in Slavery; and Expressing Intent That This Resolution Shall Not Be Used in, or Be the Basis of, Any Type of Litigation, H.R. 321, Alabama Legislature. (2007). Retrieved from http://alisondb.legislature.state.al.us/acas/.

Atoning for the Involuntary Servitude of Africans and Calling for Reconciliation among All Virginians, S. 332, Virginia General Assembly. (2007). Retrieved from http://leg1.state.va.us/cgi-bin/legp504.exe?071+ful+SJ332

Aristotle. (1991). *On rhetoric: A theory of civic discourse.* Trans. G. A. Kennedy. New York, NY: Oxford University Press.

Asante, M. K. (1998). *The afrocentric idea.* Philadelphia, PA: Temple University Press.

Brooks, R. L. (2004). *Atonement and forgiveness: A new model for black reparations.* Berkeley, CA: University of California Press.

Bakhtin, M. (1981). Discourse in the novel. In M. Holquist (Ed.), *The dialogic imagination: Four essays* (pp. 259–422). Austin, TX: University of Texas Press.

Bakhtin, M. (1986). *Speech genres and other late essays.* Trans. V. W. McGee. Ed. C. Emerson & M. Holquist. Austin, TX: University of Texas Press.

Battle, M. J. (1997). *Reconciliation: The Ubuntu theology of Desmond Tutu.* Cleveland, OH: Pilgrim Press.

Burke, K. (1961). *The rhetoric of religion: Studies in logology.* Boston, MA: Beacon Press.

Burke, K. (1966). *Language as symbolic action: Essays on life, literature, and method.* Berkeley, CA: University of California Press.

Burke, K. (1969a). *A grammar of motives.* Berkeley, CA: University of California Press.

Burke, K. (1941/1973). *The philosophy of literary form: Studies in symbolic action* (3rd ed.). Berkeley, CA: University of California Press. (Original work published 1941)

Burke, K. (1984). *Attitudes toward history* (3rd ed.). Berkeley, CA: University of California Press.

Cartwright, M. G. (1997). Wrestling with scripture: Can Euro-American Christians and African-American Christians learn to read scripture together? In D. L. Okholm (Ed.), *The gospel in black and white: Theological resources for racial reconciliation* (pp. 71-116). Downers Grove, IL: InterVarsity.

Chesebro, J. W. (1992). Extensions of the Burkeian system. *Quarterly Journal of Speech, 78*(3), 356–368.

Condit, C. (1992). Post-Burke: Transcending the sub-stance of dramatism. *Quarterly Journal of Speech, 78*(3), 349–355.

Crocker, D. A. (2006). Punishment, reconciliation, and democratic deliberation. In E. Barkan, & A. Karn (Eds.), *Taking wrongs seriously: Apologies and reconciliation* (pp. 50-83). Stanford, CA: Stanford University Press.

De Gruchy, J. W. (2003). *Reconciliation: Restoring justice.* Minneapolis, MN: Fortress Press.

De Young, C. P. (1997). *Reconciliation: Our greatest challenge—our only hope.* Valley Forge, PA: Judson Press.

Doxtader, E. (2001). Making rhetorical history in a time of transition: The occasion, constitution, and representation of South African reconciliation. *Rhetoric & Public Affairs, 4*(2), 223–260.

Doxtader, E. (2003). Reconciliation: A rhetorical concept/ion. *Quarterly Journal of Speech, 89*(4), 267–292.

Doxtader, E. (2007). The faith and struggle of beginning (with) words: On the turn between reconciliation and recognition. *Philosophy and Rhetoric, 40*(1), 119–146.

Doxtader, E., & Villa-Vicencio, C. (Eds.) (2003). *Through fire with water: The roots of division and the potential for reconciliation in Africa.* Trenton, NJ: Africa World Press.

Edwards, J. A. (2005). Community-focused apologia in international affairs: Japanese Prime Minister Tomiichi Murayama's apology. *The Howard Journal of Communications, 16*, 317–336.

Enright, R. D., Freedman, S., & Rique, J. (1998). The psychology of interpersonal forgiveness. In R. D. Enright, & J. North (Eds.), *Exploring forgiveness* (pp. 46-62). Madison, WI: University of Wisconsin Press.

Frye, N. (1957). *Anatomy of criticism: Four essays.* Princeton, NJ: Princeton University Press.

Geisler, C. (2004). How ought we to understand the concept of rhetorical agency? Report from the ARS. *Rhetoric Society Quarterly, 34*(3), 9–18.

Gibson, B. (2007, February 1). Slavery resolution rewritten: Committee passes statement of "regret." *The Clover Herald*. Retrieved from http://www.topix.com/wire/city/clover-va

Hafenbrack, J., & Kennedy, J. (2008, March 26). Florida legislature makes formal apology for slavery. *South Florida Sun-Sentinel*. Retrieved from http://www.sun-sentinel.com

Harakas, S. S. (2001). Forgiveness & reconciliation: An Orthodox perspective. In R. G. Helmick, & R. L. Peterson (Eds.), *Forgiveness and reconciliation: Religion, public policy, and conflict transformation* (pp. 51-80). Philadelphia, PA: Templeton Foundation.

Hatch, J. B. (2003). Reconciliation: Building a bridge from complicity to coherence in the rhetoric of race relations. *Rhetoric & Public Affairs, 6*(4), 737–764.

Hatch, J. B. (2006a). Beyond *Apologia*: Racial reconciliation and apologies for slavery. *Western Journal of Communication, 70*(3), 186–211.

Hatch, J. B. (2006b). The hope of reconciliation: Continuing the conversation. *Rhetoric & Public Affairs, 9*(2), 259–278.

Hatch, J. B. (2008). *Race and reconciliation: Redressing wounds of injustice*. Lanham, MD: Lexington.

Hearit, K. M. (2006). *Crisis management by apology: Corporate response to allegations of wrongdoing*. New York, NY: Lawrence Erlbaum.

Helmick R. G., & Peterson, R. L. (Eds.) (2001). *Forgiveness and reconciliation: Religion, public policy, and conflict transformation*. Philadelphia, PA: Templeton Foundation Press.

Hines, S. G., & De Young, C. P. (2000). *Beyond rhetoric: Reconciliation as a way of life*. Valley Forge, PA: Judson Press.

Jarvie, J. (2007, March 19). Formal slavery apologies debated. *Los Angeles Times*. Retrieved from http://articles.latimes.com/2007/mar/19/nation/na-apology19

Kiss, E. (2000). Moral ambition within and beyond political constraints: Reflections on restorative justice. In R. I. Rotberg, & D. Thompson (Eds.), *Truth v. justice: The morality of truth commissions* (pp. 68-98). Princeton, NJ: Princeton University Press.

Koesten, J., & Rowland, R. C. (2004). The rhetoric of atonement. *Communication Studies, 55*(1), 68–87.

Lazare, A. (2004). *On apology*. New York, NY: Oxford University Press.

Lewis, C. K. (2008). Publish and perish?: My fundamentalist education from the inside Out. *KB Journal, 4*(2). Retrieved from http://www.kbjournal.org/lewis

Lincoln, C. E. (1984). *Race, religion, and the continuing American dilemma*. New York, NY: Hill and Wang.

Lundberg, C, & and Gunn, J. (2005). 'Ouija board, are there any communications?' Agency, ontotheology, and the death of the humanist subject, or, continuing the ARS conversation. *Rhetoric Society Quarterly, 35*(4), 83–105.

McPhail, M. L. (2002). *The rhetoric of racism revisited: Reparations or separation?* Lanham, MD: Rowman and Littlefield.

Ricoeur, P. (1995). *Oneself as another*. Trans. K. Blamey. Chicago, IL: University of Chicago Press.

Ricoeur, P. (2000). *The just*. Trans. D. Pellauer. Chicago, IL: University of Chicago Press.

Ritivoi, A. D. (2006). *Paul Ricoeur: Tradition and innovation in rhetorical theory*. Albany, NY: State University of New York Press.

Robinson, R. (2001). *The debt: What America owes to blacks*. New York, NY: Plume.

S. Res. 332, Virginia General Assembly (2007) (enacted).

Salazar, P. J. (2002). *An African Athens: Rhetoric and the shaping of democracy in South Africa*. Mahwah, NJ: Lawrence Erlbaum.

Schreiter, R. J. (1998). *The ministry of reconciliation: Spirituality and strategies*. Maryknoll, NY: Orbis.

Stewart, J. (1995). *Language as articulate contact: Toward a post-semiotic philosophy of communication*. Albany, NY: State University of New York Press.

Tutu, D. M. (1999). *No future without forgiveness*. New York, NY: Doubleday.

Tutu, D. M. (2000). *No future without forgiveness*. New York, NY: Random House.

Wall, J. (2002). Moral meaning: Beyond the good and the right. In J. Wall, W. Schweiker, & D. Hall (Eds.), *Paul Ricoeur and contemporary moral thought* (pp. 47-63). New York, NY: Routledge.

Whitley, T. (2007, January 30). Slavery apology language altered: "Contrition" replaces "atone"; Potential for reparations is issue. *Richmond Times-Dispatch*. Retrieved from http://www.timesdispatch.com

Zehr, H. (1997, December). Restorative justice: The concept. *Corrections Today*. Retrieved from https://www.aca.org/publications/ctarchives4.asp

Zehr, H. (1990). *Changing lenses: A new focus for crime and justice*. Scottsdale, PA: Herald Press.

4 From Tragedy to Comedy: A Pentadic Analysis Contrasting Hillary Clinton's Health Care Reform Rhetoric, 1993–1994 and 2008

Theon E. Hill

It was called "one of the most breathtaking political comebacks in U.S. history" (Levy, 2007). When presidential candidate Senator Hillary Clinton unveiled her health care reform plan, entitled "America's Health Choices Plan," it quickly gained widespread support within the public sphere. Thanks to this plan, the senator—whose previous reform plan was castigated as "the most complicated effort since the invasion of Normandy" (Milton, 2000, p. 275)—won accolades and significant support for her reform goals. Several media outlets, many of which were among her worst critics in 1993, were clearly enamored with her proposal, describing it as "excellent" (Horowitz, 2007), as "good politics" (Levy, 2007), and as "the sort of bill that may have a chance to work" (Klein, 2007).

Hillary Clinton's name was first linked to national health care reform during her husband's presidency in 1993, when he appointed her chair of a special government task force devoted to the formation of a reform plan. In his article discussing the Clintons' reform campaign, Starr (1995) succinctly records the results: "it was one year from euphoria to defeat." The task force that began with the support of approximately two-thirds of the nation ended in shame, failing to make any tangible progress (Starr, 1995). Furthermore, the failed attempt attracted unrelenting criticism for Mrs. Clinton's apparent mishandling of the campaign (Marcus, 1994). Everything was different, however, when she made health care a key platform of her 2008 presidential campaign. The American people had forgiven her for the failures of the past. Though some remained unrelenting in their negative attitudes toward her, there was a new openness to her ideas among many others in the American public sphere. Such polarized opinions towards Clinton might explain how she could simultaneously be the "most" and the "least" trusted candidate on health care, according to polls taken in the wake of her plan's announcement (Goldstein, 2007).

The drastic changes in the public's perception and reception of Clinton in the arena of health care reform raises several questions for those interested in public discourse. Did she make key rhetorical changes between campaigns that contributed to her ability to make a strong comeback? If so, what are the implications of these changes for rhetorical theory, and for those who utilize communication to gain public support? What lessons can those embroiled in public scandals and controversies learn about regaining public trust from Clinton's rhetorical strategies? All of these questions all deal with human motivation and rhetorical processes—concerns ideally suited to analysis from the standpoint of Kenneth Burke's (1945/1969) pentad.

As will become clear over the course of this chapter, I argue that Clinton's second plan involved a strategic pentadic shift, one that aided her in three ways: (1) it allowed her to regain control of the discourse surrounding her reform plan; (2) it allowed her to reposition herself within a comic frame, as opposed to a tragic frame; and (3) it helped her reframe her own past. To substantiate these claims, this chapter uses pentadic analysis to compare Clinton's rhetoric from both campaigns, noting key changes made in her approaches to each. I draw upon speech transcripts and multiple speeches from each campaign, recognizing Birdsell's (1987) point that "root terms are likely to be considerably less well-defined in specific texts" (p. 274). I see this analysis as contributing to the ongoing scholarly conversation about pentadic shifts accomplished through discourse (e.g., Westerfelhaus, 1998) and the desirability of comic over tragic frames in recovering from public scandals (e.g., Turnage, 2009). Through this chapter, I hope to deepen our understanding of how attention to the pentad, and to pentadic shifts more specifically, can help track changes in a rhetor's discourse and in their positioning of self within the public sphere, over time. Before starting this analysis, let me first situate my approach within the relevant literature on the pentad.

PENTADIC CRITICISM

Since its systematic explication in *A Grammar of Motives*, Burke's (1945/1969) pentad has been recognized as a vocabulary for the explication of symbolic or discursive processes that influence human motivation. The pentad—Burke's

(1943) term for the five interrelated elements of Act, Agency, Actor, Scene, and Purpose—is premised on his contention that human motivation can be best understood through the eyes of drama. As a result, pentadic analysis traces the interaction and transformation of the five terms, and the specific ratios posited between terms, in particular instances of symbolic discourse.

Following Burke's lead, most scholars hold that act or action is always the core of the pentad, but that this term "may be substantially reinterpreted by featuring other terms either singularly or, more commonly by emphasizing a dominant term in a pentadic ratio" (Tonn, Endress, & Diamond, 2005, p. 204). Thus, as many rhetorical critics have argued, terms receiving the greatest emphasis reveal the framework from which the rhetor motivates an audience to action. As Crable and Makay (1972) note, "the featuring of terms implicitly features the motives within that term" (p. 14). From this standpoint, the pentad is useful to the critic by helping "to isolate persuasive resources in the speech" (Birdsell, 1987, p. 268). Furthermore, since Burke links each pentadic term with a philosophical school, a key goal of pentadic analysis is uncovering the philosophical framework the rhetor utilizes in seeking to identify an audience with his or her position.

Over the past fifty years, scholars in rhetoric and (when rhetorically-oriented) in organizational communication have utilized the pentad in a variety of ways. This form of Burkean analysis has been useful for the study of topics as varied as social movements (Brummett, 1979), public scandals (Ling, 1971; Turnage, 2009), religious controversies (Westerfelhaus, 1998), presidential rhetoric (Hahn & Morlando, 1979; Birdsell, 1987), and company picnics (Walker & Monin, 2001). In addition, scholars have made significant theoretical contributions to Burke's theory of dramatism and to the pentad as a tool for rhetorical criticism.[1] Collectively, I believe that this research advances three important points related to Burkean criticism: (1) pentadic ratios or terms that are emphasized in a rhetor's discourse make significant contributions to audience interpretations of a situation; (2) dominant ratios can shift within a particular instance of public discourse, and also over time; and (3) the ratios emphasized in discourse can facilitate the emergence of tragic or comic frames for rhetors and audiences.

First, as many Burkean criticisms have demonstrated, the dominant pentadic framing of a situation can have powerful rhetorical effects. This can be seen, for example, in Tonn, Endress, and Diamond's (2005) conclusion that scenic arguments symbolically absolved a hunter of guilt for his role in an accidental death in Maine. Blankenship, Fine, and Davis (1983) similarly probe the relationships between featured pentadic terms and their situational definitions through an analysis of Ronald Reagan's 1980 presidential campaign—a campaign, they argue, that shifted the audiences' focus from his role as an actor in the scene, to the scene in which all other candidates were contained. Scholars have also highlighted the potential of strategic pendantic shifts by rhetors to address complex situations. Ling (1970), for example, famously notes the power of Ted Kennedy's pentadic shift in his speech following the Chappaquiddick disaster; the speech redefined the situation so that, for the people of Massachusetts, forgiving their Senator appeared logical, even natural.[2] Westerfelhaus (1998) similarly exemplifies this point through his review of the changing rhetoric of the Catholic Church—a discourse that, he argues, seeks to maintain the church's opposition to homosexuality while still making space for the homosexuals among its ranks. Finally, Turnage (2009) explores the relationship between scene, act, and the tragic frame in her discussion of the highly publicized rape case at Duke University. Her analysis reveals that the scene-act ratio, combined with the tragic frame, created a situation where the potential for forgiveness and healing between the university and the surrounding community was limited. Instead, the tragic frame froze the groups into patterns of scapegoating that prevented true reconciliation.

Positioning myself in the shadow of these scholars, I seek to extend scholarship on the pentad through my analysis of Hillary Clinton's health care reform rhetoric. The work discussed above can be tied together, I contend, through analyzing a single rhetor's discursive shifts over a period of time by using Burke's pentad to trace the philosophical changes in the rhetor's framing of a situation. As a result, in the remainder of this chapter, I argue that Hillary Clinton's pentadic shift in her rhetoric of health care reform created a discursive space for her to rearticulate her failed previous attempt at reform within a comic frame, thereby symbolically armoring her against criticism and preparing her successful return to health care reform. To flesh out this argument, I first provide a background and brief rhetorical analysis of Clinton's first reform campaign. In particular, I seek to show how she utilized a pentadic ratio of agency-scene during the first campaign, conducted as First Lady. Second, I identify a new ratio of purpose-scene that emerged during her second campaign, conducted during her unsuccessful bid for the Democratic Party's presidential nomination. It is important to note that I do not claim that this rhetorical shift was the panacea, that it symbolically fixed all the problems Clinton faced. Such a claim is beyond the scope of this paper. Rather, I seek to highlight how the shift discursively repositioned her to make a dramatic comeback, to be identified as the most trusted candidate in terms of health care reform (Bright, 2007).

1993–1994 Health Care Reform History

Bill Clinton won the 1992 presidential election with only forty-three percent of the popular vote. Given his rather small margin of victory, it is clear that one key factor that put him in the White House was his campaign's emphasis on "change" in America (Holloway, 1996, p. 163). A key platform of this "change" strategy was promoting a universal health care system. He boldly promised to submit reform legislation to Congress within his first one hundred days in office. His optimism, though, was shared by the American people: At the time of his election, 68% of Americans believed the President could cure the health care crisis (Holloway, 1996, p. 159). In retrospect, setting this early deadline seems to have been a fatal mistake, because it set an unrealistic timeline for the completion of an amazingly complex task. At the time, his advisors felt that any delay would increase the likelihood of defeat by the "defenders of the status quo" (Muir & Benitez, 1996, p. 149).

In light of this impending battle, President Clinton hurriedly organized a reform task force and asked his wife to lead it, giving the first lady more power than any of her predecessors (Clinton, 2003, p. 148; Friedman, 1993). He made this appointment based on his wife's background in health care and on his desire to appoint someone that symbolized how seriously he took the issue. Upon accepting the position, however, Mrs. Clinton began receiving warnings from friends and foes about the difficulties that lay ahead. She would later admit that although she was hopeful for the possibility of reform, she "didn't fully realize the magnitude of the task" (Clinton, 2003, p. 149).

The challenges she faced included weak support from the Democratic Party, including many of President Clinton's advisors, due to the fact that many party members were frustrated at the excessive attention health care was receiving (Holloway, 1996). She also fought strong opposition from medical organizations such as the American Medical Association (AMA) and the Health Insurance Association of America (HIAA). Collectively, these organizations spent approximately sixty million dollars campaigning against her reform plan (Goldsteen, Goldsteen, Swan, & Clemena, 2001, p. 1326). Initially, Clinton shrugged off the pressure, intending to "use the public's support for her approach to attack those who opposed her" (Bernstein, 2003, p. 288). Nevertheless, her failure to gain sufficient support from the American people ultimately doomed her campaign for reform.

1993–1994 Campaign Rhetoric: Agency-Scene Ratio

During this campaign, Clinton's rhetoric promoting her husband's health care plan featured a pentadic ratio of agency-scene. Although this framing is understandable as a strategy, it left her plan vulnerable to criticism from those who sought to cast the proposal as socialist. The act she proposed for the American people was a new, universal health care system, and, rhetorically, the scene Clinton painted was that of an entire nation in peril. In her biography of Clinton, Milton (2000) describes her portrayal of America "as a nation suffering from a 'sleeping sickness of the soul'" (p. 282). In her speeches, Clinton repeatedly highlights flaws in the system, such as "a lack of choice," "discriminatory practices," and "monetary limitations." Using these key phrases, she sought to create a sense of imprisonment at every level of American life:

> As we are here today, *choice* is diminishing for most Americans. Americans are being told by their employers, who buy their insurance for them by their insurance companies if they buy directly, what doctors they can see and what hospitals they can use. . . . Under the current way health care is both being organized and developing, fewer and fewer Americans are being given *choice*. That *choice* is made by somebody else, for you. (Clinton, 1994, emphasis added)

Not only did Mrs. Clinton demonstrate these problems at the level of individual citizens, but she also reveals the ethical dilemmas the apparent crisis created for businesses:

> I was talking with some friends of mine about their small business. . . . Several years ago one of their employees had a child who was born with Down's syndrome. And all of a sudden they were faced with what so many people are faced with every day in our country. Do you want to continue to insure this family with this child? Do you want to have to pay more? Because if you continue to insure this family, the costs for all your families will go up. And my friend, whom I have known ever since high school who is a small businessman, said, "you know, what a choice for me to be asked to make, to turn my back on an employee and his family that were part of my family and my small business, or to reach down even deeper out of the wages of my employees, out of our profits, and provide health care insurance.." . . . No American should have to make that choice. (Clinton, 1993b)

To complete her sketch of the scene, Mrs. Clinton sympathizes with the concerns of misunderstood members of the medical community who had lost the ability to truly care for their patients because of restrictions the system had placed on them:

> Most doctors and other health care professionals choose careers in health and medicine because they want to help people. But too often because our system isn't working and we haven't taken full responsibility for fixing it, that motive is clouded by perceptions that doctors aren't the same as they used to be. They're not really doing what they used to do. They don't really care like they once did. (Clinton, 1993a)

This strategic portrayal of scene had two main goals: (1) she tries to show how every segment of the population is negatively impacted by the system; and (2) she positions choice as the liberator from the shackles of the current system.

This construction of the scene proved effective, and was one key victory of the campaign. Thanks to her rhetorical framing, health care became "an issue that 'people were talking about around their kitchen tables'" (Marcus, 1994). She crafts her discourse in a way that leads even insured Americans to re-evaluate their perspective of the health care system, particularly through her use of the word "choice." She positions choice as the key criterion to be used in determining the validity of reform plans that promised to release Americans from the prison of a broken system. However, she does not stop there; she also tries establishing health care as a human right:

> What we are facing now, as we look at health care reform, is the possibility of making good on the promises and the hopes of the leadership of this union of presidents, both democrat and republican over 60 years, and *making good on the fundamental promise that health care should be a right, not a privilege of a select few.* (Clinton, 1993b, emphasis added)

While scene is prominent in her rhetorical construction of the situation, it is consistently linked to agency; moreover, agency is the dominant term in this pentadic ratio. According to Burke (1969a), the underlying philosophy emphasizing agency is pragmatism (p. xxi). For this framework to be effective, the rhetor must establish the end as justified by the means. A reliance upon the agency-scene ratio, therefore, can be quite effective when it takes the form of "*x* (the scene) demands that we do *y* (the agency)." However, in elevating agency over scene within the ratio, Clinton makes crucial errors that leave her campaign vulnerable to attack and disruption. In particular, she does not sufficiently discuss the agency that would correct the scene she portrays. She explains in her speeches what the plan or agency would *do*, but she does not explain how it would *operate*. For example, in a speech to ARC, she effectively uses a criteria-satisfaction structure to match her plan to the needs arising from the current system, but she never gives specific details on how the plan would meet those needs. She assumes this end without giving her audience requisite detail:

> In the new release that the ARC issued supporting health care reform and the President, it said that the ARC wants to measure any reform against a set of five principles from a disability perspective, and these are nondiscrimination, comprehensiveness, appropriateness, equity, and efficiency.
>
> Every one of those fits into the principles that the President outlined. . . . It has to be comprehensive. And that means it has to provide a comprehensive set of benefits. It cannot discriminate against any American. It must be appropriate in the sense that we should build on what works. It should provide access to adequate quality, affordable health care in appropriate setting based upon the choices that individuals make that are best for them and their families.
>
> It must—it must have equity. And if it is comprehensive and does not discriminate, it should have equity. But it needs to have safeguards built in so that all of us feel that we are not being taken advantage of or discriminated against.
>
> And it must have efficiency, efficiency in the better delivery of health care services and more cost-effective. (Clinton 1993b)

As can be seen in the above quotations, Clinton frequently emphasizes principles instead of specifics. This was no accident; a key factor behind this rhetorical strategy is her reluctance, against the will of her advisors, to disclose any of the deliberations of the reform task force (Milton, 2000). From a Burkean perspective, it is little wonder that this approach proved problematic; despite her emphasis on agency, her secrecy limits her ability to answer questions about the functional nature of this plan for the American health care system. Furthermore, it opens her plan up to attacks from critics and lobbyists opposed to her reforms. In the absence of definite details from the Clinton camp, critics and lobbyists capitalize on the opportunity by providing their own predictions about the nature of the plan to an increasingly anxious public. They frighten the American public with claims that her plan is nothing more than "a jerry-built substitute for a Canadian-style single-payer plan" (Milton, 2000, p. 284).

Her unwillingness to offer specifics causes a disconnection to arise between the discursive reality she tries to construct and the material reality perceived by Americans. Lobbyists seize on the confusion surrounding the reform plan, organizing an extensive propaganda campaign featuring the famed "Harry and Louise" commercials. Through this campaign, lobbyists and Republican opponents shift the nature of the reform debate—from health care versus no health care to capitalism versus socialism. This polarization grew to the point that some health care professionals even labeled the President as the "Dr. Frankenstein" of health care reform (Matthews, Jr., 1993). Once the First Lady's reforms were branded as socialist, she is positioned as un-American and anti-capitalist, a difficult position to defend in America's capitalist society. She fervently tries to refute the allegations, but—without specific evidence to support her claims—her words fall on deaf ears. Clinton lost control of the discourse surrounding her reform plan, and is ultimately blamed for the nation's failure to reform the system.[3]

Her reform attempt is all but dead by 1995. The failure of Clinton's reform plan to succeed can be tied to a variety of factors. For example, Campbell (1998) argues that part of Clinton's failure is traceable to her gender; she does not enact a distinctly feminine style in her rhetoric, similar to someone like Elizabeth Dole. Nevertheless, from a Burkean standpoint, her use of agency is problematic because of the secrecy surrounding the reform task force's work; her focus on agency is also problematic in that it defines the debate as one of universal health care versus the status quo. Her opponents linked the idea of universal health care with socialism, robbing her of control of the discourse surrounding her reform plan. This identification prevents her from capturing sufficient public backing to ensure the passage of her plan.

Finally, her misuse of agency fosters the construction of a tragic frame surrounding health care, one in which she is positioned as a sacrificial "scapegoat"—a vessel carrying the guilt of all who contribute to the inability of the government to pass health care reform legislation. Having been accorded this role within the discourse of the public sphere, she loses the support of scores of Americans who are hopeful for reform. In addition, she receives scathing criticism from the press for her leadership. Many Democrats held her responsible for their party's electoral defeats, as they cost the party a majority in the House for the first time in almost fifty years (Hernandez & Pear, 2006). This frame not only affects others' views of her work on health care reform; it damages her reputation, and everyone from politicians to comedians on *Saturday Night Live* mock her.

THE 2008 PRESIDENTIAL ELECTION: A NEW HEALTH CARE REFORM RHETORIC

Despite the challenges posed by the significant losses of 1993 and 1994, several factors facilitated Hilary Clinton's dramatic return to health care reform efforts in 2008. During the fifteen years between her campaigns for health care reform, Clinton embarked on a quiet crusade to restore public trust in her leadership and vision. This crusade involved playing key roles in the formation of several pieces of smaller legislation, including the State Children's Health Insurance Program (SCHIP), the Vaccines for Children Program, and numerous programs for veterans and active military personal (Clinton, 2007a). Once sworn in as the junior Senator from New York, she began reaching out to old foes from both parties and from the business sector. These efforts were aided by external factors that also created a national appetite for reform.

As the 2008 presidential election season approached, health care remained a hot topic in the public sphere. Businesses felt greater financial strain in an employer-based system, the number of uninsured had skyrocketed, and international respect for the U.S. health care system plummeted (Boushey, 2004). In addition, views that she espoused during the first campaign had been adopted by other rhetors over the fifteen-year interlude; these views had gradually gained general acceptance in public discourse. Previously, universal health care was perceived as a trademark of socialism, but when the campaign for the 2008 presidential election began, polls showed that a majority of Americans believed that the government bore the primary responsibility in providing health care (Roberts, 2007). Also, pop culture began promoting the belief that health care is a moral right, lobbying for universal coverage by using strong emotional appeals in documentaries such as Michael Moore's *Sicko* and movies like *John Q.* These factors worked in harmony to provide Clinton with an opportunity to attempt reform a second time.

While her goal remained unchanged in 2008, Clinton's rhetorical strategy of promoting universal health care was drastically different. Unlike the previous campaign, the focus was not about her plan for universal health care (i.e., agency). Now, she focused on *why* (i.e., purpose) the nation should pursue a universal health care system. Since the conditions she described in the early 1990s remained or had worsened, scene remained an important rhetorical resource; as a result, scene is continually paired with the dominant term—purpose—in Clinton's pentadic ratio. In Burkean terms, I identify Clinton's change as a pentadic shift from agency-scene to purpose-scene. Furthermore, the pentadic shift indicates a motivational shift in Clinton from pragmatism to the philosophical school of mysticism. According to Burke (1945/1969), mysticism emphasizes the "unity of the individual with some cosmic or universal purpose" (pp. 287–288). This unity necessitates dissociation with previous linkages in the mind of the individual (p. 284). For example, in Clinton's rhetoric her pentadic shift involves dissociating universal health care from socialism and (re)associating it with fundamental human rights. The power of this shift was not lost on the media. Brooks

(2008) notes that Clinton "turned the debate . . . into a sort of philosophical holy grail, with a party of righteousness and a party of error." This shift allows Clinton to identify her plan with agreed-upon standards of morality and national pride, enabling her to accomplish three broad rhetorical goals.

First, her pentadic shift allows her to regain control of the discourse surrounding her health care reform efforts. Health care reform remained a polarizing issue during the 2008 election, but the focus of her rhetoric was no longer on her plan to overhaul the American health care system. She concentrates her speeches on the desire to provide all Americans with their moral rights. Instead of constantly fighting opponents regarding capitalism and socialism, she rests on her assertion that universal health care is simply "the right thing to do" (Clinton, 2007a). In Burke's (1945/1969) view, this pentadic shift qualifies as Clinton's attempt to generate the "mystic 'moment'" that is integral to his notion of "the grammar of rebirth"; the "rebirth" focuses on "a moment wherein some motivating principle is experienced that had not been experienced before" (p. 306). Clinton did not change her goal of universal health care, but this time, everything looked different because her rhetorical focus *was* different. Since the 1990s found her discourse limited to the level of agency, the debate was restricted to the terms of her plan. Her rhetorical shift allowed her to transcend the capitalism versus socialism debate and to draw upon commonly accepted values, on the morality of Americans. This provided a key point of identification for those who were cautious to initially support universal health care. Burke (1945/1969) notes this transcendent power of featuring purpose in discourse: "Precisely at such times of general hesitancy, the mystic can compensate for his own particular doubts about human purpose by submerging himself in some vision of a universal, or absolute or transcendent purpose, with which he would identify himself" (p. 288).

Not only did this shift in pentadic ratios allow Clinton to control discourse by transcending the previous debate of capitalism versus socialism, but it also allows her to shield herself against those who seek to renew attacks from the 1990s. Once she identified her plan with accepted standards of morality, the efficacy of "socialism" attacks is severely undermined:

> The knee-jerk response from Republicans was to smear her proposal as "socialized medicine," a fresh reminder of how illiterate, out-of-touch and irrelevant the Republicans have become on the most important domestic issue to voters. It was particularly odd coming from Mitt Romney, who should have seen in the Clinton proposal many of the same features found in the landmark Massachusetts

reform plan that he helped to negotiate as governor only two years ago. (Pearlstein, 2007)

By retaining control of the discourse surrounding health care reform, she positions herself in the minds of the American people as the most likely agent of "change" in health care in the 2008 election (Roberts, 2007).

This shift did not simply impact her ability to shape the discourse in health care reform during the presidential campaign. It also creates a discursive space for her to rearticulate a new perspective on the previous campaign. In other words, thanks to the rhetorical efforts of 2008, she is able to defend and explain her actions during 1993 and 1994. She accomplishes this, I believe, by grounding her rhetorical discourse in a comic frame. In *Attitudes Toward History*, Burke (1984) highlights several frames that rhetors utilize in discourse. Burke frequently contrasts the comic frame to the tragic frame, contending that they differ in several key characteristics:

> The tragic frame requires a sacrificial scapegoat who suffers, dies, or is banished by society in a symbolic attempt to rid itself of chaos, diseases, and impurity. In contrast to the tragic frame, the comic frame never requires the death or banishment of a scapegoat. It attempts to shame or humiliate the target into changing his or her actions. The comic frame offers hope to society because the efficacy of human agency, reason, and community are affirmed. (Christiansen & Hanson, 1996, pp. 159–160)

In her article studying the use of comic frames in social movements, Powell (1995) highlights the importance of identifying a movement's characteristic Burkean frame, noting that "since the frame a movement utilizes determines its form of symbolic action, a critic of the movement needs to know the frame in which it operates" (p. 87). Herself a public actor, one whose symbolic action substantially impacts the lives and symbolic acts of her audience, the same can be said of identifying Clinton's characteristic frame. This is even more appropriate, I believe, in that she sought to frame her new campaign for reform as a movement (Clinton, 2007b). As long as Clinton remained within the tragic frame stemming from her first failed attempt at reform, she was locked into a position as a symbolic scapegoat. As Turnage (2009) notes, the tragic frame makes forgiveness very difficult because it substitutes the search for a scapegoat for the complex resolution of conflict. In the comic frame, Clinton finds "a perspective for reducing social tension" (Powell, 1995, p. 88) because it symbolically embodies and encourages a "charitable attitude towards people that is required for purposes of persuasion and cooperation" (Burke, 1984, p. 166).

In a sense, then, the comic frame offers Clinton an alternative to playing the role of scapegoat. Instead, in the comic frame, she finds a role as a comic clown who serves to "alter consciousness of the social order" (Carlson, 1988, p. 312). In this capacity, her role enables individuals to "recognize . . . faults and work to correct them" (Powell, 1995, p. 87). As Toker (2002) explains, "only the comic frame offers a vocabulary amendable to social reform" (p. 62). Within the tragic frame, someone must accept blame and banishment for social guilt to be purged. The comic frame offers an alternative approach to guilt, in that the comic clown symbolically corrects his or her behavior and is welcomed back into society (Toker, 2002).

Clinton utilizes the comic frame to present herself as a clown who is re-formed, and had sacrificed much for society:

> I hear growing concern about the crisis in our health care system: exploding costs, declining coverage and shortcoming in care and prevention. Now, I've tangled with this issue before—and I've got the scars to show for it. But I learned some valuable lessons from that experience. One is that we can't achieve reform without the participation and commitment of health care providers, employers, employees and other citizens who apply for, depend upon, and actually deliver health care services. (Clinton 2007a)

There is another strategy at work here in her reliance on the comic frame: The comic frame allows her to describe her previous reform campaign as a stepping-stone towards a worthwhile goal and, thus, not as a failure. The language she uses to rearticulate her previous attempt at reform suggests it as a learning experience, as a necessary part of the reform process. This comic perspective allows Clinton to discuss the previous campaign as preparation for her current attempt, rather than as a failure she could never overcome. Suddenly, her 1993 campaign is not failure, but is preparatory.

She restates this same position at several points leading up to the 2008 campaign (Levy, 2007). Within a discourse featuring purpose-scene, the previous campaign is transformed; it is no longer a failed attempt or an ill-advised reform plan; instead, it is a failed attempt at providing people with their moral rights. This is a powerful strategy in overcoming the past, especially when presented in a comic frame that argues that people can move beyond past failures, that they are mistaken, as Burke says, and not criminals. Therefore, her "sufferings" and "scars" are rearticulated through this new frame, highlighting the continuous nature of her efforts on behalf of the people:

> After 1994, when people asked me if I was going to give up on health care reform, I always had the same answer. Why would I give up on

America and the American people? For so many years I have listened to their stories. I carry these stories with me every day.

And perhaps more than anyone else, I know just how hard this fight will be. But that is why I'm running for President, because I'm ready with you to help write a new story. The story about how we finally put aside our difference to face up to one of our greatest challenges. The story of how people of good faith and good will came together and worked out a solution because they cared too much about our country and their fellow citizens to let this crisis continue. (Clinton, 2007b)

The comic frame contributes to Clinton's ability to reposition herself in a favorable light with the American people, and to rearticulate her past defeat as preparatory rather than deterministic. As Toker (2002) observes, the "application of the comic strategies . . . may help create an expanded, inclusive and negotiated frame for policy practices" (p. 79). The comic frame enables her to approach reform efforts in a way that does not threaten the "status quo," but seeks to correct it (Powell, 1995, p. 87). She does this by pursuing a highly publicized strategy of "smaller steps" (Levy, 2007). Her rhetoric is more flexible and less threatening during this campaign:

[P]eople, who are satisfied with their current coverage, want assurances that they can keep it. Part of our health care system is the best in the world and we should build on it. Part is broken, and we should fix it. (Clinton, 2007a)

This strategy allows her to be clear and bold, while still identifying with the concerns of the American people.

During the second reform campaign, purpose takes center stage as her favored pentadic term. By featuring purpose, Clinton's starting point is the position that health care is a moral right, and to deny it is immoral. The language she uses calls for support from all Americans in this fight: "to truly reform health care in America, we need more than a plan. We need a movement determined to change the system who will not rest until we succeed" (Clinton, 2007b). This language is reminiscent of key points throughout history, when people banded together in the quest for equality, echoing the women's suffrage and the civil rights movements. Senator Clinton becomes the wise, comic figure suited to lead the American people in this quest. Stressing "purpose" so strongly not only allows Senator Clinton to tap into feelings of patriotism and humanity, but also imbues the reform debate with a moral imperative. By shifting to purpose as a dominant term, she taps into a higher priority among the American people than mere policy: their rights as human beings.

NOTES

1. Given the hundreds of published articles and chapters utilizing the pentad, many contributions could be highlighted within this discussion. For the sake of brevity, I focus my attention on a few areas where previous research has made observations relevant to this chapter.

2. Birdsell (1989) questions Ling's analysis, arguing that Kennedy did not shift pentadic structures, but simply positioned himself within a "more expansive, metaphysical scene" (p. 275) that Ling did not recognize. However, Birdsell acknowledges that there is a degree of ambiguity involved in interpreting the pentadic elements, and that it is a process that is heavily influenced by the goal of the analysis.

3. There were opportunities to regain control of the discourse surrounding health care reform, but Clinton vehemently refused to cooperate with members of her own party, whose reform plans aimed for a more bipartisan appeal (Brooks, 2008). By refusing to cooperate, she turns potential friends into foes. Instead of identifying with her audience, she becomes isolated. When finally released, the plan was an enormous 1,300-page document that confused average Americans to the point that even some of her own party members distanced themselves from the proposal.

REFERENCES

Bernstein, C. (2003). *Woman in charge.* New York, NY: Alfred A. Knopf.

Birdsell, D. S. (1987). Ronald Reagan on Lebanon and Grenada: Flexibility and interpretation in the application of Kenneth Burke's pentad. *Quarterly Journal of Speech, 73*(3), 267–279.

Blankenship, J., Fine, M. G., & Davis, L. K. (1983). The 1980 Republican primary debates: The transformation of actor to scene. *Quarterly Journal of Speech, 69*(1), 25–36.

Boushey, H. (2004, April 14). New evidence of worsening problems: Falling employer-based coverage. Center for American Progress. Retrieved from http://wwww.americanprogress.org/issues/2004/04/b45646.html/print.html

Bright, B. (2007). Americans want leaders to address coverage for uninsured, poll shows. *Wall Street Journal.* Retrieved from http://online.wsj.com/article/SB119014251792831362.html

Brooks, D. (2008, February 5). The Cooper concerns. *New York Times.* Retrieved from http://www.nytimes.com/2008/02/05/opinion/05brooks.html

Brummett, B. (1979). A pentadic analysis of ideologies in two gay rights controversies. *Central States Speech Journal, 30*(3), 250–261. doi: 10.1080/10510977909368018

Burke, K. (1937). *Attitudes toward history.* Berkeley, CA: University of California Press.

Burke, K. (1941). The rhetoric of Hitler's battle. In C. R. Burgchardt (Ed.), *Readings in rhetorical criticism* (pp. 188–202), 3rd ed. State College, PA: Strata.

Burke, K. (1943). The five master terms: Their place in a 'dramatistic' grammar of motives. In R. J. Young & Y. Liu (Eds.), *Landmark essays on rhetorical invention in writing* (pp. 1–11), Vol. 8. Philadelphia, PA: Lawrence Erlbaum Associates.

Burke, K. (1945/1969). *A grammar of motives*. Berkeley, CA: University of California Press. (Original work published 1945)

Burke, K. (1950/1969). *A rhetoric of motives*. Berkeley, CA: University of California Press. (Original work published 1950)

Burke, K. (1984). *Permanence and change* (3rd ed.). Berkeley, CA: University of California Press.

Campbell, K. K. (1998). The discursive performance of femininity: Hating Hillary. *Rhetoric & Public Affairs, 1*(1), 1–19.

Carlson, A. C. (1988). Limitations on the comic frame: Some witty American women of the nineteenth century. *Quarterly Journal of Speech, 74*(3), 310–322. doi: 10.1080/00335638809383844

Christiansen, A. E., & Hanson, J. J. (1996). Comedy as cure for tragedy: ACT UP and the rhetoric of AIDS. *Quarterly Journal of Speech, 82*(2), 157–170.

Clinton, H. (1993a). Remarks by the First Lady during a speech to the American Medical Association. *Speeches by the First Lady*. Retrieved from http://clinton3.nara.gov/WH/EOP/First_Lady/other/1993–06–13-first-lady-remarks-during-a-speech-to-the-arc.text

Clinton, H. (1993b). Remarks by the First Lady during a speech to the ARC. *Speeches by the First Lady*. Retrieved from http://clinton3.nara.gov/WH/EOP/First_Lady/other/1994–03–15-first-lady-address-at-washington-university.text

Clinton, H. (1994). An address by the First Lady at Washington University. *Speeches by the First Lady*. Retrieved from http://clinton3.nara.gov/WH/EOP/First_Lady/other/1994–03–15-first-lady-address-at-washington-university.text

Clinton, H. (2003). *Living history*. New York, NY: Simon & Schuster.

Clinton, H. (2007a). Hillary remarks on reducing the cost of health care. *HillaryClinton.com*. Retrieved from http://www.hillaryclinton.com/news/speech/view/?id=1789

Clinton, H. (2007b). Remarks of America's health choices plan. *HillaryClinton.com*. Retrieved from http://www.hillarclinton.com/news/speech/view/?id=3329

Crable, R. E. & Makay, J. J. (1972). Kenneth Burke's concept of motives in rhetorical theory. *Communication Quarterly 20*(1), 11–18.

Foss, S., Foss, K. A., & Trapp, R. (Eds.). (2001). *Contemporary perspectives on rhetoric*. Prospect Heights, IL: Waveland Press.

Friedman, T. L. (1993, January 26). Hillary Clinton to head panel on health care. *New York Times*. Retrieved from http://www.nytimes.com/1993/01/26/us/hillary-clinton-to-head-panel-on-health-care.html

Goldsteen, R. L., Goldsteen, K., Swan, J. H., & Clemena, W. (2001). Harry and Louise and health care reform: Romancing public opinion. *Journal of Health Politics, Policy and Law, 26*(6), 1325–1352.

Goldstein, J. (2007, September 20). Hillary Clinton: Health-care polarizer. *Wall Street Journal*. Retrieved from http://blogs.wsj.com/health/2007/09/20/hillary-clinton-health-care-polarizer/

Hahn, D. F. & Morlando, A. (1979). A Burkean analysis of Lincoln's second inaugural address. *Presidential Studies Quarterly, 9*(4), 376–379.

Hernandez, R. & Pear, R. (2006, July 12). Once an enemy, health industry warms to Clinton. *New York Times*. Retrieved from http://www.nytimes.com/2006/07/12/nyregion/12donate.html?pagewanted=all&_r=0

Holloway, R. L. (1996). The Clintons and the health care crisis: Opportunity lost, promise unfulfilled. In R. E. Denton, Jr. & R. L. Holloway (Eds.), *The Clinton presidency: Images, issues, and communication strategies* (pp. 159–187). Westport, CT: Praeger.

Horowitz, J. (2007, September 24). Hillary's universal health-care message: This plan is different. *Observer*. Retrieved from http://www.observer.com/print/57922/full

Klein, J. (2007, September 20). What Hillary has learned from '93. *Time*. Retrieved from http://www.time.com/time/printout/0,08816,1663644,00.html

Levy, L. C. (2007, September 19). Clinton's health plan is good politics. *Newsday*. Retrieved from http://www.newsday.com/news/columnists/ny-oplevy5380812sep19,0,3369107,print.column

Ling, D. A. (1970). A pentadic analysis of Senator Edward Kennedy's address to the people of Massachusetts, July 25, 1969. *Communication Studies, 21*(2): 81–86. doi: 10.1080/10510977009363002

Matthews, Jr., M. (1993, December 13). The Clinton plan—health care reform; includes public opinion of proposals—*National Review* second opinions: health-care supplement. *National Review*. Retrieved from http://findarticles.com/p/articles/mi_m1282/is_n24_v45/ai_14752866

Marcus, R. (1994, September 30). Hillary Clinton soldiers on; First Lady reshapes role after health defeat. *Washington Post*. Retrieved from www.lexisnexis.com/hottopics/lnacademic

Milton, J. (2000). *The first partner: Hillary Rodham Clinton*. New York, NY: HarperCollins.

Muir, J. K. & Benitez, L. M. (1996). Redefining the role of first lady: The rhetorical style of Hillary Rodham Clinton. In R. E. Denton Jr. & R. L. Holloway (Eds.), *The Clinton presidency: Images, issues, and communication strategies* (pp. 139–158), Westport, CT: Praeger.

Pearlstein, S. (2007, September 19). A healthy dose of Hillary. *Washington Post*. Retrieved from www.lexisnexis.com/hottopics/lnacademic

Powell, K. (1995). The association of southern women for the prevention of lynching: Strategies of a movement in the comic frame. *Southern Communication Journal, 74*(2), 86–99.

Roberts, J. (2007, March 1). Poll: The politics of American health care. *CBS News*. Retrieved from http://www.cbsnews.com/stories/2007/03/01/opinion/polls/main2528357.shtml

Starr, P. (1995). What happened to health care reform? *American Prospect, 6*(20). Retrieved from http://www.princeton.edu/~starr/20starr.html

Toker, C. W. (2002). Debating "what out to be": The comic frame and public moral argument. *Western Journal of Communication, 66*(1), 53–83. doi: 10.1080/10570310209374725

Tonn, M. B., Endress, V. A., & Diamond, J. N. (2005). Hunting and heritage on trial in Maine: A dramatistic debate over tragedy, tradition, and territory. In C. R. Burgchardt (Ed.), *Readings in rhetorical criticism* (pp. 203–219), 3rd ed. State College, PA: Strata.

Turnage, A. K. (2009). Scene, act, and the tragic frame in the Duke rape case. *Southern Communication Journal, 74*(2), 141–156. doi: 10.1080/10417940802335946

Westerfelhaus, R. (1998). A significant shift: A pentadic analysis of the two rhetorics of the post-Vatican II Roman Catholic Church regarding homosexuality. *International Journal of Sexuality and Gender Studies, 3*(4), 269–294.

5 The Good Wife (According to Dr. Phil, et al.): A Representative Anecdote of Burkean Analysis

Cathryn Hill and Richard M. Coe

The reading of a book on the attaining of success is in itself the symbolic attaining of that success. It is while they read that these readers are "succeeding" . . . What [the reader] wants is easy success; and he gets it in the symbolic form by the mere reading itself.

—Kenneth Burke, *The Philosophy of Literary Form*

Framed here as a demonstration of the power of Burke's method, this chapter analyzes the symbolic action of popular, self-help relationship guides, such as those published by Laura Schlessinger, John Gray, Phil McGraw, et al. The primary method and perspective applied in this chapter is Burke's (1954) cluster-agon discourse analysis, with which we index, cluster, and *agon*-ize (in this instance, with literal charts) the terms used by these Schlessinger, Gray, McGraw, et al. to re-present gender roles, relationship values, and conflict resolution. While such analysis readily demonstrates the ideology inscribed in the vocabulary of popular relationship guides, it is always incomplete, and may deflect attention from important aspects of a discourse's symbolic action upon its readers.[1] Put simply, Burke's perspective on perspectives leads us to suspect that many women read this genre in a way that significantly modifies its symbolic action.[2]

As Burke (1954, 1966) understood so well, the power and action of a text must be understood in terms of how it symbolically resolves tensions readers bring to that text.[3] From the perspective of symbolic action, texts need to be examined as they act upon situated readers; in pentadic terms, the *act* needs to be understood in relation to the *scene*, and readers need to be understood as co-*agents*. To begin to connect the perspectives of these co-agents to the results of our cluster-agon analysis, we conducted a set of focus groups and interviews with a sample of the genre's habitual readers. The results suggest that popular, self-help bestsellers work in a Burkean fashion as cathartic reading. Taken together, the two Burkean perspectives sublate: The perspective of symbolic action both conserves and transcends the findings of the cluster-agon discourse analysis. Taken as a methodological representative anecdote, in addition to explaining the symbolic action of popular, self-help relationship guides, this chapter offers itself as a Burkean approach that is useful for transcending the limitations of cluster-agon analysis in particular (and discourse analysis in general).

The Genre

At least in North America, self-help relationship guides constitute a socially significant genre. McGee (2005), for example, reports that between one-third and one-half of Americans buy at least one self-help title in their life-time, and adds that, in New York, one bookstore "allocates a quarter mile of shelf space to the various subcategories of self-improvement literature" (p. 11). Marketdata Enterprises (2008) estimated that the self-improvement industry was worth $11 billion in 2008, with book sales accounting for approximately $875 million. As Salerno (2005) asserts:

> Whether you follow self-help's teachings or not, you have been touched by it, because [the self-help and actualization movement's] effects extend well beyond the millions of individual consumers who preorder Phil McGraw's latest book or attend Marianne Williamson's seminar-style love-ins. The alleged philosophies at the core of the movement have bled over into virtually every area of American social conduct and day-to-day living: the home, the workplace, the educational system, the mating dance, and elsewhere. (p. 3)

According to Marketdata Enterprises (2008), the main demographic for relationship self-help is "female, middle-aged, affluent, and [living] on the two U.S. coasts" (p. 2). Yet, its influence extends far beyond those who actually read the books. Marketdata Enterprises notes the special influence of Oprah Winfrey, who often interviews self-improvement "gurus"—an influence confirmed by the women interviewed for this study. As one illustration, Harville Hendrix (included in this study) promotes himself as "Oprah's favorite therapist." The previous holder of that title, Phil McGraw (also included in this study), may have fallen from Oprah's favor, but not before she helped him launch his immensely popular daytime talk show, *Dr. Phil*.

Although we can find no study that pursues Burkean insights into self-help books, self-help relationship guides have received considerable attention from various disciplinary perspectives. Not surprisingly, many criticisms of self-help books are written by feminists, who generally find the content of the books detrimental to women's progress and to egalitarian relationships. Crawford (2004), for instance, writes that John Gray's ideology reproduces "antiquated gender roles and [reinforces] the institution of patriarchal marriage" (p. 65). De Francisco and O'Connor (1995) assert that "to call these books self-help for women is insidiously misleading and disempowering," and that it "come[s] dangerously close to furthering the oppression of women" (p. 226). Zimmerman, Holm and Haddock (2001) similarly suggest that the books "represent both the progress and tensions of current social change" (p. 130); their analysis of best-selling relationship books concludes that, despite (female) authors' resistance to gender stereotyping, the most popular books are the most disempowering. These studies are consistent with the tenor of existing literature on relationship guides, and on self-help in general. This literature is largely unanimous in suggesting that the genre is built upon cultural stereotypes, that its advice is simplistic, and that its processes are not consistent with the tenets and standards of academic research.

Despite this widespread academic disapproval, these works remain popular. As a result, more scholarly attention should be paid to the nature and source of this appeal. As it stands, critiques of these works as unscholarly or simplistic fails to provide a compelling explanation for these books' popularity with women. Though there have been some initial attempts to address this gap in the literature, these efforts often focus specifically upon the marketing these works.[4] When overemphasized or taken alone, marketing explanations reduce readers to passive victims of clever marketing strategies. Such explanations fail to recognize that readers are active agents who are motivated to read these books because they *gain* something from them. As a result, what is missing from the literature is an in-depth rhetorical analysis of how the genre works. Such an analysis would be particularly important for anyone who wants to use the genre for more feminist purposes.[5] We hope a more rhetorical, generic perspective—one informed by a Burkean notion of symbolic action—will shed additional light on what the genre of relationship guides *does* for its readers (not just what it says to them), and on *how* it does what it does. Intimate relationships are a crucial part of most people's lives, and the functioning of those relationships is of deep interest to many. A more thorough knowledge of the relationship guides as a genre would significantly contribute to understanding the current state of relationships, and would influence the perceptions and practices of relationships.

God-term: Acceptance

We engaged in a systematic process of Burkean indexing and clustering to identify the major, recurring terms in the ten books that served to represent the genre, and to identify the words that tend to appear in close proximity to these terms.[6] Seven god-terms were identified through this process: *acceptance, intimacy, communication, truth, skills, self,* and *spirituality.* In addition, our analysis identified notable clusters of words that appear in sections about gender. Discussion here revolves mainly around the god-terms *acceptance* and *intimacy,* as well as the gender clusters. Table 1 shows the cluster-agon analysis for the terms *acceptance* and *intimacy.* These terms were used by all of the authors, and the words that clustered with these terms were used by most (though not always all) of the authors.

Table 1. Cluster-Agon Analysis for Acceptance and Intimacy

Term	ACCEPTANCE	INTIMACY
Cluster words	love / intimacy	love
	respect	connection
	honor	**happy / joy / fun**
	act as if	peace / harmony
	appreciation / gratitude	friendship
	understanding	**sex / physical intimacy**
	differences	romance / passion
	trust	**commitment**
	give / receive	**trust**
	forgive	vulnerable
	critical	courage / risk
	control	positive
	reject	*negative*
	judge	*distance*
	blame	*alone / lonely*
	negative	*pain / anxiety*
		stress / tension / conflict
		fear

There was some overlap in the words that clustered with these terms (particularly *trust*), and the terms acceptance and intimacy were also sometimes found in close proximity with each other. However, focus groups and interviews with habitual readers confirm the cluster-agon analysis: the term acceptance is the primary god-term of the genre, and the term intimacy names the primary reward proffered to those who accept. Both of these terms are also prominent in the professional psychotherapy literature, albeit understood and clustered quite differently.

In the professional psychotherapy literature, the term acceptance has been gaining recognition as an important component of both individual and couples therapy. In this literature, acceptance is a complicated concept that is often paired with words such as *mindfulness, Zen, non-duality, suchness,* and *Dasein.* Bolling (1995) makes a very important distinction between three types of acceptance, the first of which involves *tolerating,* often in the service of keeping things smooth. In this sense, acceptance puts a more gracious face on enduring something negative. The second meaning of acceptance involves a kind of welcoming into a particular community, but is conditional upon one meeting the criteria of that community. The third form Bolling (1995) calls *radical acceptance,* or an acceptance that equates to "a presence—a *being present* in relations, without categorization, without judgment" (p. 217).

By contrast, in the popular self-help genre, the term acceptance is a more straightforward term. Although there are moments—particularly in Page (1994)—where popular authors seem to touch on Bolling's third meaning of acceptance (as "presence"), for the most part, it is the first (and simplest) meaning that is promoted: toleration.[7] Further, in popular, self-help relationship guides, acceptance is a highly gendered concept, one that begins with accepting traditional male behavior as a manifestation of a biologically determined male culture. Although a few of the popular authors touch on problems arising from gender inequity, the terminology of these books overwhelmingly suggests an acceptance (and sometimes even glorification) of traditional gender differences that are presented as normal and natural. For example, McGraw (2000) writes: "God didn't design us to be the same; he designed us to be *different*. He made us *different* because we have *different* jobs in this world, and yet we *criticize* each other for being who we are" (p. 261). Doyle (1999) sets up a similarly gendered binary:

> Think of the distinct *differences* between a man and a woman as *gender contrast. Opposites* really do attract, so the higher the contrast, the greater the magnetism between the couple. The more *feminine* you are, the more *masculine* your husband will be. For greatest attraction, set your contrast to high. (p. 199)

The solution to tensions arising from these *differences* is *acceptance*, undoubtedly the most important term of the genre, and the theme that our readers were most likely to mention when asked about the advice or information they remembered from the books. One self-help author puts it this way:

> Through *understanding* the hidden *differences* of the opposite sex, we can more successfully *give* and *receive* the *love* that is in our hearts. By validating and *accepting* our *differences*, creative solutions can be discovered whereby we can succeed in getting what we want. And, more important, we can learn how to best *love* and support the people we care about. *Love* is magical, and it can last, if we remember our *differences*. (Gray, 1992, p. 14)

Men and women are *different*, we are told over and over again by popular authors, and these differences are *natural, normal,* and need to be *understood*. In this context, *understanding* appears to be synonymous with *accepting*, as there are few reasoned, intelligent discussions of gender differences that might actually lead to increased knowledge and understanding of the complexities involved. Some of the non-academic authors in this study actually disparage the notion of deep understanding. McGraw (2000), for instance, asserts that "analysis is paralysis" (p. 213) and that insight is "mental masturbation" (p. 78):

> All I ask is that you follow what I ask you to do. You don't have to like it, you don't even have to *understand* it, you just have to do it day in and day out, *trusting* that the results will come. (p. 215)

As a result, these authors only help their readers *understand* by enumerating the differences many women observe in their male partners, and by describing those differences as *natural* (or biological, or God-given). The few exceptions tend to get lost in the sheer volume of exhortations to *understand*, *respect*, and *trust*—words used synonymously with *accept*. Page (1994) offers a characteristic exhortation: goodwill "includes a willingness to focus on positive qualities; an attitude of *gratitude*; mutual tolerance and *acceptance*; *respect*; *trust*; and the ability to *give*" (pp. 35–36). Within the *acceptance* cluster, then, *trust* is often paired with the words *forgive*, *give* and/or *receive*. This trend is particularly noticeable with Doyle (1999), whose book is titled *The Surrendered Wife*. The word *surrender*, as she uses it, is a synonym for *acceptance*:

> Make a point of graciously *receiving* everything your husband offers you, whether it's help with the children, a necklace or a spontaneous shoulder massage. *Accept* your husband's thoughtfulness good-na-

turedly and recognize that *receiving* graciously is the ultimate act of giving up *control*. Even if you're not sure you want the gift or think he can't afford it, *receive* it with open arms and good humor. Be on the lookout for gifts you might not have noticed before. Make *"receive, receive, receive"* your mantra. (p. 108)

In accordance with this definition of acceptance, women who experience conflicts with their spouses are, by definition, to blame. Doyle thus tells women that if husbands misbehave, their wives are responsible, generally because they are too controlling. In writing about her own life, Weiner-Davis (2001) embodies this self-critical assumption. She concludes a discussion of times for *not* approaching her husband with a request:

As you read what I've just written, you're probably thinking that Jim has a very long list of times that he is unapproachable. I'd have to agree. But there are lots of other times when he is more receptive: on the weekends before the kids wake up, over dinner when we go out together, on his car phone when he is returning from work. (p. 91)

When we discussed these books with our participants, we saw the powerful nature of this framing. The primary implication that our readers took from their reading in this genre is that women need to learn to *communicate* in ways men can understand. Men cannot be changed, they told us, and it is not in their nature to be introspective about communication. The route to achieving a lasting marriage, then, is to accept that. The other primary implication these women drew from their reading is that one should work on one's *self*, for that is all one really can control. Not surprisingly, the implicit messages found in the anecdotes and descriptions of women and men in all these books also reinforce traditional, stereotypical gender roles. Table 2 lists the terms most commonly associated with each gender.

Table 2. Gender Words

Women	Men
homemaker / housework	professional / exec / CEO
children / childcare	breadwinner / provider / earner
attractive / beautiful	successful
happy	hardworking
loving / nurturing	strong / hero / chivalrous
critical / nag / controls / bitchy	smart / intellectual / logical
rejects	sports / beer / buddies / t.v.
	withdrawn / cave

As summarized in the table above, most of the authors address gender differences in some fashion. Moreover, although their explicit arguments may differ—Gottman (1999), for instance, briefly addresses problems resulting from gender inequalities, while Gray (1992) and Doyle (1999) urge readers to amplify gender differences—the language used to describe women and men places women in the home and men in the workplace. These books suggest that an essential part of being a good homemaker is caring for *children*, and this is clearly seen as a priority for women, but not for men. Men are expected to provide financially for the family, and are typically described as *hardworking*, *smart*, and *successful*. As Gottman (1999) writes, "When their daughter Alice was born, Maggie decided to give up her job as a computer scientist to stay *home* with the *baby*" (p. 49). Weiner-Davis (2001) offers a similar narrative: "George was the *breadwinner* in the family, while Ellen was a *stay-at-home mom*. He *worked hard* to support his wife and four children and she was a very *devoted mother*" (p. 83).

Although the books often describe women as having jobs or careers, these are almost always less prestigious than that of their partners, or were secondary to the women's home interests. As a result, according to the cluster analysis, these books instruct readers that the focus of these women should be on the home, appearance, and serving others: "NO MATTER WHAT YOU'RE FEELING TODAY, only show him *happiness* and contentment. Show him someone he will want to return to" (Weiner-Davis, 2001, p. 136). Put in more explicit terms,

> Your marriage contract includes an agreement to have a mutually exclusive sexual relationship, and you owe it to your marriage to manifest your *intimacy* physically and to keep your end of the bargain. Make yourself *available* for sex at least once a week whether you feel like it or not. (Doyle, 1999, p. 206)

Doyle's advice would likely be disavowed by at least some of the authors we analyzed, but such denials would ignore the fundamental similarity in their assumptions about gender roles. The pivotal terms these popular authors use consistently portray women as putting the happiness of others in front of their own. Similarly, although most of the material in this genre is not explicitly directed at female readers, our cluster-agon analysis indicates that women are charged with fixing relationship problems (and, as noted earlier, often for causing them in the first place). This is particularly clear when one looks at the oppositions summarized in Table 2; note that the negative words in those lists apply to women, but not to men.

At worst, men were described as engaging in behavior or activities that women might not like, including *withdrawing* (or going into "the cave"), watching too much television, or drinking too much alcohol. Yet, as Doyle (1999) suggests, even this behavior must ultimately be excused, since "When men feel disrespected, they *withdraw*" (p. 39). Gray (1992) writes that wisdom emerges when this behavior is respected:

> When the Martians were completely preoccupied and in their *caves*, the Venusians also did not take it personally. They learned that this was not the time to have *intimate* conversations but a time to talk about problems with their friends or have fun and go *shopping*. (p. 41)

Markam (1999) writes about one couple that, "When they did have time together, they'd frequently run into difficulties because Simon wanted to watch a lot of sports on TV and Rachel was very upset about this" (p. 139). However, Markam insists that the solution is not for Simon to watch less television, but for Rachel to accept Simon, and to change herself so that she does not become so upset when he does this (p. 139). As this example suggests, the authors we analyzed do not sanction men for such behavior, though they do sanction women for *nagging* or being *critical* of men's behavior: "No one likes to feel *nagged* or unappreciated. No one likes to be constantly *criticized*. If you don't appreciate your spouse, someone else will" (Weiner-Davis, 2001, p. 201). On the face of it, this advice could apply equally to men and to women, but when placed in context, it is clear that it is directed at women. Within the genre, words like *critical*, *nag*, *controlling*, and *rejecting* are almost always used in reference to women.

Some authors, such as Doyle (1999), explicitly assert that there are material, as well as emotional and spiritual, rewards for women who accept, citing examples of surrendered wives whose husbands have subsequently become more financially successful. Perhaps more powerful than suggesting the emotional or financial rewards for acceptance, though, are the consequences of not accepting. These can be seen in the opposing words of the acceptance cluster. (It is also interesting to note the overlap in these oppositions, and those found in the list of gender words for women).

Gottman (1999), for example, reminds readers that "It's just a fact that people can change only if they feel that they are basically liked and *accepted* as they are. When people feel *criticized*, disliked, and *unappreciated* they are unable to change" (p. 149). Gray (1992) warns women of the dangers of failing to learn this lesson:

> In a myriad of ways she tries to change him or improve him. She thinks her attempts to change him are loving, but he feels *controlled*, manipulated, *rejected*, and *unloved*. He will stubbornly *reject* her because he feels she is *rejecting* him. When a woman tries to change

a man, he is not getting the *loving trust* and *acceptance* he actually needs to change and grow. (p. 146)

Doyle's (1999) confession provides a similar message to her readers:

> None of us feels good about ourselves when we're *nagging, critical,* or *controlling.* I certainly didn't. The tone of my voice alone would make me cringe with self-recrimination. Through *surrendering*, you will find the courage to gradually stop indulging in these unpleasant behaviors and replace them with dignified ones. (pp. 14–15)

As these passages suggest, popular works tell women who are not accepting (loving, understanding, forgiving, etc.) that they are at risk of *controlling, rejecting, blaming*, and displaying other negative traits. Although the majority of the arguments about acceptance are not overtly written to a specifically female audience, the pairing of these negative words with descriptions of women's behavior—but not men's—makes it clear who must accept and who must be accepted. Cluster-agon analysis reveals how these authors stress that women must behave well to not lose their husbands. They must not be controlling, nagging bitches, but should rather be attractive, happy, and sexually desirable. When men are strong, smart, and hardworking, they are suited to different tasks than women who are beautiful, loving, and nurturing. Appearance, at least in this genre, thus includes not only physical beauty, but also a loving and happy demeanor: "[S]how him happiness and contentment. Show him someone he will want to return to," writes Weiner-Davis (2001) because, "If you don't *appreciate* your spouse someone else will," she cautions (p. 136, 201).

DIALECTICAL TERMS AS DEFLECTION

Burke's concept of dialectical terms, the crux of *agon*-analysis, is particularly potent in relation to this genre. Burke (1950/1969) asserts that unlike terms about the world of sensation, an abstraction is understood not positively, but in juxtaposition with the term selected as its contrary. Thus, he affirms that the meaning of an abstraction changes if it is dichotomized differently (pp. 183–185). In the first two columns, Table 3 shows the dialectical oppositions used by these authors to describe facets of non-acceptance and acceptance; the right-hand column suggests alternate terms that would have danced very different attitudes.

Table 3. Dialectical Terms for the Oppositions of the Acceptance Cluster

Acceptance Oppositions	Acceptance Terms (used by authors)	Other Possible Terms (not used by authors)
Critical	Accept, understand	Uncritical, indecisive
Reject	Receive	Don't question, allow
Judge	Accept	Misjudge
Blame	Appreciate, forgive	Ignore, allow
Negative	Accepting	Neutral

As with the terms in the intimacy cluster (discussed below), the terms and oppositions of the acceptance cluster create a large divide between desirable and non-desirable behaviors. When compared to being *accepting* and *understanding*, being *critical* sounds very negative. Although there are contexts where the ability to be critical is seen as an asset (e.g., in academia and some other professions), the main context for women in the relationship guide genre is home and family; therefore, a critical woman runs the risk of being "bitchy." The importance of Burke's insight becomes evident when we juxtapose the term critical with terms such as *uncritical* or *indecisive*. Similarly *blaming*, while not as feminine as *forgiving*, might be seen as better than *ignoring*, *allowing*, or *enabling*. By looking at what terms are not juxtaposed with important terms in the genre, we get a sense of what the attention of readers is being deflected from. Table 4 provides a similar example.

Table 4. Dialectical Terms for the Self Cluster

Self-Terms (used by authors)	Oppositions (used by authors)	Possible Oppositions (not used by authors)
Strong	Weak	Vulnerable
Courageous	Weak	Cautious
Dignified	Shameful (emotional)	Authentic
Self-care	Self-neglect	Social support
True self	False self	Feeling self

Here, in the terms summarized in this table, we see an emphasis on a contained and un-needy self. Not to be *strong* and *courageous* is to be *weak*, rather than, say, *vulnerable* and *cautious*. A person who does not care for herself appropriately (as seen in her self-conduct, as *dignified*, *strong*, etc.) is *neglecting* herself. This terministic screen places emphasis on the individual to correct any "problems" without considering the social context. Within this genre, one can either be *happy, connected,* and *trusting* (in an intimate relationship), or one can be *lonely* and miserable (having lost intimacy). McGraw offers a clear example of this individualistic emphasis:

> If you have not designed and carried out your life to create or allow *distance* instead of *intimacy,* combativeness instead of cooperation, blame and rejection instead of accountability and *acceptance,* you cannot maintain the erosion and *pain* that you are now experiencing. (p. 11)

Similarly, Doyle (1999) portrays a woman's self as the route to true relational success:

> The truth is, the less you communicate your complaints, *negative* thoughts, and criticisms to your husband, the better your *intimacy* will be, and the stronger your marriage. Withholding information from your husband may feel dishonest, but it's really being mature and polite. (p. 248)

While not necessarily conscious, this choice of oppositions adds a sense of urgency: either fix your marriage or face an unhappy life. This either-or opposition deflects the possibility that a single, or even divorced, life can be a happy life, and the implications of this deflection can be highlighted by envisioning a different set of oppositions that show intimacy terms in quite a different light—the sorts of terms often attributed to men, such as *independence, freedom, self-direction,* and the like.

Primary Motive: Intimacy

Tracking the use of the word *intimacy* in the context of the term *acceptance* makes it clear that the term is used interchangeably with *love*—or, as Burke might put it, *intimacy* and *love* are convertible terms. Love and intimacy are considered both the basis of, and the reward for, marriage. Intimacy is the primary motive, the motivational god-term that names the reason for acceptance. In the intimacy cluster are found the words that essentially define what a good marriage is and why it is worth the work involved. Page (1994) provides a good example: "Our human souls cry out for two things: We want a special *connection* with another human being, specifically, *intimacy, closeness,* and unconditional *love*" (p. 200). Compare this formulation to that provided by Gottman (1999):

> At the heart of my program is the simple truth that *happy* marriages are based on a deep *friendship.* By this I mean a mutual respect for

and *enjoyment* of each other's company. These couples tend to know each other *intimately*. (pp. 19–20)

Although the term intimacy is sometimes found in (generally brief) discussions of sex, it is more often related to words that can be seen as unequivocally "positive," including the word *positive* itself. *Love, connection, romance, joy*, and *peace* are the rewards a woman can expect to reap when she does marriage properly: "You deserve a *peaceful, happy*, mutually rewarding relationship that includes *fun*, support, *sex* and *intimacy, companionship* and freedom" (McGraw, 2000, p. 299). At the same time, these rewards are not limited to women: "We believe that men and women want most of the same things in a relationship: *respect, connection, intimacy, friendship, peace*, and *harmony*" (Markman, 1994, p. 37).[8]

Prager and Roberts (2002) suggest "three necessary and sufficient conditions [for an intimate interaction]: self-revealing behavior, positive involvement with the other, and shared understandings" (p. 45). While all of the relationship guides analyzed stress the second condition, they vary in terms of the first and third. Gray (1992) implies that "shared understandings" are virtually impossible—hence the need for a dictionary to translate the different languages of men and women. Some of the books similarly discourage "self-revealing behavior," suggesting that women save their disclosures for female friends, rather than for their husbands. With two exceptions, the books do not discuss barriers to intimacy that arise if one's partner is not willing to disclose his innermost thoughts and feelings. One exception is Lerner (2001), and the other is Gottman (1999), who states: "I believe the emotionally intelligent husband is the next step in social evolution" (p. 109). His research suggests that only about 35% of married men are emotionally intelligent, and that this includes, among other things, the ability to recognize and share feelings. He offers advice to men on how to develop emotional intelligence, and he implies that living with a non-emotionally intelligent husband is miserable. However, he does not follow this argument through to its logical conclusion: For a large number of women—particularly those with partners unwilling to read the book or attend therapy—there may be no real hope of achieving marital happiness.

The ideological implications of the term intimacy is especially clear through *agon*-analysis, especially when juxtaposing the genre's oppositions to intimacy (i.e., *distance, loneliness, anxiety, stress, fear*) with potential alternatives, such as *enmeshment, burdened, boredom*, or *defeat*. The relationship guides polarize married, single, and divorced life. No middle ground or third way is projected in these books. Although they do not offer (or because they do not offer) explicit definitions, these relationship guides assume positive and unproblematic understandings of *intimacy, love,* and other terms from this cluster. Terms like *intimacy* and *romance,* in particular, are fraught with contradictions. Shumway (2003), for example, suggests that current conceptions of love are best viewed as discourses or narratives, for they are complicated terms that are not easily defined (cf. Radway, 1984; Talbot, 1997).[9] This may be one reason why relationship guides rely heavily on case examples, as they can be seen as mini-narratives, and were viewed by the readers we interviewed as essential to the genre.

Burkean discourse analysis reveals the perspectives, values, and ideologies embodied in the texts. Juxtaposed with contemporary academic psychology, it reveals the extent to which the curative processes advocated in these self-help books contradict what researchers know about effective therapeutic methods (Hill, 2007). Juxtaposed with modern feminism, it reveals that these popular, self-help books constitute part of the anti-feminist backlash. For a Burkean, there is a prior, framing question: Why do people buy and read these books in this kairotic moment? To borrow Burke's metaphor, if these books are the medicine, what is the social malady they cathartically relieve?

Reader Response

At this kairotic moment, how will these self-help books relieve the relationship woes of these readers? To answer that framing question, one cannot rely on text alone; one must interrogate the readership and analyze the social situation (Gilbert, 1994). To this end, twenty-one committed readers of this genre were interviewed in focus groups. For most, relationships were an extremely important part of their lives; they took seriously their efforts to understand and improve their relationships. At the same time, it was not easy for these readers to describe exactly what they looked for in relationships guides. Jessica said, "It's easy to feel anxious about the topics," to which Nazim added, "If you're confused, you don't want more complications."[10] Lana said that, for some relationship issues, "[you] want to be eased into it," and Lucy said, "I want to be engaged at the heart level rather than the intellectual level."

One thing that seemed to help ease anxieties and engage women "at the heart level" was the use of anecdotal examples, a key characteristic of the genre. Jessica, for example, said they were "probably the part I was most interested in reading . . . an easy way to see what the book is promising." Lily similarly explained that, for her, case examples "illustrate the point the author is making," and that their use "puts it in context." She also noted that she liked the examples because they reassured her that "someone else went through—really went through that." Tamara offered a somewhat different discussion of her reaction, saying that said the use of case examples "makes them [the books] interesting," and that it "breaks it up . . . otherwise it's stressful, feels like you're studying . . . makes it fun."

In all, our readers had two approaches to relationship guides: One was to treat the guides as true advice manuals. This generally occurred when readers were looking for assistance in solving an immediate, pressing problem. The other approach was to treat the book more like a novel. For women in the latter category, validation and hope appeared to be more important to them than specific advice or solutions to problems. As Liz said, "Even if it's not a solution, it's nice to read it . . . get some comfort from it, know that you're not crazy . . . others have gone through it." The following responses also address what women hope for in reading relationship guides:

> Linda: If you answer in a loving way, the relationship will eventually be-
> come loving. [Although this did not seem to be the case in her fifteen-
> year marriage.]
> Tamara: All marriages are difficult; I'm not the only one. Also, men and
> women are different. When I read these books it doesn't seem so bad.
> Alaine: To trust my own judgment. I found I knew a lot of what they
> were saying.
> Lucy: It depends on the book . . . . Kinda prepares you . . . one of the
> many, many things that can help a person prepare for relationships . . .
> a tool . . . like a manual.
> June: Anything's possible if you try. I mean, they're useful . . . shows you
> there are other alternatives, reasons . . . opens it up.

Comfort, peace of mind, and a feeling that "you're not the only one" were important themes across the conversations we held with readers of the genre. Particular things in the books that our participants identified as contribut-ing to a sense of validation and comfort were author self-disclosures and case examples. These points are illustrated in the following excerpts:

> Jessica: I know there must be thousands of other people with similar
> problems.
> Georgia: I'm a nosy person. I'm getting a view into something personal .
> . . . This poor slob has it worse. It feels less clinical and more personal.
> Alaine: It helps you better to identify.

Knowing that they were not alone in their struggles was sometimes all that the women felt they needed to get from a relationship guide. A number of the focus groups had discussions about men and the problems they posed in relationships. Across these conversations, it was clear that the books give them the sense that it is normal for women to struggle with this issue. The women in one group suggested that men tend to make women feel that relationship problems are their fault, and that the books provide a kind of antidote to this. Lily said, "Sometimes you think you're completely wacko—then you see something in a book that tells you you're not."

The centrality of anecdotal examples to the experience of reading relationship guides highlights the importance of the differences in gender terms identified by our cluster-*agon* analysis. Descriptions of men and women in examples in the self-help books not only reflect possibilities of how marriages are conducted and how genders are enacted, but they also reinforce these roles. One role accepted unquestioningly by the readers we interviewed was that of taking on the responsibility for relationship happiness. Although most of the women interviewed worked outside the home, they viewed relationships and home life as their main responsibility.

Further, for these readers, knowing about relationships appeared to be an essential aspect of being a woman—and relationship guides and daytime television seemed to be the main sources of their knowledge. Our readers believed themselves to be critical consumers of self-help. They certainly did not believe everything they read, nor did they believe that all the authors had honorable intentions. However, their criticisms were all *within* the genre: Throughout the course of our interviews with these women, there was no indication from them that there might be anything wrong with the genre itself. Readers appeared to have internalized much of the rhetoric of the genre, talking in terms of *self* and *spirituality*, and asserting the importance of *accepting differences* and of *communication skills*. There was little, if any, recognition neither of sexist and classist biases within the genre, nor of the contradictions inherent in the intimate/romantic version of the relationship championed in the texts. These readers aspired to be good wives, and seemed to have adopted the subject position of the good wife—ready and willing to take on the challenge of single-handedly improving the state of their own relationship.

On Burke's dialectical reading, there is a central ambiguity in Richards' definition of attitude as "incipient action": sometimes an attitude is incipient action, but sometimes dancing an attitude creates a cathartic release that itself fulfills the motive, obviating any need to act. As an illustration of this point, Burke (1941/1967) writes

> *The reading of a book on the attaining of success is in itself the symbolic attaining of that success.* It is *while they read* that these readers are "succeeding" . . . . The lure of the book resides in the fact that the reading, while reading it, is then living in the aura of success. What

[the reader] wants is *easy* success; and he gets it in the symbolic form by the mere reading itself. (p. 299)

In like fashion, our readers appreciated feeling that they were not alone in their struggles, other women experienced the same problems, and writers/experts sympathized.

Reading the books often confirmed for them that, if their relationships were not satisfactory, it was not because they did not understand relationships. Indeed, although writers like Faludi (1991) emphasize that relationship guides focus attention on what women do *wrong*, our respondents seemed to take from the books a sense that they were doing much that was *right*. No respondent noted vast and enduring improvement in their relationships as a result of reading relationship guides, but all seemed to *feel better* (if only temporarily) for having read them. When the feeling wore off, they sought another book, and this seemed the most important theme in reading relationship guides: The guides impart of sense of *comfort*. Relationship guides reinforce readers' beliefs that they are doing the right thing at the same time that they assure them that what they are doing is difficult, and that they are not alone. Women who have been primed to "do something" about their relationships are doing what responsible citizens are supposed to do: They seek guidance, and by continuing to do so, they continue to succeed symbolically.

CONCLUSIONS

One of the primary functions of relationship guides is to keep alive the ideal of romance, and to offer consolation and hope to women who perceive themselves as having failed. Relationship guides do not so much tell readers how to achieve happiness as they tell them at least one part of what that happiness is supposed to look like. Despite being dressed up in glamorous appeals to intimacy, romance, peace, and love, this portrait bears a suspicious resemblance to self-sacrifice. From a Gramscian perspective, women can be seen as collaborating in their own oppression if they adopt the "common sense" notions the genre promotes. The god-term *acceptance* is particularly potent for causing acquiescence to a position of common sense for the woman reader—especially since the only alternative portrayed is pain and suffering. The reader obtains comfort and a sense of shared misery from reading relationship guides. She is reassured that her position, though it may be difficult, is normal and a consequence of a man's nature. She is thereby also encouraged to consume the lifestyle that accompanies traditional marriage.

Relationship guides offer women a short-term solution to the dissatisfaction they feel in their relationships. The books often repeat themes that are familiar to the readers, and this is comforting in that it bolsters their sense that problems in their relationships are not their doing. The genre imparts the message that men are incapable of participating fully in relationships, and readers' frustration at this state of affairs is ameliorated by the simple act of reading. They may hope to find something to improve their situation (some way of getting the best out of their man), but mostly they anticipate being soothed. They feel better in the short term, but the cycle is perpetuated in the long term.

In this project, we approached the discourse of relationship guides in several ways. The cluster-*agon* analysis allowed us to identify the genre's god-terms and to contrast their use with that of academic psychology. While the authors of popular relationship guides use terms that are current in academic research, their clusters and *agons* produce different emphases. Terms like acceptance, intimacy, and communication are clustered with words that direct readers' attention toward the romantic aspects of relationships; this simultaneously deflects readers' attention from the complexity of the terms as recognized in academic psychology. The terms woven through the narratives also reinforce stereotypical notions of gender roles, a finding consistent with that of other researchers who have critiqued the genre. What is different about our analysis, though, is the focus on implicit rather than explicit arguments about gender. For instance, Zimmerman, Holm, and Haddock (2001) suggest that some relationship guides encourage resistance to stereotyping. Although our analysis also found a few direct arguments in the books regarding gender stereotypes, these authors negate their explicit arguments by the implicit (though possibly unintended and unnoticed) use of narratives that portray women as the ones responsible for all aspects of family and relationships. This cluster-agon analysis indicates that all of the authors, including the ones who have contributed to the academic literature, promulgate terministic screens that discourage challenges to the gender status quo.

Yet, as Burke understood so well, the power and action of a text must be understood in terms of the symbolic resolution of tensions that readers bring to the text. However much that may overlap with the ideology in the text, analysis of the text alone deflects our attention from crucial aspects of readers' uptake and their motives for reading. The readers we interviewed were motivated in large part by a felt sense of responsibility for being knowledgeable about relationships—a responsibility that was reinforced by the terministic screens of the texts. In addition to what it tells us about the genre, the research reported here is, we hope, a representative anecdote that demonstrates the power of combining Burke's techniques for analyzing discourse with his ideas about the complexity of the interaction between texts and readers.

NOTES

1. The research reported in this paper began when I (RMC) was approached by an experienced "relationship counselor," Cathryn Hill, then ABD in psychology. She was unhappy with much of what her clients were reading in popular relationship guides and was, therefore, considering writing one of her own. My response was based in the New Rhetorical genre theories (see Coe, Lingard, & Teslenko, 2002), as they focus on genres as embodying strategic responses to situations (and thus emphasize *kairos*) and on Burkean methods of discourse analysis (especially master metaphor and cluster-agon analysis). I told her about a feminist collective in Vancouver that, many years earlier, tried to reach women resistant to the movement by writing a Harlequin-type romance novel embodying feminist values. Is it possible, I asked Cathryn, to say what you want to say in this genre, or will you be silenced by generic constraints? Will you have to change the genre so much in order to say what you want to say that it will not be the same genre? Will you have to change it so much that the readers you want to reach will not want to read it because, in Burkean terms, it will not provide the emotional medicine that motivates them to read in this genre? Probably because her academic culture was shaped by psychology departments, Cathryn's cluster-agon and tropic analyses are by far the most rigorous, thorough, systematic, and detailed I have ever seen. In combination with an analysis of the genre's master metaphors, god-terms, and constructed *ethos* of the authors, this cluster-agon analysis reveals the ideology of this popular genre and demonstrates the power of Burkean rhetorical analysis (Hill, 2007). Originally, a desire to share that with fellow Burkeans shaped my motive for proposing the paper that became this chapter.

2. For Burke, of course, any one perspective is necessarily incomplete, including the perspective produced by his own method of discourse analysis. Defining himself as a perspectivist (though not a relativist), he asserts that the only way to critique and transcend any one perspective is by juxtaposing it with others. He metaphorically derived the concept of *perspective by incongruity* from the way human beings use the slightly differing perspectives of our two eyes, each of which can record only two dimensions and construct (transcendent) three-dimensional images.

3. In much of his practical criticism of literary texts, Burke explains symbolic action in relation to tensions in the lives of authors and readers. For a particularly explicit instance of the latter, see his "summarizing essay" on *Coriolanus* in *Language as Symbolic Action* (Burke, 1966).

4. Crawford (2004), for example, suggests that self-help texts are appealing because they allow for multiple readings. She claims that the "language of difference" used by Gray may mean that his books

> afford their female readers a discourse for articulating problems of inequality in relationships and for holding their partner accountable. In doing so, the readers may make visible some unexpected sites of contention and create interpretations that compete with the texts' own ideology. (p. 75)

From a somewhat different perspective, Hochschild (1994) ties the books' appeal to the difficulties women have in adapting themselves to what she calls the "stalled gender revolution"; she suggests that self-help books for women offer "psychic armor" that may be necessary for survival in today's world (p. 19). Instead, many scholars attempt to explain the appeal of these books by focusing on the successful marketing efforts behind them. Buzzard (2002) notes that an earlier version of John Gray's *Men are from Mars, Women are from Venus*, entitled *Men, Women and Relationships*, was declined by publishers. She thus attributes the success of the book to "brand marketing": "As Gray readily admits, his success today has less to do with audience satisfaction than with building a brand name that people recognize and trust, a name so reliable that Gray has been called the Coca-Cola of psychology" (p. 91). Simonds (1992) focuses less upon individual works like Gray's than on the genre as a whole: she maps the steps required by publishing firms to get a self-help book on the market. This analysis indicates that audience appeal is created by titles and book covers that promise happiness, authors who are not perceived as detached professionals (indeed, they should disclose details about their own lives), and authors who write with passion and sincerity.

5. The feminist voice may be continually shut down by Gray's texts, but women who identify as feminist still read self-help manuals. This apparent contradiction provides a space for a feminist appropriation of the genre: How do we integrate feminism into our daily lives? Perhaps, in the future, the answer to that question will be provided by books with titles such as: *How to Make your Man a Feminist in 9 Easy Steps!* or *I'm a Feminist, You're a Feminist, We're OK* (Murphy, 2001, p. 166).

6. Given the laborious and fine-grained nature of Burkean discourse analysis, we limited our focus to ten books from this genre. Although we were not concerned with providing a statistical representation of the genre, we did take care to assemble (in Burke's terms) an essential representation of it. Nine of the ten books claimed either to be a *New York Times* bestseller, or to have been written by an author who was a *New York Times* bestseller (see the Appendix for a complete list of the books analyzed in this study). The exception was a book that is fairly well-known among marriage therapists, and is the basis of a popular marriage preparation course offered in cities across North America. We also took care to ensure that we did not unduly restrict our focus to certain kinds of authors: half of the principal authors are male, and half are female; five of the books are written by current or former academics/researchers, and five by non-academics. In the pages that follow, in order to assist the reader, we have added italics to direct quotes from these sources in order to highlight the major terms recurring within them.

7. As a result, self-help literature is out-of-step with mainstream theories of psychotherapy that incorporate notions of acceptance. As Hayes, Strosahl, Bunting, Twohig, and Wilson (2004) assert, "acceptance should not be confused with tolerance or resignation, both of which are passive and fatalistic. Acceptance involves taking a stance of non-judgmental awareness and actively embracing the experience of thoughts, feelings, and bodily sensations as they occur" (p. 7). Such thoughts, feelings, and sensations allow people to know themselves and their worlds more fully, leading to higher functioning and better decision-making.

8. Jon Carlson and Len Sperry (1999), psychologists and authorities on intimacy, discuss the complicated nature of gender roles in regards to intimacy. First, they note that the communal behaviors considered desirable for women in America are more conducive to intimacy than the agentic behaviors considered desirable for men. Then, they observe:

> Because of these sociocultural norms, many women may feel more "feminine" or "womanly" when they are pursuing intimate contact while men may similarly feel more "masculine" or "manly" when resisting or minimizing their need for intimate contact. As a result, despite how painful the pursuer-distancer pattern is, and despite its destructive impact on intimacy, couple therapists may see more intimacy-hungry women and distancing men . . . because the secondary gain of this pattern is the reinforcement of behaviors that enhance sex-role identity. (pp. 25–26)

This is a sort of self-fulfilling prophecy, in which individuals, by choosing partners who are unlikely to challenge their gendered self-concept, also choose partners with whom they are unlikely to create healthy intimacy. This contradiction between what people say they want, and what they create, can also be seen in relationship guides that valorize intimacy at the same time that they emphasize gendered roles for men and women. Given that *intimacy, love,* and *connection* appear to be the basis of a good marriage, it is interesting that the authors analyzed in this study do not go into much detail regarding the meaning of these words. There are also writers within the psychological literature that discuss intimate relationships and love without defining the terms, and many of the same clusters found in relationship guides can be found in the literature (particularly *love, romance, passion,* and *commitment*). The few authors who do attempt definitions are not necessarily in agreement with one another (cf. Carlson & Sperry, 1999). Prager (1995) calls intimacy a "fuzzy" concept, and focuses on the more observable "intimate interactions," or those she describes as involving sharing (verbally or non-verbally) that which is personal (pp. 17-19). This is a practice that seems to be agreed upon (to greater or lesser degrees) by other writers (e.g., Brown & Amatea, 2000; Laurenceau, Rivera, Schaffer, & Pietromonaco, 2004; Reis & Shaver, 1988).

9. As an example of these contradictions, Shumway (2003) reminds us that, historically speaking, "romance as a discourse takes extramarital relations as its model. The discourse of intimacy, on the contrary, assumes a monogamous relationship as its paradigm" (p. 144).

10. All names of interviewees and focus group participants have been changed to ensure privacy.

References

Bolling, M. Y. (1995). Acceptance and *Dasein. The Humanistic Psychologist, 23*(2), 213-226. doi: 10.1080/08873267.1995.9986825

Brown, N. M., & Amatea, E. S. (2000). *Love and intimate relationships: Journeys of the heart.* New York, NY: Psychology Press.

Burke, K. (1954). Fact, inference, and proof, in the analysis of literary symbolism. In L. Bryson (Ed.), *Symbols and values: Thirteenth symposium of the conference on science, philosophy, and religion* (pp. 283–306). New York, NY: Harper.

Burke, K. (1966). *Language as symbolic action*. Berkeley, CA: University of California Press.

Burke, K. (1941/1967). *The philosophy of literary form: Studies in symbolic action* (2nd ed.). Baton Rouge, LA: Louisiana State University Press.

Burke, K. (1950/1969). *A rhetoric of motives*. Berkeley, CA: University of California Press. (Original work published 1950)

Buzzard, K. S. F. (2002). The Coca-Cola of self help: The branding of John Gray's *Men are from Mars, women are from Venus*. *The Journal of Popular Culture, 35*, 89–102. doi: 10.1111/j.0022-3840.2002.3504_89.x

Carlson, J., & Sperry, L. (1999). Introduction: A context for thinking about intimacy. In J. Carlson & L. Sperry (Eds.), *The intimate couple* (pp. 3-32). Philadelphia, PA: Brunner-Mazel/Taylor & Francis.

Coe, R., Lingard, L., & Teslenko, T. (2002). *The rhetoric and ideology of genre*. Cresskill, NJ: Hampton Publishers.

Crawford, M. (2004). Mars and Venus collide: A discursive analysis of marital self-help psychology. *Feminism & Psychology, 14*(1), 63-79.

DeFrancisco, V. L., & O'Connor, P. (1995). A feminist critique of self-help books on heterosexual romance: Read 'em and weep. *Women's Studies in Communication, 18*(2), 217-227.

Faludi, S. (1991). *Backlash: The undeclared war against American women*. New York, NY: Crown Publishers.

Gilbert, P. (1994). Stoning the romance: Girls as resistant readers and writers. In A. Freedman & P. Medway (Eds.), *Learning and teaching genre* (pp. 173-192). Portsmouth, NH: Boynton/Cook.

Hayes, S. C., Strosahl, K. D., Bunting, K., Twohig, M., & Wilson, K. G. (2004). What is acceptance and commitment therapy? In S. C. Hayes & K. D. Strosahl (Eds.), *A practical guide to acceptance and commitment therapy* (pp. 1-30). New York: Springer.

Hill, C. R. (2007). *Relationship rhetoric: Representations of intimacy in contemporary self-help literature*. (Unpublished doctoral dissertation), Simon Fraser University, British Columbia, Canada.

Hochschild, A. R. (1994) The commercial spirit of intimate life and the abduction of feminism: Signs from women's advice books. *Theory, Culture & Society, 11*(2), 1-24.

Laurenceau, J. P., Rivera, L. M., Schaffer, A. R., & Pietromonaco, P. R. (2004). Intimacy as an interpersonal process: Current status and future directions. In D. Mashek & A. Aron (Eds.), *Handbook of closeness and intimacy* (pp. 61-78). Mahwah, NJ: Lawrence Erlbaum.

Marketdata Enterprises, Inc. (2008). *The U.S. market for self-improvement products and services*. Retrieved from http://www.marketdataenterprises.com/FullIndustryStudies.htm#SELF

McGee, M. (2005). *Self-help, Inc.: Makeover culture in American life*. New York, NY: Oxford University Press.

Prager, K. J. (1995). *The psychology of intimacy*. New York, NY: The Guilford Press.

Radway, J. (1984). *Reading the romance: Women, patriarchy and popular literature.* Chapel Hill, NC: University of North Carolina Press.

Reis, H. T., & Shaver, P. R. (1988). Intimacy as an interpersonal process. In S. Duck (Ed.), *Handbook of research in personal relationships* (pp. 367-389). London, England: Wiley.

Rueckert, W. H. (1963). *Kenneth Burke and the drama of human relations.* Minneapolis, MN: University of Minnesota Press.

Salerno, S. (2005). *Sham: How the self-help movement made America helpless.* New York, NY: Random House.

Shumway, D. R. (2003). *Modern love: Romance, intimacy, and the marriage crisis.* New York, NY: New York University Press.

Simonds, W. (1992). *Women and self-help culture: Reading between the lines.* Piscataway, NJ: Rutgers University Press.

Zimmerman, T. S., Holm, K. E., & Haddock, S. A. (2001). A decade of advice for women and men in the best-selling self-help literature. *Family Relations, 50,* 122-132.

Appendix: Relationship Guides Analyzed

Doyle, L. (1999/2001). *The surrendered wife: A practical guide to finding intimacy, passion, and peace with a man.* New York, NY: Fireside.

Gottman, J. M. & Silver, N. (1999). *The seven principles for making marriage work.* New York, NY: Three Rivers Press.

Gray, J. (1992). *Men are from Mars, women are from Venus: A practical guide for improving communication and getting what you want in your relationships.* New York, NY: Harper Collins.

Hendrix, H. (1988/2001). *Getting the love you want: A guide for couples.* New York, NY: Henry Holt & Co.

Lerner, H. (2001). *The dance of connection: How to talk to someone when you're mad, hurt, scared, frustrated, insulted, betrayed, or desperate.* New York, NY: Quill.

Markman, H., Stanley, S., & Blumberg, S. L. (1994). *Fighting for your marriage: Positive steps for preventing divorce and preserving a lasting love.* San Francisco, CA: Jossey-Bass.

McGraw, P. C. (2000). *Relationship rescue: A seven-step strategy for reconnecting with your partner.* New York, NY: Hyperion.

Page, S. (1994). *Now that I'm married, why isn't everything perfect?: The 8 essential traits of couples who thrive.* Boston, MA: Little, Brown & Co.

Schlessinger, L. (2001). *Ten stupid things couples do to mess up their relationships.* New York, NY: Cliff Street Books.

Weiner-Davis, M. (2001). *The divorce remedy: The proven 7-step program for saving your marriage.* New York, NY: Simon & Schuster.

6 Transcendence by Colonial Perspective: Bureaucratization, F. Max Müller, and the *Sacred Books of the East* (1879)

Abigail Selzer King

Exploring the Colonial Archive with Kenneth Burke

On September 17, 1857, Karl Marx published an article in the *New York Tribune* criticizing the British government for using torture to collect overdue taxes from Indian subjects. This practice was so widespread that he described torture as a "financial institution of British India." Marx argued that institutionalized torture flourished because of the dysfunctional appeal system that denied redress to victims while protecting perpetrators from censure. In this early example of colonial critique, Marx points to both the violent and the juridical injustices of colonial politics. It is important to consider, however, that colonial powers were not limited to these means for establishing and maintaining imperial domination. In particular, the English language, the written word, and the vast catalogue of knowledge amassed by colonial agents were powerful elements of the apparatus that secured colonial control.

In the specific case of the British Empire, scholars and colonial bureaucrats alike organized a substantial collection of observations, histories, lists, maps, and dictionaries to provide the knowledge needed to underwrite colonial administration (Van der Veer, 2001).[1] This body of work was wide-ranging in topic, and filled a vital gap in English knowledge; without precise information about Indian geography and people, the British colonial bureaucracy would be dysfunctional. Quite simply, the British authorities needed to count the Indian body politic before they could rule and tax them. As a consequence, this collection of knowledge, and the books they filled, are what Michel Foucault (1972) might call an *archive*; they embody "a practice that causes a multiplicity of statements to emerge" (p. 129). In this case, the practice is colonial rule, and the statements that emerge from it are the studies of topics such as Indian geography, flora, fauna, laws, and religious practices. Thus, much of this discourse takes the form of quantifiable, scientific observations—a form that also functions to conceal its role in the metropole/colony relationship. Although colonialist practice has come under attack from a number of scholarly directions, I contend that the textual contents of this archive present a unique opportunity to study the *rhetorical* nature of colonial discourse. Kenneth Burke (1984) writes that words "contain attitudes much more complex and subtle than could possibly be indicated in the efficient simplifications of a 'practical' dictionary" (p. 329). Viewed in Burkean terms, the contents of the colonial archive become an indication of the textual reach of the Empire, and a window into the subterranean attitudes that permeate its discourse.

This chapter joins a conversation in progress; indeed, one quite far advanced. Postcolonial scholarship has transformed our view of the "naturalness" of historical practices and texts, and has not overlooked the use of language as a tool of colonization. At the same time, this work has rarely been joined to the work of rhetorical scholars and critics.[2] Although there are some interesting areas of overlapping emphasis, Burke's rhetorical theory has not been widely used in the literature of this field. One advocate for the integration of rhetoric, colonial critique, and Burkean thought is anthropologist James A. Boon. His volume *Affinities and Extremes* (1990) leverages Burkean thought to contend with questions of motive and the role of language in "histories, narrative, social formations, and ideological constructions" of the Hindu-Balinese culture during colonization (p. 54).

In addition to providing a rhetorical guide to the concerns of postcolonial contexts, Boon (1990) explicitly draws upon Burke's explanation of logology to critique Antonio Pigafetta's linguistic reconstruction of the Malay culture. In 1525, Pigafetta published a list of Malay words with Italian translations, a publication that represented the first extensive translation between the Malay language and any European language (Boon, 1990, p. 10). This list, Boon argues, belies the ways in which the Malay culture was understood by colonizers from Europe. Even though his study is not solely focused on Burke, in a significant section, Boon divides the words in Pigafetta's list according to Burke's (1966) four terministic pyramids: words for the natural, words about words, words for the socio-political realm, and words for the supernatural. Boon finds that Pigafetta's list reflects a colonial vision of the Malay-speaking lands as one that is focused on "cloves, mace, paradise birds, and proper kingship" (p. 12). Boon's exercise in the application of logology to a colonial artifact thus demonstrates the potential value of combining Burkean theory with colonial critique.

Within scholarly literature in the field of communication, Cheree Carlson (1986) has been one of the strongest voices advocating the use of Burkean theory to study colonial politics. Her study of the anti-colonial protests and social movement activism of Gandhi uses Burke to theorize the comic nature of social movement organizations that practice civil disobedience. Carlson finds that the differences between using a comic and a tragic frame for studying social movements have important consequences for understanding a movement's goals and outcomes. For example, Carlson explains that in movements understood through a tragic frame, "no social change is possible without some form of violence" (p. 447). For the study of non-violent movements and civil disobedience, Carlson argues, a comic frame allows the critic to see the ways in which the movement identifies the "evil acts of good people" without antagonizing the opponent (p. 452). Gandhi's work exemplifies this characteristic, she writes, and clarifies his methods of fostering identification between members of his movement and their opponents. Carlson's use of Burkean thought expands the possibilities for understanding the enduring the political ramifications of Gandhi's form of resistance.

Combined, the work of Boon and Carlson indicate that Burke's corpus contains valuable theoretical constructs for studying colonial politics. This essay aims to extend such efforts, gaining further insight into the rhetorical nature of colonial discourse by making programmatic use of Burke's rhetorical theory. Where Carlson examined resistance to colonizers, this chapter considers an artifact that contributed to the development of an expansive colonial discourse. Specifically, I focus upon the *Sacred Books of the East* (*Sacred Books*) series as an exemplar from the colonial archive. *Sacred Books of the East* is a fifty-volume series of texts translated into English from six sacred traditions: Brahmanism, Taoism, Janism, Zoroastrianism, Buddhism, and Islam. Edited by Oxford philologist and Orientalist F. Max Müller (1823–1900), this series was a massive undertaking that had enduring consequences. Although not well-known in our own twenty-first century, this series was a decisive moment in the creation of our present; it produced critical editions of texts that were, in many cases, previously unavailable in written form.

The series is prefaced by an essay in which Müller lays out his editorial aim and discusses some of the difficulties of compilation and translation. Müller's preface is included in the first volume of *Sacred Books*, and is broad in scope: It considers the contents of that first volume and foreshadows the entire series.[3] If read through the terms of Burkean theory, the prefatory materials of the *Sacred Books* series reveals Müller's connection with the imperial

British project in India. Specifically, the *Sacred Books* series advances colonial interests through the use the written word and the English language.

This chapter undertakes two primary tasks: First, I conduct a rhetorical analysis of Müller's preface to highlight, in Burkean terms, the role of the *bureaucratization of the imaginative*. This bureaucratization, I argue, is accomplished through stabilizing localized, oral traditions into a standardized, textual form. Next, I describe this bureaucratization as a perspective that enables Müller to articulate a transcendent position regarding the relationship between the Christianity of the metropole and the religions of the colonies. I conclude by arguing that this transcendence is vital to the colonial discourse of comparative religious studies; through a "rational" and "scientific" ordering that marginalized other sacred practices, Müller reifies and naturalizes Christian thought as a whole.

BUREAUCRATIZING THE IMAGINATIVE: *SACRED BOOKS OF THE EAST*, HINDUISM, AND THE INFLUENCE OF TEXT

Early in the preface, Müller (1879) writes that "in order to have a solid foundation for a comparative study of religions of the East, we must have before all things complete and thoroughly faithful translations of their sacred books" (p. xi). This statement stakes out two of Müller's concerns: a commitment to disseminating *faithful* or *true* translations, and a commitment to developing the requisite materials for comparative religious study. In this passage (and in the preface as a whole), Müller positions *Sacred Books* as the authoritative source for English translations of these works. He accomplishes this by distinguishing his volumes from previous translations that were authored by "dilettanti," who gave incomplete or overly optimistic representations of these sacred texts. He argues that these previous works "have removed the study of religion from that wholesome and matter-of-fact atmosphere in which alone it can produce valuable and permanent results" (p. x).

In addition to this blanket condemnation of the genre, Müller (1879) also identifies specific dangers that arise from the flippant treatment of religious texts. First, Müller argues that such treatments lead readers to believe that the sacred texts of Eastern religions are overflowing with insights that provide enlightenment. In addition, he writes that these treatments raise unfounded fears about the teachings contained in these texts. As a result, Müller proposes that the study of religions be reclaimed by the academic elite—those who can provide a methodical, rational study of this complex and consequential material. He thus offers his series as a way to "place the study of ancient religions of the world on a more real and sound, on a more truly historical basis" (p. ix).

From a Burkean perspective, this "real and sound" intent of Müller's project reveals a bureaucratizing perspective, one that requires an ordering of knowledge about Eastern, sacred traditions. In Burke's (1984) terminology, this is understood as an example of the bureaucratization of the imaginative, a rhetorical construct that points to the interaction of conceptual and material factors and the social processes of stabilization in history and their consequences, both intended and unintended. In this case, the social process is Müller's editorship of the *Sacred Books* series and its consequences that, as we will see, involve significant support for the British colonial apparatus.

Burke's concept of the bureaucratization of the imaginative accents the dialectical relationship between texts and documents and the establishment of social control. His twist on "bureaucratization" draws upon the ambiguity contained within the term itself. It can be understood in two ways: (1) as the institutional process through which public offices consolidate power for themselves as a group, and (2) as the process through which individual officials attempt to appropriate power for their particular bureaus and for themselves (Simpson & Weiner, 1989, Vol II, p. 665). Here, "bureau" references a department within an organization and an Anglicization of the French *bureau*, literally meaning "a desk." Although this is not made explicit within Burke's discussion, I call attention to the role of the written word in this definition. The process of bureaucratization on the intra-institutional and inter-institutional levels is a practice that is facilitated by the power of the written word, and is predicated upon the textual appropriation of power. Yet, Burke is not only interested in organizational politics. The imaginative that is bureaucratized is abstract, unstable, and changeable. This kind of imagining—individual or shared—is captured by bureaucratizing forces and is shaped by them.

This discussion of bureaucratization offers vital insight into the colonialist dimensions of Müller's *Sacred Books* series. We clearly see the bureaucratization of the imaginative accomplished through the translation of the Rg-Veda that Müller himself completed for the first volume of the series. The process through which Müller's Rg-Veda emerges is both intellectual and material: The manuscripts of the Rg-Veda first needed to be compiled and translated, and then formed into a book. A closer, Burkean inspection of the creation of Müller's Rg-Veda indicates the presence and consequences of bureaucratization.

Müller faced a large, if not daunting, task in compiling an English Rg-Veda. The Rg-Veda had never previously been written down. Prior to its publication within Müller's volume, the imaginative tradition of Brahmanism did not exist as a coherent body of texts. Instead, it was comprised of sacred practices that were locally diverse, and had both textual and oral traditions.

It is important to note that, at the time, oral elements of the Vedic tradition were not accidental or due to illiteracy. In Brahmanism, Sacred knowledge was *deliberately* transmitted orally. This practice was designed to ensure that the information it contained could be more closely controlled by those who were meant to have access to it (Van Lohuizen-de Leeuw, 1954). With the English translation of the Rg-Veda, then, there are two notable shifts that are produced. First, Müller's work to collect and edit the Vedic tradition as it was represented in the extant manuscripts required the bureaucratization of a diverse, imaginative tradition through its use of the stabilizing powers of textuality (Van der Veer, 2001). Second, the compilation and publication of this critical edition made this sacred tradition *publicly accessible*. From this point forward, the only prerequisites for access to the Vedas were a working knowledge of the English language and access to Müller's volume.

The homogenization of the decentralized, heterogenous Vedic tradition was accomplished using the Lachmann method (Van der Veer, 2001). This process entails creating a hierarchy among extant texts—in essence, developing a genealogical link between manuscripts to identify the oldest version (Shepard, 1930). The Lachmann method allows translators to map the relationships between versions of texts through identifying separative and conjunctive errors (Timpanaro, 2005). Separative errors indicate which versions of a specific text belong to separate parts of the stemma, while conjunctive errors indicate the relationships between versions. The critical assumption driving this method is that identifying the oldest version reveals the most authoritative version, the one that contains the *True* text. Despite the method's façade of empirical inquiry and objectivity, the translator therefore exercises a substantial amount of authority in constructing the text. The rhetorical nature of the Lachmann method becomes evident here: In choosing which edition represents the original and true version, other versions are rejected. Here, then, lies the danger: Through the Lachmann method, translators' selections may truly be, as Burke cautions, deflections.

Moreover, through this method, the compilation of critical editions facilitates the bureaucratic determination of the parts of an imaginative tradition that become sanctioned and preserved. Further, this process separates these sanctioned, authoritative elements of the tradition from those that are undesirable and, thus, not preserved. At the end of this process, one version is compiled from many; one articulation of the imaginative is bureaucratized, while others are forgotten. In postcolonial terms, as Van der Veer (2001) notes, establishing authoritative editions through the Lachmann method allowed Orientalists to avoid the "messiness of localized native interpretation" (p. 115). Unstable, local interpretations were replaced by a concrete, reformulated, religious book.

The book, therefore, serves as a key material object in the creation of Müller's (1879) Rg Veda specifically, and in the bureaucratization of sacred eastern traditions more generally. Müller's focus on the production of books privileges that which is written, casting doubt upon information that is transmitted orally. This privileging is displayed in his teleological account of the tradition: "most of the ancient sacred books have been handed down by oral tradition for many generations before they were consigned to writing" (p. xiii). In addition, he claims that oral traditions are unable to resist change, meaning that the transmission of knowledge in this form is "not without its dangers" (p. xv). The reasoning here is as follows: Sacred texts must remain static since they present the revealed truth—a model that Müller imports from Christianity. If the text is altered, it no longer represents this sacred truth. The Christian distinction between canonical literature and apocryphal texts is superimposed on this scholarly process of consolidation and translation.

Müller (1879) explains that there is nothing in the east "corresponding to what we would call literature," since proverbs were transmitted haphazardly through the oral tradition (p. xiii). Stories become sacred because of their association with ancestors—not because they are an officially recognized element of any established canon, as in the West. As a consequence, the process through which eastern traditions articulate the boundaries of their teachings is, from Müller's perspective, unacceptably unsystematic. He notes that

> the idea of keeping the original and genuine tradition separate from apocryphal accretions was an idea of later growth, that could spring up only after the earlier tendency of preserving whatever could be preserved of sacred or half-sacred lore, had done its work and wrought its own destruction. (p. xvi)

In this formulation, oral traditions allow for the knowledge to be corrupted; when these traditions are written down, whatever truth is left is secured as a text.

The privilege associated with the written word increases the efficacy of Müller's bureaucratization of the imaginative. The codification of or capturing the imaginary transmutes the changeable into the static, much in the same way oral traditions are captured when they are written down. The rhetorical dimension of bureaucratization becomes important here: Stabilization requires that one expression of the imaginary is privileged over another—or, as Burke (1984) writes, "call the possibilities 'imaginative.' And call the carrying-out of *one* possibility the *bureaucratization* of the imaginative" (p. 225). The bureaucratization of the imaginary occurs, then, when the unstable geographies of the imaginary are articulated through screens that privilege the concrete. Within the pages of *Sacred Books*, the bureaucratization of the imaginative occurs through the written codification that changes the nature of these traditions. Thanks to Müller's volumes, the written manifestations of these traditions now appear as "sacred texts," fixed and authoritative doctrines that are separated from the ritual practices within which they had been embedded.

Müller's (1879) insistence on documenting the true versions of these sacred texts is seen throughout the preface. He states that the objective of *Sacred Books* is the compilation of "complete and thoroughly faithful translations" (p. xi). In this formulation, the word "faithful" is a striking terminological choice, one that he does not explicate further. His use of the word, however, raises an interesting question: To whom or to what does Müller intend these translations to be faithful? The *Oxford English Dictionary* indicates that the word *faithful* is linked to the words *allegiance, religious belief,* and *fact* (Simpson & Weiner, 1989). These key terms situate faithfulness as an allegiance to three loci of power: state, church, and empirical inquiry (respectively). Within the context of *Sacred Books*, I contend, these three allegiances combine to situate this project as more hegemonic than disinterested scholarship. To the extent that these pillars of Müller's colonialist translation have combined interests, their strategies are integrated but distinct.

Central to Burke's concept of the bureaucratization of the imaginative is the assumption that stabilization facilitates the consolidation of power. As such, the *Sacred Books* series provides part of the needed knowledge to underwrite (quite literally) the colonial apparatus. Specifically, it represented one of the key strategies used to extend the power of the British Empire. Little wonder, then, that *Sacred Books* was partially funded by the British East India Company (Sharpe, 1979, p. 36). The British East India Company's complicated role in India began, at its name indicates, as a trading monopoly in the seventeenth century (Kulke & Rothermind, 1998). Over time, it developed into a monopoly that allowed the British to establish colonial power across wide swaths of territory, while protecting the government from extensive liability (Kulke & Rothermind, 1998). As the Company—and England's need for the company—changed, political power was transferred from the British East India Company to a British-run government in India. Following this transfer of power, the Queen of England was named Empress of India in 1877, and the Company returned to its original, mercantile role (Strachey, 1911). Throughout its various incarnations, the British East India Company thus formed an important arm of the British imperial project—making their funding of Müller's text a significant indicator of the colonialist function of his project. The link between the Company, the Crown, and *Sacred Books* is further indicated by Müller's dedication.

The entire series of *Sacred Books* is dedicated to the Marquis of Salisbury (1830–1903), who had, until just prior to the books' publication, been the Secretary for the State of India (1866–1867). As Van der Veer (2001) notes, "in order to colonize India the British had to acquire empirical knowledge about India's population, geography, languages, and customs" (p. 113). Imperial power was, in this way, built upon and consolidated through the processes of bureaucratization. The empirical process through which data was compiled and catalogued created a form through which the British understanding of India was written. Ascertaining what, exactly, the Indians believed was a central part of this undertaking. However, the formulation of this inquiry discloses the Imperial assumption that there was one answer to the question—when, given India's heterogenous traditions, there was no single answer.

Müller explicitly understood his scholarly work as an effort to find this one answer—an answer that would allow him to properly *order* the people and beliefs of the East. As Inden (2000) notes, "Müller assumes that nature is ordered according to a unitary principle and that the order 'out there' is discovered by the investigator and not constructed" (p. 14). As the ideological foundation for *Sacred Books*, this hegemonic faithfulness combines with an unshakeable essentialism to generate a naturalized vision of an orderly eastern world. Müller (1879) assures the reader, for example that "our translations are truthful, that we have suppressed nothing, that we have varnished nothing, however hard it seemed sometimes even to write it down" (p. xx). The order Müller presents to his reader is not, however, one found in nature, but is found in a construct that supports the hierarchies that were central to British colonial rule.

In this way, Müller's project of bureaucratization also displays systematic classification processes of hierarchy that were so central to Burke's definition of the hu-man. In *Language as Symbolic Action*, Burke (1966) famously identifies one implication of our symbolic abilities: We are "goaded by the spirit of hierarchy" or "moved by a sense of order" (p. 15). From a Burkean perspective, as a result, *Sacred Books* can be viewed as a bureaucratization of an imaginative that maintained and extended the hierarchical relationship between England and India, between Christianity and other religions, and between essentialist truth and the truthfulness of relativism. Burke's use of the words "goaded" and "moved" indicate that hierarchy is an ordering that simultaneously functions as a motive for action. In the case of Müller, this motive is manifested throughout the volumes comprising *Sacred Books*.

Inden's (2000) discussion of hegemonic agents and texts is useful here in extending Burke's consideration of the human animal as the creator of hierarchy. Inden defines hegemonic agents as the "writers and institutions that have dominated the public discussions about others, not simply in a constraining or coercive sense, but also in the sense that they have been accorded positions of leadership" (p. 36). Here Inden's Müller's descriptions resonate. Müller did not hold a position of leadership in the East India Company, nor in the British-run Indian government. In fact, Müller never went to India at all (Van der Veer, 2001, p. 116). However, as the first chair of comparative philology at Oxford, a position that was created for him, he exerted considerable influence in the field, an influence that was enhanced by his creation of *Sacred Books* (Van der Veer, 2001).

As such, Müller's work shaped what Inden (2000) calls "the public discussions about others" (p. 36). Indeed, Müller's work was intended to accomplish precisely that. In the preface, recall that Müller (1879) expresses dissatisfaction with the current status of British knowledge of eastern religions; the production of this knowledge has, he says, been dominated by dilettanti (p. x). His goal—one he hopes *Sacred Books* will accomplish—is the study of eastern religions in a "more discriminating, in fact, a more scholarlike spirit" (p. x). The intent of *Sacred Books*, in Inden's (2000) terms, is thus to create a hegemonic text that "appears to speak for and to not only the interest of rulers but also those who are ruled" (p. 43). The hegemonic agent, as the writer of a hegemonic text, institutionalizes and provides the documentation of the systems of hierarchy that, according to Burke, define the hu-man.

TRANSCENDENCE BY COLONIAL PERSPECTIVE

Burke (1984) offers his view of transcendence in an oft-quoted passage of *Attitudes Toward History*: "When approached from a certain point of view, A and B are 'opposites.' We mean by 'transcendence' the adoption of another point of view from which they cease to be opposites" (p. 336). Although this quote is often used in reference to Burke's comic frame, for the purposes of this chapter, I contend that it is the colonial "point of view" that is being constructed through Müller's symbolic act of transcendence. The first step of this transcending process is the grouping of the six distinct and, at times, conflicting sacred traditions—Brahmanism, Taoism, Janism, Zoroastrianism, Buddhism, and Islam—into one transcendent category, named "Eastern Religions." As is discussed below, the attribution of the word "religion" here may be rather imprecise. Moreover, I point out the imperial perspective on the geographic identification of these texts as all having come from the "East." To the Taoists of China, for example, the territories lying to the east are Japan, followed only by the American continent. However, the oppositions that exist between these six traditions are transcended by a colonial perspective in which all Eastern religions can be understood together and, thus, cease to be opposites.

Once the differences between these traditions are transcended, the religions of the East become A, and those of the West (primarily Christianity) become B. Through *Sacred Books* and Müller's scholarly perspective, these distinctions are transcended by a colonial, rational, literate endeavor that folds eastern and western traditions into a unified category, named *religion*. This transcendence has two steps: First, Müller symbolically generates a transcending perspective through his use of bureaucratization. Second, Müller draws upon this symbolic act of transcendence to contribute to the comparative study known as comparative religion.

Müller's editorship provide him with many symbolic resources for the creation of transcendence in that he designed this series, set the table of contents, and ordered the texts into a collection of religious artifacts. As editor, Müller creates and compares the positions that Burke might call A and B. However, in the case of the traditions translated into these volumes, the points could be more appropriately identified as A through F—that is, one point for each religion treated in the *Sacred Books* series. As discussed above, prior to Müller's series, these six religions had never been ordered into a category named "eastern religions." Through *Sacred Books*, however, these six points of view are articulated and documented in books, and thereby transformed. They become discernable positions; they are: fixed religious systems that share an "Eastern" orientation, but display divergent teachings and traditions; united by their common participation in the series; and simultaneously separated from each other (quite literally) by the front and back covers of each volume. From the vantage point created by this editorial process, Müller can survey the field of religions. To complete this process, he places Christianity within the field of perspectives to be transcended—though this process is, from the first, weighted in favor of Christianity.

This next level of colonial transcendence is institutionalized as and through the study of comparative religions. Indeed, one of Müller's goals in producing the *Sacred Books* series was to both enable and legitimize this line of scholarly inquiry. The Victorian study of comparative religion was a system of inquiry that studied non-Christian practices, but was predicated upon a presumption of Christianity's superiority. In so doing, it established a hierarchy of world religions that placed Christianity at its apex (Van der Veer, 2001, p. 111). In this formulation, studies of comparative religion analogized sacred traditions to Christianity so that they could be, ultimately, subjugated to it. The establishment of this hierarchy, however, required the codification of practices in the East as "religions" that could be written, stabilized, and studied. It required, in other words, a very particular kind of bureaucratization—and Müller's work was vital to the legitimization and completion of this process.

The *Sacred Books'* renaming of *practice* as *religion*, as Burke might suggest, is more consequential than it initially appears. Within this context, for example, the extension of the term *religion* is made problematic by the word's definition and etymology.[4] The word *religion* is defined both as a state of life in service to a particular religious order, and also as the systems of worship that constitute this life (Simpson & Weiner, 1989). Translating the term into other languages cannot, therefore, be described as straightforward process; it is one that involves reinterpreting and reconstructing foreign phenomenon. For example, as McCutcheon (2003) points out, "English-speaking Indians have no difficulty conceiving of what we call Hinduism as being their 'religion'—although, technically speaking, to a person we might call a Hindu, 'Hinduism' is not a religion but is, rather, *sanatana dharma*" (p. 253). Thanks to writers like Müller, the *sanatana dharma*—the cosmic order of duty—has been, for the purposes of the West, categorized as a religion and systematized through the terminology of its attendant definition. Similarly, to the extent that the sacred practices included in *Sacred Books* were, prior to this critical edition, unsystematic, their inclusion in the category named *religion* is rhetorically significant and consequential.

Müller believed in the existence of a universal religion: He believed that if all sacred traditions could fit into the category named *religion*, then the essence of religion itself could be assessed (Harrison, 1969, p. 206). Importantly, universal religion for Müller provided the point of origination for all religions. Harrison refers to a passage in one of Müller's lectures where he states that religious discourse is not given by God to one chosen people; rather, the study of comparative religion shows that "the highest attributes which we claim for the Deity are likewise ascribed to it by the *Sacred Books* of other religions" (as cited in Harrison, 1969, p. 206). His commitment to discovering the nature of universal religion is also articulated in the preface to *Sacred Books*. Within it, Müller (1879) writes that "there is no lesson which at the present time seems more important than to learn that in every religion there are such precious grains" (p. xxxviii). Here his use of the term *religion* is motivated by a process that privileges analogical argument—an analogy through which the systematic nature of religion becomes not just a salient characteristic, but a prerequisite.

KENNETH BURKE AND COLONIAL CRITIQUE

In sum, this chapter has considered the *Sacred Books of the East* series as an example of the process Burke calls the bureaucratization of the imaginative:

It united, codified, and ordered religious practices from the east. This bu-reaucratization, I have argued, facilitated a symbolic transcendence in which a colonial perspective compared and reduced Eastern religions—thereby showing, ultimately, the enduring supremacy of Christianity. More gener-ally, however, this chapter has taken its inspiration from another goal: to explore Burkean thought as a resource for developing critiques of colonialism and postcolonialism.

In this context, Burke's strengths are in his focus on the power endemic to symbolicity—a power that has an important and influential role in enacting and institutionalizing colonial politics. Previous work has explored some of the ground necessary to extend Burkean scholarship into postcolonial topics. For example, Cheney, Garvin-Doxas, and Torrens (1998), in their survey of some of Burke's most prominent works, identify what they term an *implicit theory of power*. Burke, they contend, addresses power in the context of lan-guage, since his "theory of human relations centers on language" (p. 135). They find in Burke's writings theoretical tools for understanding the func-tions of power when it is wielded by the collective. Cheney et al. explain that conventional descriptions of power situate it within the individual, whereas Burke more properly conceives it as a process of socialization and hegemony (p. 141).

For those interested in extending his work into critiques of colonialism, Burke's theoretical position on the collective wielding of power may provide a valuable contribution. In this chapter, I focused upon his discussion of the force of language in creating hierarchies and in facilitating a transcendent, colonial perspective. Although Müller was the primary object of my analysis, the *Sacred Books* series was also a collaborative undertaking: Müller edited manuscripts collected by his associates in India, and the project found finan-cial backing in the East India Trading Company. In isolation, Müller's trans-lations would have done little to influence the metropole/colony relationship. It is through his connections with the scholarly community in England as well as the colonial bureaucracy in India that his work was published, dis-seminated, and thereby contributed to England's colonial practices.

In the example of the Rg Veda, in Müller's hands, Hinduism became a religion, was documented and stabilized in English, and was eventually returned to India in that form. Van der Veer (2001) notes that Müller gave copies of the *Sacred Books* series to the Prince of Wales, who brought them to India on a diplomatic visit (p. 112). During his time in India, the Prince of Wales gave these copies to Indian rajas as gifts. The metaphorical im-plications here are strange and too complicated to track. Sacred Sanskrit texts were brought to England, translated, published in English, and then returned to Indian royalty in an anglicized and bureaucratized form. Indeed, it is hard to imagine what the rajas would have made of "their" religion upon opening these volumes.

In the context of Burkean scholarship, this chapter has traced a specific mode of transcendence—one that is politicized and used as a tool of repression. Here, transcendence represents less a mode of reconciling conflict than it does as a mode for ordering and enforcing hierarchy. Burke (1984) explains that "one may 'transcendentally' organize his interpretation of human motives by the following broad emphases: a human act is done for God, for an ideal (humanity, culture, justice, truth), for a corporate grouping (political or otherwise), for oneself" (p. 338). In the *Sacred Books* series, we find a transcending organization of religions, offered in the service of the corporate grouping, "empire." This transcendence by colonial perspective points to the utility of using Burkean thought to unwind and explicate the collective wielding of power that flourished in colony/metropole relationships. Moreover, the specific case of the imperial apparatus may prove to be a valuable example for drawing out a new, and heretofore unrecognized, dimension of Burke's political thought.

NOTES

1. For examples of this body of literature, see Laham (1851) and Martin (1857).

2. Pennycook (1998) and Suleri (1998) represent two notable examples of postcolonial scholarship focused upon topics of interest to rhetoricians. Although both of these volumes trace connections between language and colonialism, neither uses Burke's theory specifically to develop their key arguments. Yet, postcolonial scholars are not solely to blame for this lack of synergy between the rhetorical and the postcolonial. For example, Shome's (1996) call for rhetorical scholars to integrate postcolonial concerns into their work has largely been ignored.

3. Each volume, including the first, has an introduction to the specific texts it translates. Even though only one volume of the series was published in 1879, the preface in the first volume considers the entire series. At the time, Müller anticipated that the series would include twenty-four volumes. As his editorship continued, *Sacred Books of the East* grew to include fifty volumes, and was not complete until 1910, ten years after Müller died.

4. As McCutcheon (2003) notes, scholars who have investigated the word's origins have found more confusion than clarity. For example, there is no root word for "religion" in the Greek New Testament (p. 253). Although its Latin root, *religio*, appears later, there is no synonym for "religion" in languages not derived from Latin (p. 252).

REFERENCES

Boon, J. A. (1990). *Affinities and extremes*. Chicago, IL: University of Chicago Press.

Burke, K. (1984). *Attitudes toward history*. Berkeley, CA: University of California Press.

Burke, K. (1966). *Language as symbolic action*. Berkeley, CA: University of California Press.

Carlson, A. C. (1986). Gandhi and the comic frame: *"Ad bellum purificandum."* *Quarterly Journal of Speech, 72*(4), 446–455.

Cheney, G., Garvin-Doxas, K., & Torrens, K. (1998). Kenneth Burke's implicit theory of power. In B. Brock (Ed.), *Kenneth Burke and the 20ᵗʰ century* (pp. 133–150). New York, NY: State University of New York Press.

Foucault, M. (1972). *The archaeology of knowledge and the discourse on language*. New York, NY: Pantheon.

Harrison, C. (1969). The liberalism of Max Müller. *Contemporary Review, CCXIV*, 206–209.

Inden, R. B. (2000). *Imagining India*. Bloomington, IN: Indiana University Press.

Kulke, H., & Rothermund, D. (1998). *A history of India*. London: Routledge.

Laham, R. G. (1851). *The ethnology of the British colonies and dependencies*. London: John van Voorst.

Marx, K. (1857, September 17). Investigation of tortures in India. *New York Tribune*. Trotsky Digital Archive. Retrieved from http://trotsky.org/archive/marx/works/1857/09/17.htm

Martin, R. M. (1857). *The British colonies: Their history, extent, condition and resources*. London: The London Printing and Pub. Co.

McCutcheon, R. T. (2003). *The discipline of religion: Structure, meaning, rhetoric*. London: Routledge.

Müller, F. M. (1879). *Sacred books of the East*. Ed. F. M. Müller. Vol. 1. Oxford: Oxford University Press.

Pennycook, A. (1998). *English and the discourses of colonialism*. London: Routledge.

Sharpe, E. J. (1975). *Comparative religion: A history*. London: Duckworth Press.

Shepard, W. P. (1930). Recent theories of textual criticism. *Modern Philology, 28*(2), 129–141.

Shome, R. (1996). Postcolonial interventions in the rhetorical canon: An "Other" view. *Communication Theory, 6*(1), 40–59.

Simpson, J. A., & Weiner, E. S. C. (1989). *Oxford English Dictionary* (Vols. II, VII). Oxford: Clarendon.

Strachey, J. (1911). *India: Its administration and progress*. London: Macmillian & Co.

Suleri, S. (1998). *The rhetoric of English India*. Chicago, IL: University of Chicago Press.

Timpanaro, S. (2005). *The genesis of Lachmann's method*. Trans. G. W. Most. Chicago, IL: University of Chicago Press.

Van Lohuizen-de Leeuw, J. E. (1954). India and its cultural empire. In D. Sinor (Ed.) *Orientalism and history* (pp. 35–67). Cambridge, UK: Heffer.

Van der Veer, P. (2001). *Imperial encounters: Religion and modernity in India and Britain*. Princeton, NJ: Princeton University Press.

7 TRANSCENDENCE AFTER DIALOGUE

Gregory Clark

The most striking feature of contemporary moral utterance is that so much of it is used to express disagreements; and the most striking feature of the debates in which these disagreements are expressed is their interminable character.

—Alasdair MacIntyre

In my reading of its ancient and modern theory, rhetoric invites hope through its emphasis upon the transcendent capacity of dialogue. That is, definitions of rhetoric locate persuasive language in the context of discursive exchange—where people offer to others differing or opposing ideas about what is or ought to be, with an eye toward establishing some sort of agreement. Whether that agreement follows from exchanges that are cooperative, competitive, or even coercive, rhetorical theory generally assumes that people determine the direction of collective actions and develop shared conceptions of a common reality through an exchange of assertions and responses. This, in short, is dialogue; and the end of dialogue is agreement, enabling people to transcend their prior differences.

Dialogic rhetorical exchanges can take the form of agonistic argument or cooperative conversation. Either way, when rhetoric is understood as dialogical in its function, it teaches us that our words are capable of bringing us together. That lesson is founded upon faith in a rational sort of transcendence—upon a belief that people can rise above their differences, and even their conflicts, to agree upon beliefs and actions by reasoning together. The accomplishment of that reasoning through the processes of discursive exchange is the dialogical work of rhetoric.[1]

The problem, of course, is that we know from experience that dialogue can fail. It can fail, for example, in the absence of a common language, the raw material for constructing agreement. It can also fail in the absence of shared values, the motivators that prompt people to persist in the difficult and frustrating process of reaching agreement with others. Without a common language or shared values, people who differ simply cannot complete the transcendent work of rational dialogue. They cannot move from their different points of origin to a place where they can cooperatively articulate agreement. We have all been there—to that *other* place—where disagreement seems to be the only destination talk can take us. That is the place where we stop talking; it is the place where, if we can, we part ways with those with whom we differ. If the circumstances we share do not allow that parting of ways, then the best we can hope for is to share that place in silence. Here, rhetoric seems to be out of business, and I would argue that this is what experience teaches us—a lesson that most of our rhetorical theory implicitly confirms. As a consequence, what we know about rhetoric suggests that the limits of dialogue do indeed mark the limits of rhetoric and, logically, the outer boundary of the unifying work of rhetorical transcendence.

Kenneth Burke's writings about rhetoric also confirm that suggestion. To put it simply, a conception of rhetoric that situates rhetorical exchange within language alone cannot operate when dialogue fails and people fall silent. My project here is to suggest that a careful reading of Burke's conception of rhetoric and its implications for rhetorical transcendence reveals a different possibility: that there are rhetorical prompts to agreement that do not depend on dialogue. Indeed, Burke's concept of rhetoric indicates that rhetorical resources for transcendence remain available after dialogue fails. To be specific, Burke reaches beyond dialogical reasoning and discursive language to include communicative resources that are aesthetic in their form, and potentially transcendent in their effect. Despite his emphasis on dialogical words—remember, for example, his allegory of the parlor conversation as a model for human rhetorical experience—Burke teaches us that aesthetic experiences do rhetorical work that can prompt people to understand their differences as transcended, even when conversation in the parlor has fallen silent.

With that overall purpose firmly in mind, let us turn to Burke's rhetorical theory. As he describes it in *A Rhetoric of Motives*, Burke's (1969) work on rhetoric engages two related projects: The first is a project he describes as "reclamation": "we would . . . rediscover rhetorical elements that had become obscured when rhetoric as a term fell into disuse," and when "esthetics sought to outlaw rhetoric" (p. xiii). The second project is the explicit expansion of rhetoric beyond its "traditional bounds": "There is an intermediate area of expression that is not wholly deliberate, yet not wholly unconscious," an area located "midway between aimless utterance and speech directly purposive" (p. xiii). To facilitate these two projects—projects that revised our understanding of what counts as rhetoric; indeed, of what is rhetorical— Burke proposes that the work of rhetoric should be understood as prompting identification. That is how, as he suggests, the traditional, rhetorical work of persuasion proceeds. More radically, however, by proposing the rhetorical as a prompt to identification, Burke provides himself as "an instrument" to "mark off the areas of rhetoric, by showing how a rhetorical motive is often present where it is not usually recognized, or thought to belong" (p. xiii). Because the work of *identification* encompasses persuasion as it is conventionally understood, and also situations where "people earnestly yearn to identify themselves with one group or other," rhetoric and the rhetorical are given a "wider scope" (Burke, 1951, p. 203). I would add, though, that often it is less that we yearn than that we are *prompted* to so yearn, influenced rhetorically from "a partially dreamlike, idealistic motive, somewhat compensatory to the real differences or divisions, which the rhetoric of identification would transcend" (Burke, 1951, p. 203).

For Burke, rhetoric enables people to identify with each other in ways that transcend differences and divisions that are inherent to human interaction. He locates the moment of that transcendence in what he describes as dialectic—the primary working element of his rhetoric. It is true that many of Burke's descriptions of dialectic, like those of rhetoric, frame that process as discursive, but like the notion of identification, the notion of transcendence itself is described in ways that do not locate it exclusively in discourse. In contrast to most interpreters of Burke, I read that as an invitation to consider rhetorical resources that do not require the use of language.

Burke (1984) offers a simple but expansive description of transcendence in his early book, *Attitudes Toward History*: "When approached from a certain point of view, A and B are 'opposites.' We mean by 'transcendence' the adoption of another point of view from which they cease to be opposites" (p. 336). That statement, I would emphasize, does not specify discourse as the means by which those alternate points of view are adopted. Later, Burke adapts that description in *A Rhetoric of Motives* (*Rhetoric*) to describe how identification proceeds; but, again, he uses terms that do not limit this rhetorical work to language. Burke (1969) famously writes in *Rhetoric*:

> A is not identical with his colleague, B. But insofar as their interests are joined, A is *identified* with B. Or he may *identify himself* with B even when their interests are not joined, if he assumes they are, or is persuaded to believe so. (p. 20)

Though Burke rarely discusses the possibility directly, these statements certainly allow readers to locate a variety of non-discursive experiences that are well within the "range" of the rhetorical.[2]

The idea that rhetoric is not limited to language is not new to contemporary scholarship, working as we do in a field where visual rhetoric is an important part of our study. Burke's rhetoric of identification and his dialectic of transcendence can help us understand how non-discursive resources do rhetorical work, what non-discursive rhetorical resources are available for that work, and how those resources (particularly those inherent in aesthetic experience) become effective rhetoric. When Burke writes about rhetoric, he often describes its effect as aesthetic, and when he writes about the aesthetic—often calling it *poetic*—he tends to describe its effect and function as rhetorical. This convergence suggests that, in his mind at least, experiences prompted by aesthetic encounters might provide rhetoric with the power of transcendence in communicative situations where dialogic discourse has failed. Certainly the rhetorical work done by an aesthetic experience is of a different order of precision and practicality than the work done by rhetorical dialogue. The reverse possibility, suggested by Burke, is nonetheless worth exploring: that shared experiences of feeling—the sort offered by aesthetic experience—can enable people who have failed to articulate common ground to experience themselves as standing together.

When Dialogue Fails

In reading Richard Weaver (2001), we are reminded that rhetoric describes, above all, an interpersonal project of influence where much is often at stake. As Weaver puts it, "We have no sooner uttered words than we have given impulse to other people to look at the world, or some small part of it, in our way" (p. 1360). That influence is a moral act. Whether the morality of an act of influence is slight or profound, it remains inherent in rhetorical interaction. Burke (1979) reminds us that people "derive purposes from language, which tells them what they 'ought' to want to do, tells them how to do it, and in the telling goads them with great threats and promises, even unto the gates of heaven and hell" (p. 274). For Burke, as for Weaver, we cannot *not* engage in dialogue, and cannot *not* feel as a moral imperative. "If men were not apart from one another," Burke (1969) writes, "there would be no need for the rhetorician to proclaim their unity" (p. 22). Given all that, we experience the failure of dialogue as a moral failure. We proclaim our unity, for that is what we must do, one way or another. For us, "identification is compensatory to division" (Burke, 1969, p. 22). Identification is the compensation—in the sense of recompense—that helps us to recover from the frightening experience of conflict, and from division, an experience that threatens to leave each of us alone. We always seek—sometimes desperately—the compensation of identification.

Our modern failure to find this compensation is Alasdair MacIntyre's (1984) topic in *After Virtue*. For him, the failure of dialogue, as he describes it in the epigraph to this chapter, is fundamentally a *moral* problem. Dialogue fails frequently in modernity. In MacIntyre's explanation, the fragmentation of human culture has followed from what we call globalization, a predicament that leaves us—probably permanently, MacIntyre concludes—with neither the common values nor the common language to enact dialogue that would transcend our differences. Lacking the resources necessary to resolve our conflicts dialogically, MacIntyre argues that we find them "interminable"— a form of the same word that Burke (1984) uses to describe the trajectory of his paradigmatic parlor conversation that never resolves or ends (p. 6). There is quite a difference between these two conceptions of "interminable." For MacIntyre (1984), interminable conflict is the moral and rhetorical reality shared by those who must live together "after virtue," in the era that follows the breakdown of agreement upon what is good. For him, the only hope that remains is the limited rhetorical project of constructing "local forms of community within which civility and the intellectual and moral life can be sustained through the new dark ages which are already upon us" (p. 263).

The violent state of our intensely interdependent world renders this conclusion hopeless and dangerous. The fact is, we often must continue to interact with those to whom we have nothing left to say. According to MacIntyre, this indicates the point at which we must separate ourselves from them; however, for most of us, most of the time, separation is not a realistic option. MacIntyre recommends that we withdraw into insular communities of the like-minded, spaces where we can sustain the transcendent work of dialogue. This is a problematic choice, though, at a time when human survival increasingly depends upon global cooperation. This, I contend, is where Burke provides us with vital resources for grappling with our current situation. Burke's ideas about communication in the context of conflict acknowledge that we are likely to fail to agree *and* that we need to keep trying to agree, despite our failure. Burke assumes that dialogue often fails, but that, even in the face of failure, there are rhetorical resources that enable us transcend our differences. These resources are implicit in Burke's definitions of rhetoric.

The first definition of rhetoric Burke (1969) offers in *A Rhetoric of Motives* is a moral one: "Rhetoric is concerned with Babel after the Fall. Its contribution to a 'sociology of knowledge' must often carry us far into the lugubrious regions of malice and the lie" (p. 23). A few pages later, Burke provides another definition—this one is more practically descriptive. The "the basic function of rhetoric," he writes, is "the use of words by human agents to form attitudes or to induce actions in other human agents" (p. 41). Here Burke describes inherently dialogical work that is "rooted in an essential function of language itself, a function that is wholly realistic, and is continually born anew; the use of language as a symbolic means of inducing cooperation in beings that by nature respond to symbols" (p. 43). This definition is much more neutral than rhetoric located in those "lugubrious regions of malice and the lie," but Burke understands that those regions are where most of us, at least some of the time, must necessarily reside. It is certainly where public discourse was residing in the United States during the years in which he wrote *A Rhetoric of Motives*—those years after World War II when the Cold War and its attitudes of fear saturated the national culture. Even without overt malice and lies, most of us, most of the time, are on the outskirts of those regions; we feel alienated from others and a need to connect.

This frank observation that "rhetoric is concerned with Babel after the Fall" is hard to take when we want the reassurance of identification that follows from the compensation of transcendence. Yet, the biblical story of Babel teaches us that this compensation is difficult to come by. Let us review that story, here in the language of the *King James Bible*:

> And the whole earth was of one language, and of one speech. . . . And they said, Go to, let us build us a city and tower, whose top may reach unto heaven; and let us make us a name, lest we be scattered abroad upon the face of the earth. And the Lord came down to see the city and tower, which the children of men builded. And the Lord said, Behold, the people is one and they all have one language; and this they begin to do; and now nothing will be restrained from them, which they have imagined to do. Go to, let us go down, and there confound their language, that they may not understand one another's speech. So the Lord scattered them abroad from thence upon the face of all the earth. (Genesis, 11:1–8)[3]

As Burke observed in his initial definition of rhetoric, this post-Babel state is our human predicament. Whether by divine edict or by happenstance, language renders us incapable of fully understanding each other, and that may be a good thing. We are too shortsighted, and we are often too arrogant to constructively use the collective power that follows from pure agreement. While the individual "Fall" that another biblical story locates in the Garden of Eden might explain the state of our souls, this collective "Fall" offers a way to explain the state of our societies. Whether we consider it scripture or useful fable, the story of Babel teaches us this: Rhetorical interaction is natural and necessary for humans, and doomed to fall short of full success. We cannot help but seek, through rhetoric, the dialogical exchange that would enable us to transcend the differences, misunderstandings, mistrust, and conflicts that divide us. Regardless of how hard and hopefully we work in our reasoned talk to realize that transcendence, dialogue often fails. At least part of the reason for that failure is that, as Burke (1984) puts it, "people are *necessarily* mistaken," that "*all* people are exposed to situations in which they must act as fools," because "*every* insight contains its own special kind of blindness" (p. 41).

These quotes from Burke describe the way things are most of the time; these are some of the "facts of life" that disrupt dialogue. Of course, there are also genuinely bad intentions that get in the way—those that take form of the "malice and the lie"—that rhetorical theory has long acknowledged. As Michael Leff (2003) notes, John Witherspoon—that democratic Scot who signed the Declaration of Independence and then taught rhetoric and theology to generations of students at Princeton—insisted to his students that "the highest achievement in the art of speaking must coincide with 'the greatest reserve and self-denial in the use of it, otherwise it will defeat its own purpose'" (p. 138). A much more recent teacher, Wayne Brockriede describes rhetoric as communication "'in which a speaker seeks to have his way with an audience'" (as cited in Leff, 2003, p. 136). George A. Kennedy (1997) has been similarly candid about the matter, observing that "rhetoric has its origin in the instinct for self-preservation and is a form of energy transmitted through signs to persuade an audience to act in securing or preserving the best interests of the speaker" (p. 230). These are the realities of self-interest, if not of "malice and the lie," that are unavoidable after Babel. They can keep dialogue from succeeding; though, when dialogue does fail, what rhetorical options remain?

Kenneth Burke's Aesthetic Rhetoric

Although less often recognized, much of what Burke said about rhetoric encompasses poetics. His writings suggest that rhetoric influences people in their beliefs and intentions toward identifying with others in ways that transcend differences, but that this work is accomplished through shared aesthetic experience. Essentially, he indicates that rhetorical transcendence often happens aesthetically. Indeed, the idea that aesthetic experience can wield the rhetorical power of influence is implicit in Burke's (1969) shift from describing rhetoric from *persuasion* to *identification*; it is a shift that enables us to understand how "a rhetorical motive is present where it is not usually recognized, or thought to belong" (p. viii). Most of Burke's examples of those other places where rhetoric resides are aesthetic; more specifically, they are *poetic*.

To understand how rhetorical work can be done through aesthetic means, we need to look at another shift in our thinking about rhetoric that Burke invited: from a focus on rhetoric as a prompt to action, to rhetoric as a prompt to *attitude*. Traditionally, rhetoric does the work of transforming persuasion into action; but, if we understand rhetoric instead as identification, we can recognize the project of rhetoric as considerably wider in its influence, as one best summarized as persuasion to attitude. Burke (1969) writes, "Insofar as a choice of *action* is restricted"—as it certainly is when dialogic discussion of actions are not appropriate or possible—"rhetoric seeks rather to have a formative effect upon *attitude* (as a criminal condemned to death might by priestly rhetoric be brought to an attitude of repentance and resignation)" (p. 50). Indeed, Burke tells us in *Rhetoric*, "This shift corresponds to a distinction between act and attitude (attitude being an incipient act, a leaning or inclination)," and the idea of the rhetoricality of persuasion to attitude, without immediate reference to action, "permit[s] the application of rhetorical terms to purely *poetic* structures" (p. 50). It is precisely this application "of rhetorical terms" to "*poetic* structures" that Burke explores in much of his work.

Furthermore, this idea of persuasion to attitude—with attitude understood as an incipient act—is implicit in classical rhetorical theory. Aristotle's description of epideictic rhetoric suggests that, in contrast to deliberative or forensic rhetoric, the epideictic can be understood as non-dialogic because, unlike legislative and judicial discourse, it does not make assertions that require public answers. Rather, epideictic rhetoric offers vivid depictions of subjects deserving praise or blame, thereby prompting the audience to reflective contemplation. Of rhetoric, Aristotle (1991) wrote that "it is necessary for the hearer to be either a spectator or a judge," and in the case of epideictic rhetoric, the audience functions clearly as spectator (p. 47). In his translation of Aristotle's *Rhetoric*, Kennedy (1997) emphasizes that "the audience in epideictic is not called upon to take a specific action," but is rather called upon to modify or strengthen a belief in response to the rhetoric. Further, he writes that while the category seems vague in Aristotle's work, "later ancient rhetoricians regarded it [epideictic rhetoric] as including poetry and prose literature, and since Renaissance times it has sometimes included other arts like painting, sculpture, and music as well" (Aristotle, 1991, p. 48). In a like fashion, Perelman and Olbrechts-Tyteca (1969) suggest that epideictic rhetoric has more in common "with literature than with argumentation" (p. 48), since it does the rhetorical work of intensifying the "adherence" of the audience "to certain values" they have in common in order to prompt a "sense of communion" (pp. 48-49). Consequently, they conclude, "every device of literary art" might be rendered rhetorical (p. 51).

I would emphasize that these passages do not refer to a "pure" kind of literature or art; this is aesthetic work that has been harnessed for a rhetorical purpose. Burke (1966b), for his part, was long-attuned to the overlap of rhetoric and poetics—the rhetorical and the aesthetic; he recognized that these two categories "readily become confused because there is a large area which they share in common" (p. 302). The common ground shared by the rhetorical and the aesthetic, as traditionally defined, is the prompting of attitude. Burke is explicit in his contention that poetic language can accomplish identification in attitude, if not in action. He is not as explicit, though, about the fact that the rhetorical power of the aesthetic is not dependent upon language. What he writes about rhetoric and the poetic suggests that language is not always essential to the work of transcendence that follows from the experience of rhetorical identification. For Burke (1966a), *transcendence* is the project of "building a terministic bridge whereby one realm is *transcended* by being viewed *in terms of* a realm 'beyond' it" (p. 187). The language of that description, like his various descriptions of the rhetorical work of identification, allows the inference that such bridges need not only be terministic: They can also be experiential. Experience, specifically shared, aesthetic experience—I suggest—is the rhetorical resource we have left after dialogue has failed. I explain this suggestion further, but first I offer an example of an aesthetic experience that accomplishes rhetorical ends.

The Reluctant Sextet

A few years ago, I observed a highly selective summer workshop designed to launch accomplished young jazz musicians into professional careers. It was organized by a friend of mine, a man respected internationally in jazz circles as both a musician and an educator. Joining him as workshop faculty were a premier jazz bassist, one of the idiom's foremost guitarists, one of its leading and most versatile pianists, an accomplished and well-known drummer, and a prominent and innovative trumpeter. The specific purpose of the workshop was to give students an opportunity to be mentored in performing jazz music from a rich and diverse set of perspectives. As the workshop progressed, it became apparent that those perspectives were more diverse than expected. For the students, the diversity was creating intellectual inconsistencies, as they tried to reconcile the differences presented to them in instruction; for the faculty, the diversity of perspectives was creating open conflict.

That conflict emerged in interactions between my friend, who is a saxophonist, and another faculty member, a trumpeter. Together with the other four faculty members, they constituted a sextet. However, within that sextet, the conflict was located in the dominant sound—the horns. My friend, as an educator and performer, is a jazz historian; he began his career working as musical director for an aging Benny Goodman. For him, at its best, jazz music has a continuous and evolving tradition that is a century old. His pedagogical approach within the workshop grew out of this perspective: He hoped to teach students to find in that tradition, as well as in the classical tradition that preceded it, elements they could consolidate in their own improvisational work to advance jazz music. By contrast, the trumpeter believed jazz music to be constituted entirely of acts of innovation. He began his professional career working with Miles Davis, at a time when Davis took his band into the realm of experimental rock. For him, innovation and experimentation are the only traditions worth preserving in jazz music. So, his pedagogical project for the workshop was to teach students trained in jazz to break out of its traditional forms. For my friend, jazz is about progressive continuity. For the trumpeter, it is about revolution.

During the early days of the workshop, the two tried to talk through their differences. After a number of these conversations proved fruitless, they quit trying. It had become clear to them that further attempts at dialogue regarding the central task of the workshop would be pointless. My friend felt that the trumpeter was undermining his work with the students; the trumpeter felt the same way about my friend. Their way of dealing with this intractable conflict was to spend the days of the workshop working in isolation from each other. This was not a successful solution, however, since the students could not be so isolated. The students were meant to work with both the saxophonist and the trumpeter, and were becoming increasingly troubled by the conflict. As apprentice jazz musicians, they had difficulties finding a workable place for themselves within the ideological territory of the workshop.

As the workshop neared its end, the saxophonist and the trumpeter were forced to confront each other. That occurred when the six faculty met to rehearse for the closing concert they were to play, as a sextet, for the students. This was a stellar ensemble, but one that would not have come together in any other setting; not surprisingly, the rehearsal did not go well. Tense and terse discussions were followed by abortive attempts at music; the trumpeter tried to push the ensemble well beyond the principles my friend had taught all week. For his part, my friend pulled them all back with equal energy. The other four faculty—comprising one of the best rhythm sections I have ever heard—tried, in argument and in performance, to fill in the empty ideological and musical space between the two horns and hold things together. All told, it was an hour of little talk; some truncated playing, and a surprising amount of uncomfortable silence. The rehearsal broke up without even an agreement on a playlist for the concert.

When the six of them reunited, it was on the bandstand as students filled the room. The bassist called a standard tune they all would know, and they playing. They followed jazz convention, playing a familiar tune together, in an unfamiliar, improvised harmony. They then accompanied each other successively—each taking a turn improvising a solo from the tune's chord changes, and then playing the tune together again. For people who know jazz, such a format is familiar and, unless interesting things begin to happen, it can get boring. Interesting things certainly happened. The trumpeter pushed hard, both in his accompaniments and his solos, and the saxophonist pushed back. Using creative connective tissue, the other four worked to fill in the spaces that the conflict between the two horns opened up in the music. It was strenuous playing for them all—unexpected and unpredictable.

The music worked for the audience. The sextet played for a full hour, all standards, and their students, who packed the house, were transfixed. This audience understood the music, knew the musicians, and—because they had come to understand the stark philosophical conflict being played out before them, if not how to resolve it—recognized what was at risk in the performance. They knew what they were witnessing: inventive, eloquent jazz being played at the edge of dissolution. The audience knew they were doing more than just listening—they were *experiencing* the music and identifying themselves with what the musicians were having to do. Understanding the issues that were shaping the music, they were sharing with their mentors the conflicting feelings being expressed as that music took shape. Since the music maintained its shape despite the musicians' differences, the students recognized in a very personal way the kind of aesthetic work that the best jazz musicians must do. The conflict on stage could have broken the music in pieces, but as the six faced together the responsibility that the situation demanded of them—both as individuals *and* as an ensemble—they asserted themselves in all their differences. The performers created an experience of the most precarious and satisfying harmony for their audience.

When the sextet finished, the students were on their feet, celebrating a memorable experience of aesthetic transcendence, a musical transcendence of a hopeless conceptual conflict. In terms of dialogic rhetoric, hopelessness remained even after the performance; but, in the aesthetic experience of the performance itself, conflict was transcended. The students, however, had aligned themselves ideologically in the days preceding this concert. On the night of the concert, the students found themselves sharing a transcendent experience of music. They left the concert unified, with an attitude of hope, as they considered jazz and their own prospects within it. The musicians left the stage sharing a very different attitude. For them, the performance had done little more than continue aesthetically what they still recognized as a hopeless conflict.

THOUGHTS ON AESTHETIC TRANSCENDENCE

What does this example teach us? First, it teaches that, among those who share them, aesthetic experiences do the rhetorical work of prompting attitudes and, thereby, resolving conflicts immune to dialogue. It also teaches, though, that such resolutions might not be as durable as those achieved dialogically. In this case, despite the new attitude that followed from the shared experience of the audience, the real conflict they witnessed (and been implicated in) remained unresolved in the realm of reason. This was where the faculty musicians remained: For the members of the sextet, the disagreement that divided the saxophonist and the trumpeter persisted within, and also followed, the performance. Pressed by the exigence of playing together, and also by their shared commitment to the project of making the performance work for their students, they joined—almost despite themselves—in the project of making coherent and, for the audience at least, satisfying music.

That music was particularly satisfying for the audience because it was *not*, as Burke might put it, stripped of attitudes. The emotions inherent in their opposing convictions were openly expressed in the musicians' performance. Yet, because the situation they shared required them to make music as an ensemble, these musicians found themselves as exemplars in managing that expression in ways that rendered their work harmonious rather than dissonant, and unified—though enriched with tension—rather than fragmented. The result was a performance that enabled the audience to experience for themselves, as Burke (1973a) might put it, "a perspective atop all the conflicts of attitude" (p. 148). That was a transcendent perspective that provided these students, who had struggled themselves with a conflict that divided their faculty, with an attitude of hope. They left the concert united, hoping for the capacity of the music to mediate individual expressions as collective, aesthetic statements, and for their own capacity to play it together, despite their differences. For them, that hope eclipsed the professional anxiety with which they had struggled before the concert. For the faculty, though—and especially for the contending horn players—the dialogical failure they had confronted for days remained their primary shared experience, a failure that eclipsed the success of the performance: When it was over, they knew that nothing had been truly resolved for them.

This anecdote suggests some of the limits of aesthetic transcendence. An aesthetic experience of transcendence is, indeed, epideictic; it is not deliberative or forensic. Epideictic rhetoric cannot codify collective decisions. Rather, it affects individual attitudes that can be collectively shared. Dialogue, though, is precisely a project of codification, of making and communicating rhetorically what Burke (1973a) calls "semantic meaning," and describes as "a vocabulary that gives the name and address of every event in the universe" (p. 141). Such a name and address is empirical, rational, and characterized by "the elimination of attitude." It presents, as Joe Friday used to say, "Just the facts." Burke's point is that "poetic meaning" can be much more rhetorically powerful, and that we often influence others more effectively through the "full moral act" of presenting them with "a perspective atop all the conflicts of attitude" (pp. 147–148). That is, more powerful than an agreement reached dialogically is the experience of sharing an attitude that transcends rational differences and conflicts, and that binds people together through a transformative feeling. It is sharing this feeling, I believe, that enables identification. Simply put, the rhetorical assertion of what Burke calls poetic meaning enables people to *experience* attitudes—and, consequently, feelings—that are shared. Even though such experiences are often ephemeral, like that of the sextet's audience, they can sometimes bring people together when dialogue cannot.

Burke provides some evidence for this claim in "Poetics, Dramatistically Considered," and essay that traces the roots of the word *poetry* to a verb meaning "to make," of the word *aesthetic* to a verb meaning "to perceive," and of the word *artistic* to a verb meaning "to join." Through his recovery of those roots, Burke locates the rhetorical power of aesthetic experience. In terms of my story, the reluctant sextet *made* coherent music from the very elements of their conflict, doing so in a way that enabled people they cared about to collectively *perceive* the conceptually dissonant as aesthetically harmonious, and to *join* together in response in a common attitude of hope. The musicians did not explicitly agree to do that. Rather, bound by a common commitment to a professional project, they could not help but do such rhetorical work in the process of making music for an audience. Their music thus embodied Burke's (1968) highly rhetorical definition of aesthetic form in *Counter-Statement*. "Form," he writes, involves "the creation of an appetite in the mind of the auditor and an adequate satisfying of that appetite" (p. 30). The aesthetic is an "an arousing and fulfillment of desires" that is, indeed, "a way of experiencing" (pp. 124, 143).

This idea of experience as a way of knowing and acting in the world is rooted in the culture that Burke, born an American at the end of the nineteenth century, inherited. Ralph Waldo Emerson began his long essay, *Nature*, by altogether rejecting the project of dialogue in matters of true importance, recommending instead an epistemology and an ethics constituted of encounters with the world external to individual intellect. In a later essay,

"Experience," Emerson (2003) puts that position in terms more directly pertinent to my point. "Life is not dialectics," he writes, and an "intellectual tasting of life will not supersede muscular activity" (pp. 293–294). William James (1997), writing from within this Emersonian tradition, describes religion not as theology, but as an immediate personal and non-rational experience: "Religion shall mean for us the feelings, acts, and experiences of individual men in their solitude, so far as to apprehend themselves to stand in relation to whatever they may consider divine" (p. 29). For John Dewey, who followed from James, and whose work Burke read carefully, that kind of experience is the basis of art and intellectual action. "Instead of signifying being shut up within one's own private feelings and sensations," Dewey (2005) wrote in *Art and Experience*, experience "signifies active and alert commerce with the world; at its height it signifies complete interpenetration of self and the world of objects and events" (p. 18). That statement seems to align with Burke's (1984) early description of transcendence in *Attitudes Toward History* as "the adoption of another point of view from which ['opposites'] cease to be opposites," a process that results in a "new sense of identification (a new way of defining the individual's identity with relation to a corporate identity)" (p. 337).

Finally, here is Burke's (1973b) concept of aesthetic transcendence articulated in explicitly musical terms. "'Transcendence,'" Burke writes, "is the solving of the logical problem by stretching it out into a narrative arpeggio, whereby a conflicting element can be introduced as a 'passing note,' hence not felt as 'discord'" (p. 99–100). The conflicting notes remain, but in effect, their dissonance is transcended by the aesthetic experience that the whole presentation creates. It is a presentation of a narrative sort, one that takes those who witness it on an experiential journey that makes not so much rational, but an aesthetic sense. Such an arpeggio transcends the harmonic conflict that is simply irresolvable if one "collapse[s] the arpeggio of development by the nontemporal, nonhistorical forms of logic," and presents the notes in a "simultaneous 'polarity'" (p. 99). That is because, if one "introduces into a chord a note alien to the perfect harmony the result is discord. But if you stretch out this same chord into an arpeggio having the same components, the discordant ingredient you have introduced may become . . . but a 'passing note'" (p. 99). The arpeggio can be *experienced* as harmonious, while the chord cannot. This is because the arpeggio *makes* something that can be experienced as harmony out of the very materials of dissonance, an aesthetic act with rhetorical impact and consequence.

In my story, the musicians in the sextet left the stage without hope. Even though their collective performance was, for their audience, an experience that transcended the conflict with which they struggled—and even though, in the process, the meaning they communicated to those students was profoundly hopeful—the attitudes of the two horn players remained deeply dissonant because their beliefs were hopelessly opposed. When they played together for their apprentice students, respect for the music and for their audience led them to make a rich and tense arpeggio out of a bad chord. What they made transcended their conflicting ideas. In effect, their performance told the students a hopeful story about the complex unity that an ensemble of differing and conflicting people can create. For the musicians, on the other hand, the bad chord, not the arpeggio, was foremost in their minds. As a result, the conflict remained—applying a term used by both Burke and MacIntyre—*interminable*.

Where does that leave us? Perhaps it leaves us understanding that the work of rhetoric—the work of bringing people together in attitude and in action—can be accomplished aesthetically. Poetic meaning has the power to push people past their differences and conflicts, beyond their intentions and their capacities, when shared circumstances of living and working together demand it. At least it can do that temporarily. That understanding can be hopeful when we find ourselves stuck living and working together in situations where dialogue fails. It can help to know what the faculty sextet learned: When we have to give up on talk, on the aspiration to agreement, and just take care of business together, we can sometimes offer experiences to others that prompt them to transcendence and to hope, even if we do not experience that transcendence ourselves.

Although the story of the reluctant sextet suggests that our rhetorical acts might be more powerful for others than for ourselves, there is also a more optimistic understanding we can take from this story. Sometimes the experience of joint action—even mundane action, taking care of business together—can bind people together in a common understanding, a common cause, and a common identity that, once experienced, is sufficient to render their unresolved "semantic" conflicts less relevant than they might otherwise have been. These are some of the lessons we can piece together from what Kenneth Burke writes about the aesthetic work of rhetoric, the rhetorical work of the aesthetic—and the possibility that we might, even after dialogue has failed, use rhetoric in a variety of other ways to transcend differences and enable people to come together.

NOTES

1. For an excellent recent study of dialogic rhetoric, see Zappen (2004).

2. In his own work of rhetorical criticism, Burke put that expanded definition of rhetoric into practice when he treats poetry, drama, and even music—as evident in his music criticism—as rhetorical.

3. In his account of this event, Flavius Josephus (1737) fills out the story:

> Now it was Nimrod who excited them to such an affront and contempt of God. . . . He also gradually changed the government into tyranny, seeing no other way of turning men from the fear of God, but to bring them into a constant dependence on his power. He also said he would be revenged on God, if he should have a mind to drown the world again; for that he would build a tower too high for the waters to be able to reach! And that he would revenge himself on God for destroying their forefathers! Now the multitude were very ready to follow the determination of Nimrod, and to esteem it a piece of cowardice to submit to God; and they built a tower, . . . and by reason of the multitude of hands employed in it, it grew very high, sooner than anyone could expect. . . . When God saw that they acted so madly, he did not resolve to destroy them utterly, since they were not grown wiser by the destruction of former sinners; but he caused a tumult among them, by producing in them divers languages, and causing that, through the multitude of those languages, they should not be able to understand one another.

References

Aristotle. (1991). *On rhetoric: A theory of civic discourse.* Trans. G. A. Kennedy. New York, NY: Oxford University Press.

Burke, K. (1951). Rhetoric—Old and new. *The Journal of General Education, 5,* 202–209.

Burke, K. (1966a). I, eye, ay—Concerning Emerson's early essay on "nature" and the machinery of transcendence. In *Language as symbolic action: Essays on life, literature, and method* (pp. 186–200). Berkeley, CA: University of California Press.

Burke, K. (1966b). Rhetoric and poetics. In *Language as symbolic action: Essays on life, literature, and method* (pp. 295–307). Berkeley, CA: University of California Press.

Burke, K. (1968). *Counter-statement.* Berkeley, CA: University of California Press.

Burke, K. (1969). *A rhetoric of motives.* Berkeley, CA: University of California Press.

Burke, K. (1970). *The rhetoric of religion: Studies in logology.* Berkeley, CA: University of California Press.

Burke, K. (1973a). Semantic and poetic meaning. In *Philosophy of literary form* (pp. 138–167), 3rd ed. Berkeley, CA: University of California Press.

Burke, K. (1973b). The philosophy of literary form. In *Philosophy of literary form* (pp. 1–137), 3rd ed.Berkeley, CA: University of California Press.

Burke, K. (1984). *Attitudes toward history* (3rd ed.). Berkeley, CA: University of California Press.

Burke, K. (2001). Watchful of hermetics to be strong in hermeneutics: Selections from "Poetics, dramatistically considered." In G. Henderson & D. C. Williams (Eds.), *Unending conversations: New writings by and about Kenneth Burke* (pp. 35–80). Carbondale, IL: Southern Illinois University Press.

Dewey, J. (2005). *Art as experience.* New York, NY: Penguin.

Emerson, R. W. (2003). Experience. In L. Ziff (Ed.), *Nature and selected essays* (pp. 285–311). New York, NY: Penguin.

James, W. (1997). *The varieties of religious experience.* New York, NY: Signet Classic.

Josephus, F. (1737). Antiquities of the Jews. In W. Whiston (Ed. & Trans.), *The works of Flavius Joseph.* Retrieved from http://sacred-texts.com/jud/josephus/

Kennedy, G. A. (1997). *Comparative rhetoric.* New York, NY: Oxford University Press.

Leff, M. (2003). Tradition and agency in humanistic rhetoric. *Philosophy and Rhetoric, 36*(2), 135–147.

MacIntyre, A. (1984). *After virtue: A study in moral theory* (2nd ed.). Notre Dame, IN: University of Notre Dame Press.

Perelman, C., & Olbrechts-Tyteca, L. (1969). *The new rhetoric: A treatise on argumentation.* Trans. J. Wilkinson & P. Weaver. Notre Dame, IN: University of Notre Dame Press.

Weaver, R. (2001). Language is sermonic. In P. Bizzell, & B. Herzberg (Eds.), *The rhetorical tradition: Readings from classical times to the present* (pp. 1351–1360), 2nd ed. Boston, MA: Bedford/St. Martins.

Zappen, J. P. (2004). *The rebirth of dialogue: Bakhtin, Socrates, and the rhetorical tradition.* Albany, NY: SUNY Press.

8
Kenneth Burke and the Dark Side of Transcendence: Localism, Wendell Berry, and the New Southern Agrarians

Andrew King

ate on a warm spring night, my county agent phoned to tell us that the price of wheat had climbed to twenty dollars per bushel. His voice crackled with excitement as he explained that several dry years in the Ukraine, Australia, and Russia had pushed the price from the miserable four dollar level of three years ago to its new stratospheric high. "We could all make a little money, and it really is too bad we didn't go organic when we had the chance. Those clever growers will get twenty-nine to the bushel," he expostulated, his voice slurred by cupidity.

There was more. My agent had other stranger news: "You know, there is another odd thing happening lately. The boys are coming home. There is a steady trickle back in all of our river counties. For the first time since 1976, our survey shows more farmers in the Red River Valley than the previous five years. You might have to turn your slate equipment shed back into a school house."

That night, I dreamed of earlier expatriates, the poet-farmer-agrarian crusader, Wendell Berry, who had returned to rural Kentucky from New York. My dream went deeper, all the way to the Back-to-the-Landers of the Great Depression, and finally to the Southern Agrarians and their northern forerunner, Kenneth Burke. During the agricultural trough of the 1920s, Burke dreamed of an agrarian renaissance. Fittingly, during his last years, he knew about and approved of the work of the Agrarian Localist Movement, led by

Wendell Berry and Wes Jackson. As an environmentalist who believed in community and sustainability, he was heartened by the return of our exiles, and he would have reminded us that he had been in the vanguard of the agrarian's odyssey eight decades ago. Burke was always a prophet and a seeker. He once told me that he had read Vachel Lindsay's (1926) poem about the Phantom Buffalo and the coming of the Great Northern railroad. We talked about the retreat of the farms in the great Western plains, and Burke agreed that "it might be a good thing to bring back the prairie grass in those arid places." Today, in western and central Dakota, Lindsay's (1926) "tossing, blooming, perfumed grass" has supplanted the former wheat fields, and the phantom bison have returned. Burke and I have had several, imaginary conversations about the return of the wild, and he has pronounced it good.

EMERSONIAN TRANSCENDENCE

In *Language as Symbolic Action*, Burke (1966) included a very rich, fifteen-page chapter on transcendence (pp. 186–201). It is a chapter that evokes strong responses from readers. The late Dale Leathers (1988) called it "moonshine, an impenetrable mish-mash of quasi-religious syntax." On the other hand, the late Mark Van Doren (1964) footnoted the chapter in his *Portable Emerson*, recommending it to his readers as "a rather novel interpretation of what Emerson truly meant by the idea of transcendence" (p. 17). Hugh Duncan was even more sanguine, asserting that "through the idea of transcendence Burke discovered the common ground that allows the social order to manage its differences in race, social class, and economic status in a creative and productive manner," going on to say that, "as a result of his adoption of transcendence, Burke better than Parsons, Mills, or Max Weber has built a vocabulary to explain social change" (personal communication, September 9, 1970).[1]

Burke (1966) himself defines transcendence as "a rival sort of medicine to the cycle of victimage and redemption" (p. 186). Transcendence, Burke writes, is "more than weapon in the arsenal of the priest"; in fact, he calls it "the ultimate priestly function" (p. 186). The priest transforms the victim through sacrifice, but the priest is also pontiff, the bridge—the agent who links visible and invisible worlds. In a brief reply to an offer for a speaking engagement at my university in 1972, Burke links transcendence to transformation. He refers briefly to a midsummer night's party he had recently attended, calling the Summer Solstice "an ancient celebration of transcendence, a night when old European pagans lighted signal fires on hilltops in order to travel between visible and invisible worlds" (personal communication, September 9, 1970). Burke's own writings are rich with the imagery of the transformative journey: crossing and returning, exile and homecoming, the Upward and Downward Way, Losing and Binding Sin, Death as the transcendence of life, losing one world to find another, and so on (e.g., Burke, 1950, p. 11).

Transcendence, Burke (1966) famously writes, is "the building of a symbolic bridge whereby one realm is viewed in terms of a realm beyond it" (p. 196). Burke also speaks of different modes of transcendence; thus, one kind of transcendence is rugged or tough-minded—like Hegel's notion of cooperative competition. Here, in Burke's view, new worlds emerge from the bone-crushing confrontation of opposites. Yet, his writings contain discussion of another sort of transcendence, one that he calls tender-minded, or merely dialectical. This is an Emersonian sort of transcendental mechanics, in which the reformer tends to lose sight of many of the adversarial terms that had been doing battle on the barricades. Burke (1966) holds in contempt this tender-minded sort of transcendence, commenting: "The scheme amounted to this: Show how evils will have good results, but play down the reciprocal possibility where good might have evil results" (pp. 188–189). In this way, Emerson, like Whitman, could "look upon traveling salesmen and see a band of angels" (p. 189).

One is reminded of George Bernard Shaw's famous saying that "criticism is autobiography," since Burke's criticism of Emerson's transcendence is that it is simple-minded, naively optimist, and filled with ingratiating imagery. That is to say, Burke faults Emerson's lack of a sense of evil. This criticism has been made of Burke, too. William Marchland (1977), for example, accuses him of "picking off scabs and then hurrying past the sufferer," while Bill Bailey notes that "in his critical work Burke often exposes the rottenness of society, but like the masked Silenus treats it less as an evil than as an intellectual mistake or an error in perception" (personal communication, January 9, 1976).[2] Sharon Whately (1999) similarly notes:

> Burke's remedy for deadly confrontation is comic detachment in which he had an almost mystical faith. It seems to me that comic detachment, like Gandhi's non-violence might often play into the hands of the oppressor. Burke's condemnation is shallow and cerebral, not heartfelt and muscular.

Again, the late William Bailey has noted that Burke was like Emerson in many other ways. As he wrote me following one of Burke's lectures,

> Burke and Emerson seem like two horses from the same stable. Their delight in phrase-making, their constant digressions, their fear of emotional commitment, their hit and run criticism and their giddy

optimism in the face of intractable problems are familiar hallmarks.
(personal communication, January 9, 1976)

Burke and Emerson are alike in an even more fundamental way: Kenneth
Burke and Ralph Waldo Emerson are both advocates of the poetic view of
life. Both romanticized agrarianism and saw it as a means of spiritual transformation. Both mistrusted institutions, and often dismissed industrial civi-
lization as dull, regimented, and ugly. Neither was unique in this regard; they
were members of a well-established intellectual tradition.

BURKE'S AESTHETIC WARRIORS

Distracted by his stylistic ticks, we tend to exaggerate Burke's originality. He
was a thing of a type, a so-called Bohemian Agrarian. Earlier voices inspired
him and spoke through him. Coleridge and the Romantic poets were there
before him. As early as the 1830s, Romantic poets lamented that their green,
English countryside was being rendered hideous by a great swath of newly
built mills that stretched from Manchester, in the midlands, to Swindon, on
the Welsh border. The feared that such an ugly landscape must produce a
corresponding ugliness in the English soul, Richard Burton worried that we
would become choleric as the industrial revolution drew us all indoors (as cited in Gallagher, 1993, p. 13). Of course, Coleridge, whom Burke greatly ad-
mired, published pamphlets on behalf of Robert Peel's relief bills. Coleridge
was greatly distressed over the degradation of both the human and the environmental resources of the nation. Against the ugliness and degradation of
the industrial revolution, the Romantics opposed an ideal Eden: the sacred
groves of Britain's vanishing rural heritage (e.g., Coleridge, 1951). Students
of the nineteenth century are familiar with Leigh Hunt's restorative walks,
and the Lake poets regularly refreshed themselves from immersion in the
cesspool of London by returning to the unspoiled lake country.

Emerson (2009), in his essay on farming, was over the moon about the
transformative powers of farming, fishing, and forestry. He was effusive in
describing how "the care of bees, of poultry, of sheep, of cows, the beautiful
dairy, and the care of hay, of fruits, orchards and forests give to us a strength
and dignity like the face and manners of Nature" (p. 673). By contrast with
this aesthetic vision, Emerson paints a picture of the sufferer in the textile
factories of New England, who returns to wholeness, and resolves: "'Well,
my children, whom I have bred, we shall go back to the land, to be recruited
and cured by that which should have been my nursery and now shall be my
hospital'" (p. 673). Recall also his friend Thoreau's (1910) famous metaphor
for the creative influence of immersion in nature, when Thoreau compares
the high period of his imagination to his famous and oft-repeated metaphor:

"like corn growing in the night" (p. 147). Today, ecologists weary of fighting bruising battles with developers have begun to embrace the poetic approach to nature in order to recruit the larger public. While developers marshal evidence for a particular assault, the ecological movement seeks to outflank them by creating a green-thinking general public that can be mobilized as a third party in every ecological confrontation between local citizens and developers.

The Machinery of Transcendence

Burke's beau ideal was Freud. Burke once confessed to me that he wanted to do on a societal level what Freud had done for the individual. As Freud brought clarity to the individual, Burke's criticism would puncture oppressive ideas for the larger society, and make them aware of the probable consequences of their choices. Yet, like Freud, Burke had an exaggerated idea of the power of enlightenment. Burke felt that mere public exposure of the self-interested lies of the powerful would free us from their oppressive influence. Sadly, pre-Freudian and post-Freudian agrarians have not shared this faith in the educative powers of criticism.

Two of Burke's greatest mentors, John Ruskin and William Morris, masters of Arts & Crafts and organic architecture, were also masters of the strategies of identification and division. They showcased the ugliness of England's factories and mass-produced products, and contrasted their anonymity and shoddiness with the time-honored aesthetic of organic craftsmen. They championed restoring the hand-made life of rural England as a remedy for the inorganic, destructive, mind-numbing life of the imperial technology of the nineteenth century. Whatever we think of their overheated rhetoric—Morris, for example, predicted that Arts and Crafts would restore native culture, smash imperialism, decentralize unions, create communal loyalty, and crush corporate capitalism—their movement endured and, like Banquo's ghost, it will not lie down.[3] Exploiting the widespread revulsion with mass-produced products, homes, and art, Ruskin and Morris developed the international Arts & Crafts movement, a movement that died in the trenches of the Great War, only to be called to a second life at the beginning of the twenty-first century.

For Ruskin, the theorist, and Morris, the guild master, aesthetic praxis was a central part of the machinery of transcendence. Both men went far beyond consciousness raising or intellectual critique. They practiced an organic aesthetic for the masses. Through the daily practice of architecture, town planning, public murals, garden design, and the crafting of garden and household tools, these practitioners believed that they would bring about an inner transformation—thereby changing alienated workers to profoundly involved citizen-artisans and artists. The point was not to make a handful of great artists, but to join together a mass of people working to make their community beautiful and distinctive. In his open-air lectures, Ruskin constantly reminds his auditors that the achievement of a public aesthetic involves a journey of the soul. William Morris, in particular, was a man of action. He had the driving, hands-on determination that Emerson and Thoreau lacked; he built a social movement. Through his craft, he constructed a community of active participants. He was a man of the barricades. He had the instinct of a drum major.

The late blooms of the agrarian movement have come from organizers and practitioners as well. Wendell Berry despaired of the educative powers of critique. He wrote:

> In 1976, I felt that my book, *The Unsettling of America*, would make a difference. My book argued that a concerted program deliberately orchestrated by land grant colleges, agri-business, and factory farmers had pushed millions of American from the land. I described the logic, the rhetoric, and coercive farm policies through which family farm had been eliminated by America's agricultural czars. Although they had not used overt violence, they had disposed us of our heritage and culture just as surely as Stalin had forced millions of kulaks on to the Soviet Union's collective farms. The book was nearly uniformly praised, and I felt that I might be a catalyst in the restoration of rural America. (personal communication, May 16, 2005)

Berry's disillusionment was swift in coming. He was invited to important forums. Deans of land grant universities patronized him, and they agreed with his strongest criticisms. They went further, freely admitting that the consolidation and industrialization of American farms had smashed community, impoverished our soil, poisoned our rivers, and crushed the small town. They believed in his message, they accepted his ideas, and they saluted his courage. Even today, members of Congress from the so-called "farm states" routinely invite representatives of small farmer's groups to suspiciously expensive luncheons at foully expensive clubs. As my county agent once quipped, these servants of the great fertilizer and chemical companies—champions of our bought-and-sold researchers in the land grant universities—routinely confess their enthusiasm for Wendell Berry's books, and cluck approvingly over the hectoring criticisms of Wes Jackson and the land institute.

Of course, Berry points out, they speak another message down into their sleeves. They say:

> What you ask is correct but it is too difficult to do. Who can turn the Queen Mary on beech muck or pull a rope of sand uphill? It is too late to restore the family farm and the autonomy of the local community. The ship has sailed. (personal communication, May 16, 2005)

Berry no longer bothers with them. Gods of the local household have spoken to him, and he, long ago, began a different journey. This new journey is a grass-roots odyssey, one that takes his message to small farmers and intact communities and initiates social and economic and cultural practices that fly directly in the teeth of corporate agriculture. Today, his doctrine of localism is more than an idea; it is a *social praxis*, constantly modified to meet new challenges. One of its institutional arms, the Farmer's Market, has been successfully planted all over North America, and Berry has recruited millions of urbanites by getting them interested in the source of their food. It is truism that one of the most powerful identities in a culture is its food: "'the suet pudding' English, the 'frog eating' French, the 'sausage eating' Germans—these tags note the divisive and uniting powers of national patterns of consumption" (Berry, 1970, p. 73).

As a novelist and a poet, Berry pays attention to the transcendent aspect of food production and farming. He makes local production and consumption a spiritual act. He links localism to the Slow Food movement worldwide. He appropriates the transformational rhetoric of Ruskin and Morris, and hurls his rhetorical bayonets at an updated version of William Blake's "satanic mills": globalism.

A RIVAL TRANSCENDENT

Unlike Burke—who, from an early age, knew that technology had a siren song of its own—Berry came late to understanding the power of its attraction. The young Burke was deeply marked by the work of Thorstein Veblen, and he knew the power of the objective spirit, the seductive promise of an infinitely receding future of technological progress, the intrinsic value of quantification, the sweetness of pecuniary alienation, and the utopian charisma of technology. Burke lectured us on the power of agency as the newly-dominant member of the pentad in New Harmony, Indiana, and noted that technology was firmly in the saddle.[4] The technological is, after all, an endeavor that promises to transcend the limitations of the planet—an endeavor that holds out the promise of a kind of eternal life by offering to transcend the weakness of the body (envisioning the human as a constantly renewed cyborg). Burke predicted that technology would continue to appropriate religion's promises of redemption, eternal life, and the end of suffering. As a scion of the industrial community, Burke knew what Berry did not.

Following three decades of struggle, Berry has learned not to fight the technocrats in their symbolic strongholds. He is Burkean in method, if not in formal allegiance. As a novelist, lecturer, and teacher, he has used the agrarian poetic. He has gotten a good drama going, a drama in which the embattled, small farmer and the wealthy, cultured urban voluptuary have gained forces against the enemy: land grant universities, the United States Department of Agriculture, Monsanto Chemical and Fertilizer Company, Midland cooperatives, and other jackals of the corporate, agriculture establishment. He understands the symbolic power of his adversaries, and—despite his suspicion of technology—allows his fighting squadrons to use the global Internet on behalf of localism. He has learned to fight the syphilitic jackals of the agricultural establishment with their own weapons. He allies with Wes Jackson (1996) of the land institute, author of that famous book, *Becoming Native to this Place*, a mythopoeia researcher who is one the best practicing rhetoricians of our time. He renewed his acquaintance with the surviving communities of the Southern Agrarians and the Fugitive Poets, Richland's in Tennessee, Sand Mountain Redoubt in Alabama, and Home Place near Walker, Louisiana.

Long ago, a member of Samuel Johnson's Thursday Club, a poor Anglo-Irish poet named Oliver Goldsmith invented the vocabulary of localism in two works: *She Stoops to Conquer*, a play, and "The Deserted Village," a long poem about the destruction of local tradition and folk culture by the newly-ascendant national gentry. These provided Thomas Jefferson with a language he used to champion the American yeoman. Goldsmith equates local ownership with accountability. Community and virtue—the message of Wes Jackson, Wendell Berry, and Cary Dawson—are but glosses upon Goldsmith's story of the disinherited, rural proletariat and the fall of the nation. Berry (1970) has tried to evoke "private responsibility in a country that has nearly destroyed private life"; this sense of crafting our new communities is, he emphasizes, "the task of the environmental movement" (p. 73). Bill McKibben (2007), author of *Deep Economy*, the runaway bestseller on environmental action, outlines the many steps needed to embrace the hand-made life. He notes that "progress toward the local economy will come not from grand visions but from a series of incremental changes" (p. 158). He does not underestimate the difficulty of such an effort. One fundamental challenge, he points out, is that Americans "define freedom" almost entirely in terms of "autonomy and mobility" (p. 225).

Both Berry and Burke understood that the poetic selling of agrarian localism has a problem not faced by Goldsmith, the Romantic poets, or even

Emerson. Today, only two percent of Americans live on farms. Their "greenness" owes more to Walt Disney than to direct experience with nature. Burke complained about the wall of technology separating us from nature, and Berry was appalled at the ignorance of the urban population, of their ungroundedness. People deal with the miracles of technology every day, every hour, and every minute. They seldom see the miracle of the earth: the old bargain that we have made with the Great Mother.

What kind of experience ought they have? The kind of experience that allows people to make sense of agrarianism. I would have people see humane farming practices, and I would have them experience the seeding and first emergence of a crop. That is, people need to experience the poetry of the earth. That would be an experience of transcendence worthy of our nature and our responsibility as wordlings of this world, as earthly bodies that learn language.

Notes

1. These quotes are taken from a letter from Hugh Dalziel Duncan concerning Burke's appearance as part of the George Sparks Lecture Series.

2. This evaluation was offered from William Bailey in response to Burke's appearance at the Harvest lectures at the University of Minnesota.

3. For a rich but succinct discussion of the Arts and Crafts movement and the leadership of Ruskin and Morris, see Sommer and Rago (1995, pp. 6–21).

4. New Harmony was, of course, the site of the inaugural meeting of the Kenneth Burke Society in May, 1990.

References

Berry, W. (1970). *A continuous harmony: Essays cultural and agricultural*. Washington, D.C.: Shoemaker and Hoard.

Burke, K. (1950). *A rhetoric of motives*. New York, NY: Prentice Hall.

Burke, K. (1966). *Language as symbolic action: Essays on life, literature and method*. Berkeley, CA: University of California Press.

Coleridge, S. T. (1951). Social confidence. In K. Coburn (Ed.), *A Coleridge reader* (pp. 351–365). New York, NY: Pantheon Books.

Emerson, R. W. (2009). Farming. In B. Atkinson (Ed.), *The essential writings of Ralph Waldo Emerson* (pp. 673-681). New York, NY: Random House.

Gallagher, W. (1993). *The power of place*. New York, NY: Poseidon Books.

Jackson, W. (1996). *Becoming native to this place*. New York, NY: North Point Press.

Leathers, D. (1988). Kenneth Burke as a stylist: Was obscurity his greatest virtue? (Unpublished paper.). Speech Communication Association Convention, New Orleans, LA.

Lindsay, V. (1926). *The flower-fed buffaloes*. Retrieved from http://www.poetryfoundation.org/poem/242582.

Marchand, W. (1977). Commitment, social action, and the American literary establishment. (Unpublished lecture.). William Harvest Lectures, University of Minnesota, Minneapolis, MN.

McKibben, B. (2007). *Deep economy: The wealth of communities and the durable future*. New York, NY: Henry Hold & Co.

Sommer, R. L., & Rago, D. (1995). *The Arts and Crafts movement*. New York, NY: Barnes and Noble.

Thoreau, H. D. (1910). *Walden*. New York, NY: Thomas Crowell & Company.

Van Doren, M. (Ed.). (1964). *The portable Emerson*. New York, NY: Viking Books.

Whately, S. (1999). Burke at the barricades: A moderate feminist view. (Unpublished paper.). Triennial Meeting of the Kenneth Burke Society, Iowa City, IA.

Contributors

Gregory Clark is University Professor of English at Brigham Young University. As this book is published, he is president-elect of the Rhetoric Society of America, serving previously as RSA executive director and editor of *Rhetoric Society Quarterly*. His work explores questions of rhetorical aesthetics, the inquiry that first led him Kenneth Burke. Clark's two books that explore Burke's particularly American rhetorical aesthetic are *Rhetorical Landscapes in America: Variations on a Theme from Kenneth Burke* (University of South Carolina Press, 2004) and *Civic Jazz: America's Music, Kenneth Burke, and the Art of Getting Along* (University of Chicago Press, 2015).

Richard M. Coe retired as Professor of English at Simon Fraser University, where he was the 1984 recipient of the Excellence in Teaching Award. Since retirement, he has lost interest in scholarly pursuits unrelated to Kenneth Burke, but is also the author of *Toward a Grammar of Passages* (Southern Illinois University Press, 1987), *Process, Form, and Substance* (2nd Ed., Longman, 1990), *Critical Moments in the Rhetoric of Kenneth Burke: Implications for Composition*, with Martin Behr (Inkshed Publications, 1996), and a number of essays on Kenneth Burke, appearing in journals such as *JAC*, *Rhetoric Review*, and *College English*.

Bryan Crable is Professor of Communication and Director of the Waterhouse Family Institute for the Study of Communication and Society at Villanova University. He is the author of *Ralph Ellison and Kenneth Burke: At the Roots of the Racial Divide* (University of Virginia Press, 2012), has twice received the Charles Kneupper Award from the Rhetoric Society of America, and in 2011 received the Kenneth Burke Society's Lifetime Achievement Award. His essays have appeared in *The Quarterly Journal of Speech*, *Rhetoric Society Quarterly*, *Rhetoric Review*, *Argumentation & Advocacy*, *Human Studies*, *Communication Quarterly*, and *Western Journal of Communication*.

John B. Hatch is Associate Professor of Communication Studies at Eastern University in St. Davids, Pennsylvania. His monograph *Race and Reconciliation: Redressing Wounds of Justice* (Lexington Books, 2008) received the top single-author book award from the National Communication Association's Communication Ethics division in 2009. He has published essays on racial reconciliation, slavery apologies, dialogic rhetoric, and hip-hop. Other research interests include communication ethics, the rhetoric of music, and religious discourse.

Cathryn Hill has worked as a psychologist in Vancouver, British Columbia, for over twenty years. Finding that her graduate training in clinical psychology did not fully prepare her for the political and social challenges that can arise within therapy sessions–especially those involving couples and families–she pursued an interdisciplinary doctorate that blended her interests in psychology, sociology, popular culture, and rhetoric. She is currently in private practice with a focus on couple therapy, and continues to pursue her love-hate relationship with self-help culture.

Theon E. Hill is Assistant Professor of Communication at Wheaton College. His research explores the relationship between rhetoric and social change. Specifically, he examines the role of radical rhetoric as a crucial form of civic engagement and public advocacy. His previous work on rhetoric and social change in political, social movement, and religious contexts has appeared in edited collections and scholarly journals. Currently, he is working on a book-length manuscript examining the relevance of Martin Luther King, Jr. in the Age of Obama.

Andrew King is Professor of Communication Studies at Louisiana State University. He studied under Robert Scott of the University of Minnesota, in the days when three quarters of the graduate students were recent military veterans and Scott was our beloved Major Domo. Andy's dissertation was on the civil rights movement, and he was one of the few young scholars who met and corresponded with Martin Luther King, Jr. He has served at Buffalo State University College, Arizona and LSU, directing more than thirty theses and dissertations. He is also one of the few gray eminences who actually knew Burke, having invited him for college lectures in 1971. He and his wife Ellen are currently at work on a new book, *Living in the Active Voice*.

Abigail Selzer King is Assistant Professor of Technical Communication and Rhetoric at Texas Tech University. Her research examines the intersections of organizational communication and rhetoric, specifically focusing on the rhetorical constitution of identities, genders, and nationalisms. Selzer King's work has appeared in journals including *Argumentation & Advocacy* and *Visual Communication Quarterly*.

James F. Klumpp is Professor of Communication at the University of Maryland. He is coauthor with Bernard L. Brock, Mark Huglen, and Sharon Howell of *Making Sense of Political Ideology: The Power of Language in Democracy* (Roman & Littlefield, 2005), a Burkean consideration of ideology in the political spectrum. A rhetorical critic and contemporary rhetorical theorist, he has written over twenty essays elaborating Burke's work and its implications on rhetoric as a tool of politics and social change. He was the winner of the National Communication Association's Douglas Ehninger Distinguished Rhetorical Scholar Award in 2013.

John S. Wright is the Morse-Amoco Distinguished Teaching Professor of African American & African Studies and English at the University of Minnesota, and is the Faculty Scholar for the Archie Givens Sr. Collection of African American Literature & Life. His *Shadowing Ellison* (University of Mississippi Press, 2006) provides a Burkean reading of Ralph Ellison's work within the context of American democracy. In addition to articles, presentations, and chapters, his other books include *A Ralph Ellison Festival* (coedited with poet Michael Harper; Carleton College, 1980), and *A Stronger Soul within a Finer Frame* (with Tracey E. Smith; University of Minnesota Press, 1990).

Index

pentad, 31, 69, 85, 93, 98, 115–117,
128, 193; analysis, 86, 98, 115–116,
128, 130–131; pentadic term, 27,
116, 132; ratios, 116–120, 123–124;
shifts, 115, 117, 123–124; terms, 27,
116, 127, 132
perfection, 12, 22, 24–26, 39, 50,
53–56, 59–60, 62, 63, 65, 97, 154,
183; perfectionism, 50, 54; principle
of, 24, 53–54, 62
Perinbanayagam, Robert, 4
perspective by incongruity, 7, 40, 42,
45, 46, 59, 150
perspective of perspectives, 15, 95
perspectivism, 150
persuasion, 18–19, 67, 69, 86, 125, 172,
176, 177
planned incongruity, 40
Plato, 5, 14–21, 29, 30, 55, 68, 70;
Phaedrus, 70
plurality, 14, 70, 72
poetic ideal, 88, 107
poetic structure, 177
point of view, 36, 39, 165, 172
politics, 26, 34, 37, 39, 66–68, 70–73,
76, 78, 83–86, 88–89, 114, 130, 155,
157, 159, 167, 199; binary, 36
populism, 35
positive terms, 16, 68–69, 81, 84
postcolonialism, 167
power: theory of, 167
pragmatism, 120, 123
Prairie Home Companion (Keillor), 38
prayer, 11, 33–34, 45, 60, 74, 76
priestly function (ultimate), 21, 48, 58,
177, 188
Prince of Wales, 167
progressivism, 54
psychogenesis, 46
psychotherapy literature, 136
Pulchinello (*commedia del arte*), 59
purification, 35
Purpose, 27, 93, 98, 116

quality, 12, 15, 17, 82, 92, 121
Quasimodo (*The Hunchback of Notre
Dame*), 59

race, 4, 26, 33, 38, 39, 41, 43–45,
47–53, 56, 64–65, 71–72, 77–78,
87–89, 99, 102, 104–107, 111–112,
188, 197–198; ritual, 48–49, 51–53
racism, 88, 101, 103–105, 112
Raglan, Lord: *The Hero; A Study in
Tradition, Myth, and Drama*, 47
Randolph, A. Philip, 47
Reagan, Ronald, 83, 85, 116, 128
realism: cynical, 91
realism (linguistic), 67, 70, 84, 99,
100, 103
reality, 6–7, 13, 19, 36, 48, 56, 60,
78–79, 97, 121, 170, 174; social, 7
realms, duality of, 17, 23
realpolitik, 89
reconciliation, 21, 26, 75, 87–102,
105–113, 117, 198
Reconstruction, 103
redemption, 34–35, 41, 46, 50, 57, 60,
62, 89–90, 96–97, 105, 188, 194
redress, 84, 88, 155
rejection philosophy, 92
relationship guides, 132–134, 136,
144, 146–150, 152
relationships, 7, 27, 49, 90–91, 116,
134, 145–150, 152, 154, 160, 168
religion, 31, 34, 40, 61, 64, 85, 94,
110, 112, 153, 158, 164–169, 183,
185, 193
reluctant sextet, 28, 182, 184
Renaissance, 177
repentance, 91, 97, 100, 105, 177
Republicanism, 39
restorative justice, 27, 90, 98, 107, 112
restorative truth, 98
Rg-Veda, 159
rhetoric, 6, 15, 17–19, 26–28, 31, 34,
36, 39, 41, 52, 54, 60–61, 64, 67–
69, 71, 74, 81–82, 84–86, 88–89,
94, 96–100, 106–108, 110–113,
115–118, 120–125, 127, 129–131,
134, 147, 150, 153, 156–161,
168–178, 181–186, 191–193, 195,
197–199; dialogic, 89, 180, 184,
198; epideictic, 89–90, 94, 101,
108, 177, 181; political, 67, 72

www.ingramcontent.com/pod-product-compliance
Lightning Source LLC
Chambersburg PA
CBHW032350280326
41935CB00008B/512